MARYLAND

A History of Its People

MARYLAND

A History of Its People

THE JOHNS HOPKINS UNIVERSITY PRESS

Baltimore and London

To our sons and daughters
and all sons and daughters of Maryland

The Johns Hopkins University Press
701 West 40th Street
Baltimore, Maryland 21211
The Johns Hopkins Press Ltd., London

∞
The paper used in this publication meets the minimum requirements of American
National Standard for Information Sciences—Permanence of Paper for Printed
Library Materials, ANSI Z39.48-1984.

LIBRARY OF CONGRESS CATALOGING-IN-PUBLICATION DATA
Main entry under title:

Maryland, a history of its people.

   Bibliography: p.
   Includes index.
   Summary: An introductory high school textbook surveying the history of Mary-
land, with emphasis on the blacks, women, immigrants, and other special groups
contributing to the variety of its population.
   1. Maryland—History. [1. Maryland—History] I. Chapelle, Suzanne Ellery
Greene.
F181.M317   1986   975.2   85-19888
ISBN 0-8018-3005-2 (alk. paper)

Contents

CHAPTER 1

Maryland's Formative Years, 1634–1763   3

CHAPTER 2

The Revolutionary War Era, 1763–1789   49

Reo Touring Car $1000

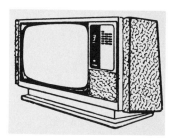

List of Maps, Graphs, and Tables

A Word to Readers

The history of Maryland is the story of its people: men, women, and children; Indian, black, and white; wealthy, middle class, and poor. Over the centuries, Marylanders—all of them—helped build this state we live in. Maryland began as a tiny settlement in the wilderness in 1634 and grew to be a thriving technological society. Marylanders shaped their state with hard work, courage, and wisdom, and they also settled many conflicts along the way.

No large group of people can live together very long without disagreeing over what is right. Much of history is the working out of priorities. Struggles for power, for political and economic domination, grow out of the varying needs and desires of different groups of people. Studying history is really looking at the conflicts and compromises, the achievements and failures, of the many people who have lived before us.

Maryland has been described as "America in miniature" because of its widely varied people and landscape. Maryland's culture has elements of the North and elements of the South; its landscape is partly urban and partly rural; and its geography contains both coastal plain and mountain peaks. Much can be learned about how the United States developed by studying how Maryland developed.

Maryland has played a role in most major national events. Its history also is unique in many ways. This book will make clear some of the connections between the national and the local, between broad trends and individual events, between the resources of the earth and the people who depend on them.

As you read, remember that senators and slaves, bankers and seamstresses, farmers and social workers are all part of the state's history. Whether they lived in the seventeenth century or the twentieth, they all wanted a decent life for themselves and their families. They all wanted enough liberty to be able to control their own fate. These people were not very different from the people you know today.

The history of Maryland is the story of its people. Some will be familiar to you. The unfamiliar people will, perhaps, help you to understand better the people you already know.

MARYLAND

A History of Its People

MARYLAND		THE NATION AND THE WORLD
Spanish visit the Chesapeake Bay	1524	
	1587–1604	War between Spain and England
	1607	Virginia settled
John Smith explores the Bay	1608	
	1612	New York settled
	1619	First slaves in Virginia
	1620	Plymouth Colony settled
	1630	Massachusetts Bay Colony settled
Trading post established at Kent Island	1631	
George Calvert dies Cecilius Calvert is granted a charter	1632	
Ark and *Dove* land at St. Clement's	1634	
	1642	English Civil War begins
Ingle's Rebellion	1645–1646	
Act of Toleration	1649	Charles I executed
	1660	English monarchy restored
	1676	Bacon's rebellion in Virginia
	1681	William Penn is granted Pennsylvania
	1688	Glorious Revolution in England
Proprietor overthrown	1689–1697	King William's War against France in the northern colonies
Maryland becomes a royal colony	1691	
Anglican church established	1692	
	1693	College of William and Mary founded
King William's School founded	1696	
	1702–1713	Queen Anne's War against Spain and France throughout the colonies
Proprietorship restored	1715	
First issue of *Maryland Gazette* published Baltimore Town founded	1729	
Paper money legislation passed	1733	
Continuous publication of *Maryland Gazette* begins	1745	
Tobacco Inspection Act	1747	
Maryland census taken	1755	
	1756–1763	Seven Years' War in America and Europe (French and Indian War)

CHAPTER 1

Maryland's Formative Years, 1634–1763

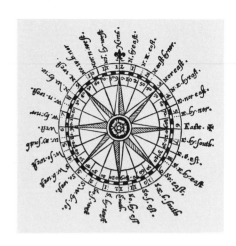

In 1634 a small group of settlers, most of them men, landed at what is now St. Mary's City, in the new colony of Maryland. They had spent three months crossing the wide and sometimes turbulent Atlantic Ocean before sailing into the Chesapeake Bay in search of a suitable place to land. Seeing safe harbor and virgin forest, they envisioned the town they would build.

The landscape that confronted the pioneers bore no resemblance to their old country. They saw no houses, only the huts of Indians. They found no stores or markets, craftsmen's shops, churches, schools, courts, or legislature. They had no newspapers, books, music, inns, or theaters. But before any of these could be created, the basic necessities—food and shelter—had to be provided.

Explorer Captain John Smith had written of the Bay area in 1608, "Heaven and earth never agreed better to frame a place for man's habitation." The wealth of woodlands and fields, the fertile soil and plentiful wildlife, and the bounty of the waters held great promise for these adventurers. They had chosen to seek a new life in the American wilderness. Some would succeed beyond their wildest dreams. Others would not survive the colony's early years.

Many of the first settlers or those who followed them died soon after their arrival. Others were held in bondage and had no opportunity to work for themselves. The search for greater opportunity led many people to move on, and by the end of the colonial period, settlement had spread across the colony.

The history of Maryland in the early colonial years is largely the story of how the settlers adapted the society and government of England to their new environment. The institutions they built provided a framework of stability and order for them. Other men and women joined the early settlers and their descendants, and together these people built a new society in the colony of Maryland.

Queen Henrietta Maria, wife of King Charles I, in whose honor George Calvert named "Terra Mariae," Maryland.

The Founding of Maryland

The founding of a colony in Maryland was not an isolated or a unique event. It took place during a period when many European countries were spending much effort and money to establish colonies in the New World.

European Exploration and Colonization

For Europeans, the fifteenth and sixteenth centuries were an age of exploration and overseas trade and settlement. Portuguese sailors explored the coasts of Africa and India. Dutch and English traders formed companies that followed the Portuguese lead.

Christopher Columbus, an Italian, set out on expeditions for the Spanish Crown. After Columbus discovered the Americas in 1492, Spaniards sailed to the New World to conquer its inhabitants and settle there.

Frenchmen and Englishmen fished the waters off Newfoundland in the sixteenth century, while French fur traders built trading posts in North America. In the late 1500s Englishmen failed in several attempts to settle colonies in Newfoundland and at Roanoke, North Carolina.

War between Spain and England interrupted colonization for several years, but after 1604, overseas trade and colonies again commanded attention. Englishmen formed groups to promote settlement in Ireland, Newfoundland, Virginia, New England, and elsewhere. These investors included court officials, merchants, and gentlemen, among them George Calvert.

As a secretary of state in the court of King James I, George Calvert had many opportunities to become involved in the colonization taking place in Ireland, North Carolina, and Newfoundland. In 1621 George Calvert began a settlement in Newfoundland.

In 1625 disputes over policy and his conversion to Catholicism forced Calvert to resign his offices. James I rewarded him for his years of service by giving him the title Baron of Baltimore, a title in the Irish nobility. Even though he had a title and therefore would be called Lord Baltimore, George Calvert had lost an important source of income, so he looked to North America for opportunities. He traveled to Newfoundland in 1627, but, finding the climate there too harsh, he decided to look farther south for a place to build a permanent colony.

A Charter for Maryland

George Calvert arrived in Virginia in October 1629, but he was not well received there, so he went back to England to obtain a new site for a colony. Because the land Calvert wanted had already been granted, King Charles I gave him land north of Virginia: present-day Maryland. Calvert was to receive his land through a charter, or grant, that defined his powers as the proprietor, or owner, of the land.

The chartering process begun by George Calvert was not completed until shortly after his death. Thus, the charter went into effect under his son Cecilius, Maryland's first proprietor. The grant gave Lord Baltimore and his heirs power in Maryland equal to the power of the king in England.

The proprietor could defend his province by raising an army and waging war against his enemies. He could encourage trade and economic growth by founding towns, building forts, establishing ports, and imposing customs duties. He could establish courts, appoint justices and other government officials, and enact laws with the agreement of the freemen of the colony. He could himself grant land to settlers, who would hold it as his subjects. He could give the title of lord to those who held large grants, or manors, and authorize the lords to hold courts to govern their tenants. The charter gave Lord Baltimore a vast territory and broad powers. In return, he owed the king only two Indian arrows each year and one-fifth of all precious metals found in Maryland.

Cecilius Calvert, the second Lord Baltimore, portrayed here with his grandson and a servant, completed the chartering of the Maryland colony after his father died.

Terms of Settlement

Every settler who joined Calvert's colony would receive 100 acres of land for himself and 50 or 100 acres for every person he brought with him. Anyone who brought in five or more men would receive at least 1,000 acres of land for every five men of working age. Large investors in the colony would also receive 10 acres of land in the city that was being planned as the capital of the colony. This system governed land distribution until 1683. After that date, new owners had to buy their land.

George Calvert also offered settlers shares in a company that would control fur trading with the Indians. Profits from furs, he hoped, would provide income for the investors, including himself, while the land was being developed.

The offerings to the early potential settlers had two purposes. First, they would provide Lord Baltimore with steady income. He would collect rent on all land granted to settlers and duties on furs and agricultural products sold to Europe or elsewhere. Second, they would form a basis for political leadership and organization. Because large investors depended on Baltimore for their grants of land, offices, and titles, Baltimore could expect them to be loyal to him. George Calvert also expected that ordinary settlers would follow the leadership of these wealthy men. Thus, an orderly and obedient colony would grow and prosper, for the benefit of both settlers and proprietor.

Religious Toleration

The settlement in Maryland was also intended as a refuge for Roman Catholics. George Calvert and his heir Cecilius did not seek to establish Maryland as a Roman Catholic colony. Rather, they wanted persons of all faiths to be able to practice their religion in private, and without persecution, discrimination, or exclusion from political life. Catholics as well as Protestants would be able to vote and to hold office, which Catholics could not do in England. The Calverts hoped that Catholics would be able to worship in their faith without suffering any penalties in the new colony.

George Calvert did not live to see his plans for his colony carried out. He died in April 1632, leaving his eldest son, Cecilius, to complete the chartering of the Maryland colony. The charter granted in June 1632 gave Cecilius Calvert the land between the Potomac and Delaware rivers, as far north as the fortieth parallel, and as far west as the headwaters of the Potomac. The grant included only "parts of America not yet cultivated or planted," thus excluding the lower Eastern Shore, which had already been settled by Virginians. A trading post at Kent Island in the Chesapeake Bay remained within Maryland. It would be a source of dispute for many years.

The First Settlers

Cecilius Calvert had his charter. Now he needed to find men to settle his colony. He attracted to his venture a group of 17 gentlemen, mostly younger sons of wealthy Roman Catholic families. An order of Catholic priests, the Jesuits, also made a major investment in the first voyage. In all, nearly 150 settlers set sail from England in November 1633 on two small sailing ships, the *Ark* and the *Dove*. Most of the passengers were indentured servants, nearly all of them men and Protestants. These passengers signed an indenture, or contract, in which they agreed to work for a gentleman for a set

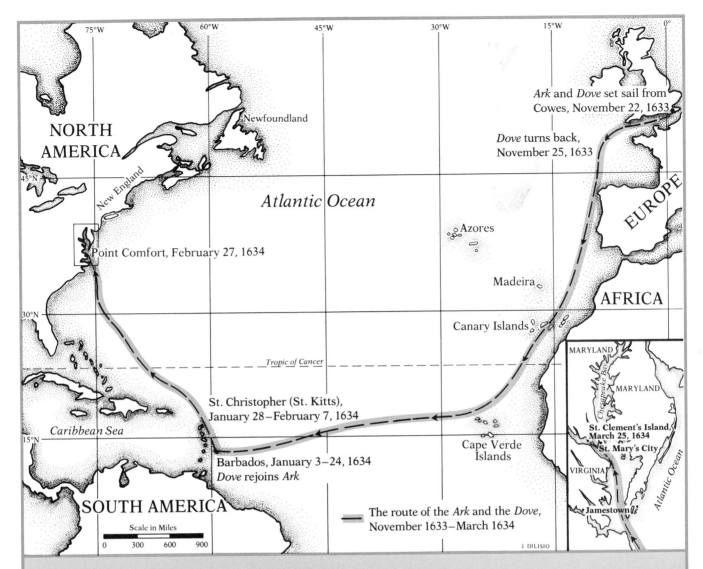

Ark and *Dove* set sail from Cowes, November 22, 1633

Dove turns back, November 25, 1633

NORTH AMERICA

Newfoundland

New England

45°N

Atlantic Ocean

EUROPE

Point Comfort, February 27, 1634

Azores

Madeira

AFRICA

30°N

Canary Islands

Tropic of Cancer

St. Christopher (St. Kitts), January 28–February 7, 1634

Caribbean Sea

15°N

Cape Verde Islands

Barbados, January 3–24, 1634
Dove rejoins *Ark*

SOUTH AMERICA

Scale in Miles
0   300   600   900

The route of the *Ark* and the *Dove*, November 1633–March 1634

J. DILISIO

MARYLAND

MARYLAND

St. Clement's Island, March 25, 1634

St. Mary's City

VIRGINIA

Atlantic Ocean

Jamestown

THE VOYAGE OF THE *ARK*

The first colonists traveled to Maryland on the *Ark*. Their fifteen-week voyage was cramped and uncomfortable, like all ocean travel in the seventeenth century. Only the gentlemen might have had separate cabins. The other passengers spent most of the voyage confined to the lower deck, where they slept, ate, and lived together without any privacy. Each day they faced water-soaked bedding, monotonous food, fear of pirates, and seasickness.

Early in the voyage, two storms broke the routine. During the second storm, the colonists "were in fear of imminent death all . . . night." Ships traveling to the Chesapeake sailed south to Africa before turning west to cross the Atlantic. Calm weather during the long reach across the ocean could also be fatal, as food and water would run out if a ship was becalmed too long.

Passengers on the *Ark*, instead, suffered from too much drink when they celebrated Christmas day. Some drank too much wine, and 30 fell ill with a fever, which killed about 12.

The *Ark* and the smaller *Dove* carried not only provisions for the voyage, but also supplies the settlers would need once they arrived. Colonists were advised to bring food (meal, peas, oil, vinegar, salt, sugar, and spices), several sets of clothing, bedding, muskets, powder and shot, hoes, axes and other tools, iron cooking pots and pans, and seeds for their crops. They carried cloth, clothing, wine, sugar, raisins, and honey to trade for cows, pigs, and horses in Virginia. Whatever they did not bring or could not buy, they would do without until the next ship arrived from England.

One of the two ships that carried the first settlers to Maryland in 1634 was the Dove. *This replica, the* Maryland Dove, *is docked at St. Mary's City.*

TWO PASSENGERS OF THE *ARK*

Mathias de Sousa

Mathias de Sousa, Maryland's first black resident, arrived at St. Mary's on the *Ark* in 1634. Of mixed African and European descent, he was an indentured servant of one of the Jesuits. Like other indentured servants, he later became a freeman of the colony. He was hired as skipper of a vessel that was engaged in trade with the Indians. He exercised his political right to attend the General Assembly. At some later time, however, he became an indentured servant again.

Father Andrew White

At age 54, Father White, an English-born Jesuit priest, was probably the oldest passenger on the *Ark*. His "Brief Relation of the Voyage unto Maryland" is our most vivid account of the voyage of the *Ark* and the *Dove* and of the founding of the colony. Once he arrived in the colony, Father White conducted missionary work among local Indians. He learned their language, compiled a dictionary and a grammar, and wrote a catechism for the instruction of Indian converts. In 1645 a Protestant rebel captured Father White and took him back to England in chains.

term of years in return for free passage. Once they completed their years of servitude, they, too, would be freemen, and they might acquire land of their own in America.

The two ships made stops in the West Indies and Virginia, and then, in early March, after a voyage of more than three months, they sailed into the Chesapeake Bay and up the Potomac River. Here the passengers hoped to locate a site for their settlement.

The New World

When the colonists on the *Ark* and the *Dove* sailed through the mouth of the Bay at Capes Henry and Charles, they encountered one of the most distinctive features of Maryland's geography. The Chesapeake Bay, the submerged mouth of the Susquehanna River, is the largest inlet on the East Coast. The Maryland portion of the Bay stretches 195 miles in length and includes an area of nearly 2,000 square miles. By comparison, the colony contained about 10,000 square miles (or 7 million acres) of land.

The Geography of Maryland

Numerous rivers drain into the Bay on both shores, forming large necks of land on the Western Shore and many smaller fingers of land on the eastern side. More than 150 rivers, creeks, and branches feed into the Bay. This water network gives Maryland a tidal shoreline of about 3,000 miles, roughly equal to the distance between Maryland and England. The rivers and creeks served as roads for the early settlers and allowed them to trade from their own home docks, or landings, directly with England. Large vessels, for example, could sail 110 miles up the Potomac River (to present-day Georgetown) and 55 miles up the Patuxent River.

Maryland has three major geographical regions. The land on both sides of the Bay forms the coastal plain, or tidewater, region, a low, flat area with light, sandy soils, swamps, and tidal marshes. West of the coastal plain lies the Piedmont region. It extends from the fall line, the first series of rapids on the rivers, to the Blue Ridge Mountains. This area is marked by rolling hills and fertile soil. Finally, the Appalachian region is a forested, mountainous area covering the western portion of the state from the Blue Ridge

Mountains to Garrett County. Here the valleys provided passages through the mountains for the settlers who were moving west.

The land supported a variety of plants and animals. Virgin forests of oak, walnut, pine, cedar, poplar, hickory, maple, black gum, elm, ash, and chestnut trees covered the colony. Strawberries and raspberries, sorrel and other herbs, grape vines and fruit trees, grew in abundance. Bears, elk, deer, wolves, and wildcats roamed the woods. Squirrels, rabbits, wild turkeys, foxes, and other small game animals were plentiful. Flocks of geese, ducks, cranes, and wild pigeons filled the sky. Terrapin, crabs, and oysters were there for the taking; shad, herring, bass, and many other species of fish swam in the waters of the Bay and its tributaries.

Promotional literature put out by Cecilius Calvert, Lord Baltimore, in 1633 promised settlers "many other commodities, which time, industry and Art will discover, the fruites whereof may be easier tasted, then beleeved." The natural environment of the Chesapeake region did not disappoint the Europeans who settled there.

Maryland Indians

Long before the colonists arrived, Indians had been living around the Chesapeake and enjoying the region's natural abundance. The first Indians reached Maryland 13,000 to 10,000 years ago, during the glacial period. These semi-nomadic people, known as Paleo-Indians, moved through the area hunting the large game animals—mammoths, great bison, and caribou, for example—that could survive the cold climate. They also ate nuts, berries, and fish.

When the climate warmed and the glaciers melted, about 10,000 years ago, the big game animals died out. Forests replaced grasslands, and smaller game animals like deer became the main sources of food and clothing. During this period, known as the Archaic, Indians gathered into more permanent villages. They depended more heavily on fish and wild plants for their food.

About 1000 B.C., the Woodland period began. Agriculture played a major role in the Indian food supply, and corn became the most important crop. Indians also raised beans, peas, squash, sunflowers, and tobacco. Women and children gathered wild plants, berries, and nuts. The men hunted wild birds and game animals and fished the Bay and rivers for crabs, shrimp, oysters, eels, and fish.

By the seventeenth century about 40 Indian tribes lived in the area that formed Lord Baltimore's province. Nearly all were part of

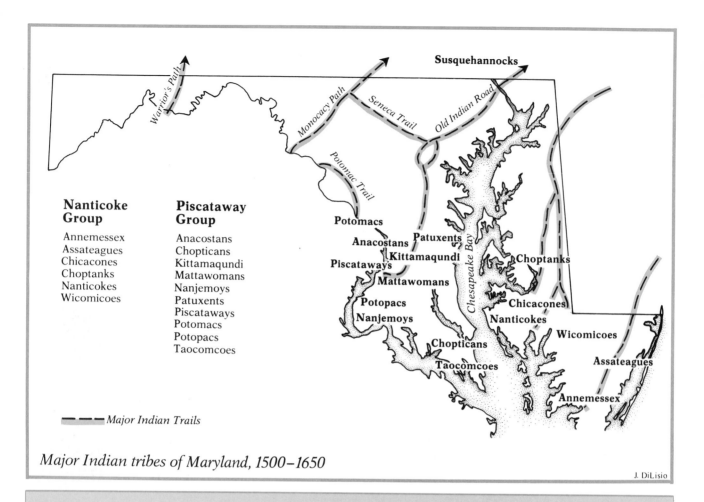

Nanticoke Group

Annemessex
Assateagues
Chicacones
Choptanks
Nanticokes
Wicomicoes

Piscataway Group

Anacostans
Chopticans
Kittamaqundi
Mattawomans
Nanjemoys
Patuxents
Piscataways
Potomacs
Potopacs
Taocomcoes

Potomacs
Anacostans
Patuxents
Kittamaqundi
Piscataways
Mattawomans
Choptanks
Potopacs
Nanjemoys
Chicacones
Nanticokes
Chopticans
Wicomicoes
Taocomcoes
Assateagues
Annemessex

Chesapeake Bay

Warrior's Path
Monocacy Path
Seneca Trail
Old Indian Road
Potomac Trail

‑ ‑ ‑ *Major Indian Trails*

Major Indian tribes of Maryland, 1500–1650

J. DiLisio

WOODLAND INDIAN LIFE

In 1608, Captain John Smith depicted this Susquehannock brave carrying his bow, his club, and the animal he killed during the hunt.

Indian women and children raised crops of tobacco and corn and other vegetables. Women loosened the soil with a crude hoe and planted the seeds, while children were responsible for weeding. Young boys were also "living scarecrows." They sat on sheltered platforms, ready to scare away birds that tried to eat the crops. Indian women also wove mats and baskets and made clay pottery for cooking and holding water. Indian men hunted and fished to supply meat and skins.

The wigwams in which the Indians lived usually held one large room that was shared by several families. The rooms were arched, and generally were 20 feet long, 15 feet wide, and 10 feet high. In winter the Indians built fires on the dirt floor, and the smoke escaped through a hole in the roof. Low benches, lining the wall and covered with mats, served as beds.

Indian clothing, made of deerskins, consisted of an apronlike garment worn by both men and women. Long cloaks and leggings were added in colder weather. Indians also wore ornaments made of beads, shells, animal teeth and bones, and copper. In addition, Indians sometimes decorated their bodies with tattoos or painted designs. Both men and women wore their hair long, but men usually had more elaborate hairstyles and dressed more colorfully.

Indians believed that in addition to human beings, water, stone, fire, and animals also possessed a spirit. They made sacrifices to these spirits in order to bring themselves good luck. Woodland Indians had several religious ceremonies in which they performed special songs and dances and said prayers.

the Algonquin stock that extended from the Carolinas to Hudson's Bay in Canada. Lower Western Shore tribes, such as the Choptico, Mattawoman, and Patuxent, belonged to a loose federation. The Piscataway were the dominant tribe, and their chief acted as the tayac, or emperor, of the federation. On the Eastern Shore, the Nanticokes formed the largest tribe, with about 1,500 members. They provided leadership for smaller tribes such as the Choptank, Pocomoke, and Wicomico. A third group, the powerful Susquehannocks, lived at the head of the Bay and were members of the Iroquois nation. In all, the Indians numbered about 8,000 to 10,000 people.

Typically, Woodland Indians were village dwellers. They lived in wigwams made of a frame of tree limbs covered with bark or grass mats. Within the villages, the hereditary chief and his advisors enjoyed a higher social status than the rest of the tribe. Each village also recognized the leadership of the tayac.

The tribes of the Chesapeake region traded goods with one another in networks that reached as far as the Ohio valley. Trade was made easier by the use of a form of money known as wampum, from the Algonquin word meaning "white strings." Peak, the more valuable form of wampum, consisted of strings of polished dark purple or white shells. Roanoke, worth only one-half to one-third as much, was made of broken pieces of unpolished shells. Bark canoes and log dugouts carried Indians up and down the region's rivers to trade furs and other goods. A network of foot trails, mostly running north and south, connected hunting lands and villages and served also as trade routes.

European Exploration

Europeans visited the Indians of the Chesapeake region as early as the sixteenth century. Spanish explorers left records of visits in 1524, 1525, and 1561 in which they described the Chesapeake as the best and largest port in the world. The first lengthy exploration of the Maryland portion of the Bay occurred in 1608, when the English Captain John Smith led two expeditions from Jamestown, Virginia, that probed the rivers on both sides of the Bay. Smith used the knowledge gained on these trips to draw the first detailed map of the Chesapeake, which he decorated with a drawing of a Susquehannock warrior.

After Smith's visit, the Maryland tribes continued to have occasional contact with Europeans who came to trade or to explore the region. Settlers moved in as well. Virginians began to settle Accomac and Northampton counties on the lower end of the Eastern Shore. In 1631, William Claiborne set up a trading post on Kent Island. As many as 100 people lived there by 1634. There were unfriendly encounters also. Indian uprisings in Virginia in 1622 set off raids against the Piscataway and other tribes. A more important source of trouble for the Algonquin tribes, however, was raids by the warlike Susquehannocks that Smith had pictured on his map.

These experiences with white settlers and Indian groups in Virginia and on the Eastern Shore of Maryland affected the way Western Shore Indian tribes received the colonists on the *Ark* and the *Dove*. While the Indians were suspicious of these newly arrived Europeans, they also looked on them as potential allies against the Susquehannocks and thus allowed them to settle peacefully.

Early Years of Settlement

St. Mary's City, the first settlement in Maryland, was built on land that had already been cleared by local Yaocomico Indians. The Indians helped the colonists cultivate their first crops.

The *Ark* and the *Dove* landed at St. Clement's Island in the Potomac River on March 5, 1634. Lord Baltimore's younger brother, Leonard Calvert, who was the governor of the colony, led a small party of men up the river to meet with the tayac of the Piscataway federation. The tayac did not invite the English colonists to stay in his territory but, remembering the Susquehannocks, neither did he ask them to leave. Instead, he gave them permission to settle where they wished. Calvert and the others then rejoined the ships anchored off St. Clement's Island, and there, on March 25, the Jesuits offered a mass of thanksgiving. The day is still celebrated annually as Maryland Day.

St. Mary's City

Calvert and his men set off again to look for a place to settle. They struck a bargain with the Yaocomicos, a peaceful farming and hunting tribe, for their village land. The settlers gave the Indians cloth, hatchets, and hoes; in exchange, the Indians agreed to turn half the village over to the settlers immediately, and to give them the rest of the village the following year. The Indians would stay for one year to help the colonists grow their first crops and to teach them the skills they would need to live in the New World.

Three days later the rest of the colonists arrived at the site, which they named St. Mary's City, and immediately built a fort to add to the site's natural defenses. Over the next few years, they added about 10 houses, a storehouse, a mill, a Catholic chapel, and a blacksmith's forge. The settlers never built the town they had planned, however. The fur trade proved to be a failure and they did not find the gold or silver that many colonists had hoped for. Instead, Maryland settlers quickly turned to agriculture and made tobacco their cash crop. To grow tobacco, which was too bulky and fragile to be carried far over land, profitably, planters needed easy access to waterfront landings. Reliance on tobacco led to scattered settlement, not the growth of towns.

Settlement Patterns

The large investors took land for their manors along the main bodies of water: the bay itself, St. Mary's River, and the Potomac and Patuxent rivers and their branches. Ordinary freemen located their plantations near the manors. As these banks filled up, the same process was repeated along new rivers. Colonists did not begin settling the interior of an area until the waterfront lands were claimed.

Population grew slowly during the early years and depended on immigration for its growth. By 1642 there were probably between 340 and 390 people in the colony. These settlers were the survivors of the 500 or more people who had immigrated since 1634. Nearly all immigrants underwent a period of sickness, known as seasoning, and many died, most likely from malaria and dysentery. Others were left too weak to survive later illnesses. Thus, more than one of every five persons who came to Maryland seeking opportunity found only death.

By 1642 settlers had claimed only 37,000 acres of the 7 million in the colony. Ownership was unevenly divided. Sixteen manors accounted for 31,000 acres, while many smaller freemen held the other 6,000 acres. The average size of the smaller plantations was only 125 acres. Despite these claims, very little of the land was cleared for growing crops. Much of the land remained as it had been before the colonial grant, marked only by the villages and trails of the Indian tribes who lived there.

St. Mary's City functioned as the seat of the colonial government from 1634 to 1694. This replica of the colonial State House was built in 1934.

The Government of the Colony

Although the colonists had barely made a mark on the vast wilderness, they were not isolated from European civilization. Ships that came to Maryland to collect tobacco brought new settlers and news from home. They carried supplies of tools, cloth, salt, and other essentials that were not made in the colony. Marylanders also maintained ties with England by establishing a familiar pattern of government.

Leonard Calvert served as the governor of Maryland and three gentlemen appointed by Lord Baltimore served as his council of advisors. A secretary kept the colony's records and oversaw the distribution of land. Together these five men made up the executive branch of the government.

The judicial branch was formed by the governor and the council, who met as the Provincial Court. Englishmen who came to Maryland brought with them English common law and a long legal tradition. The Provincial Court settled disputes over land and collection of debts, quarrels between neighbors or husband and wife, questions of inheritance, and many other matters.

The charter had given Lord Baltimore the power to make laws with the agreement of the freemen, and it was also practical to consult with the colonists to encourage their acceptance of the government and its actions. Thus, a legislature, called the General Assembly, or the Assembly, was established.

By 1650 the Assembly had assumed the form it would keep for the remainder of the colonial period. The governor and council made up the Upper House. Delegates to the Lower House were elected directly by voters in each county. In the earliest years of settlement, all freemen could vote for delegates. Eventually, however, restrictions concerning religion and ownership of land or other property limited the right to vote.

Daily Life

Whether living in a household of their own or as servants in someone else's home, most early settlers spent a life with few comforts. Maryland never experienced the "starving time" of the first settlements in Virginia and New England, however. The colonists grew corn as their main source of food, and they also grew beans, peas, squash, and other vegetables. Within a few years there were enough cattle and pigs to feed both residents and newcomers. Tobacco provided a small income for buying goods that had to be imported.

When they could spare time from working in the fields, settlers had to build homes for themselves. In the earliest years, their homes were usually small, one-story wood-frame buildings covered with split boards or a mixture of clay and twigs. Houses like these had only one or two rooms and few furnishings: a mattress of straw or cattails (but no bed frame), a chest or two for storage, perhaps a crudely made table and some benches, a few iron pots, and wooden bowls and utensils.

Servants were mainly expected to clear land and raise crops and livestock, so most of the servants brought into the colony were young men. Until well into the seventeenth century, the population of Maryland consisted mostly of young, single men. Masters did not allow their servants to marry. Not even all the freemen could find wives, however, for there were few women in the colony.

As indentured servants became free, their places were taken by new indentured servants who arrived by ship. However, former servants did not easily join the ranks of landowners. Often they continued to work for their former masters and live with them while trying to save money. They needed cash or credit to pay the costs of surveying and patenting, or filing claim to, land. They needed money to build a house and stock a plantation with tools, livestock, and other necessities.

The task of creating a society out of a wilderness proved to be a difficult one. Many of those who attempted to make a life for them-

The Godiah Spray Tobacco Plantation in St. Mary's City recreates a small house and garden like the ones the early settlers lived and worked in. Women tended the garden, growing vegetables and herbs, while men worked in the fields to produce tobacco and corn.

selves in the New World died before they had any success, while few of those who survived a normal life span became rich. Nonetheless, the first settlers, both rich and poor, established a toehold that later generations could build on.

A "Time of Troubles"

Cecilius Calvert, Lord Baltimore, originally planned to sail with the first expedition to Maryland. However, attempts were made in the early 1630s to block his charter, and he was convinced that it would not be wise to leave England. Similar concerns prevented later visits, and Cecilius died in 1675 without ever having visited his colony. Although he was unable to join the settlement, Cecilius protected his charter and outlasted his enemies by staying in England.

Challenges to Lord Baltimore

Initial opposition to Lord Baltimore's grant came from the "Virginia interests," a group of English merchants and Chesapeake planters. They fought Baltimore's grant because it included land that they considered to be part of Virginia. They also feared that a colony in Maryland would slow Virginia's growth and threaten their control of the Chesapeake economy. While they did not stop Baltimore from getting his charter, they did keep the lower Eastern Shore in Virginia.

Kent Island was another source of conflict. William Claiborne argued that his trading post there was a cultivated settlement and, because the charter had given Baltimore only "uncultivated" land, that his post should be exempt from Baltimore's rule. A combination of force and rewards finally gave the government at St. Mary's control over the Kent Island settlers. By 1638 Kent had become a second county and sent delegates to the Assembly, but Claiborne and his supporters did not accept the proprietor's rule for many years, and they occasionally rebelled to regain control of the island.

Maryland's harmony was further disrupted when civil war broke out in England in the 1640s. The war concerned both religious and political issues. Anglicans, Catholics, Puritans, and other Protestants had many deep-seated disagreements. Politically, Parliament vied with the king for power. In 1642 fighting broke out, and for a while the Puritans prevailed. In 1649 they beheaded King Charles I, then took control of the English government. Only in 1660 was royal power restored.

Fighting among different groups in England inevitably spilled over into Maryland. With a Catholic proprietor and governing elite and a mostly Protestant population, Maryland could not avoid being drawn into the fight. A Puritan ship captain, Richard Ingle, and his men attacked the colony in 1645. Governor Leonard Calvert and other settlers fled to Virginia. In 1646 Leonard Calvert recruited soldiers in Virginia and used them to recapture the province. Those who lived through the nearly two years of Ingle's Rebellion called the period the "time of troubles" or the "plundering time."

MARGARET BRENT: VOICE FOR WOMEN'S RIGHTS

Margaret Brent was one of the first women to settle in early Maryland. The daughter of Richard Brent, a wealthy English Catholic landowner, she arrived in the colony in 1638, when she was about 37 years old, with her sister and two brothers. She and her sister settled in St. Mary's City, where Margaret Brent became an active member of the community. Suits concerning the sale of imported servants or the collection of debts brought her into court, and, because she was unmarried, she could appear in court on her own behalf. Margaret also owned property on Kent Island, where she had several houses and a mill, as well as servants, who raised tobacco and looked after livestock.

Maryland's first governor, Leonard Calvert, named Margaret as the executor of his will. She had to manage his property, pay his debts, and turn the estate over to his heirs. Margaret assumed this role during a time of crisis, as soldiers who had helped Calvert win back the colony during Ingle's Rebellion now demanded their pay, and the colony faced a shortage of food. The Assembly gave Margaret, as the governor's executor, authority to act as Lord Baltimore's attorney. She sold cattle belonging to the Calverts in order to pay the soldiers, buy food, and avert the crisis.

In 1648 she appeared before the Assembly to demand two votes, one for herself as a landowner and one as Lord Baltimore's attorney. The delegates refused her request, although they praised her efforts to resolve the crisis. Lord Baltimore's anger over the sale of the cattle caused Margaret to leave Maryland, and the Brents moved across the Potomac to Virginia, where Margaret died by 1671.

Puritan Settlement

After Leonard Calvert died in 1647, Cecilius Calvert, Lord Baltimore, tried to ease religious tensions in the colony by naming a Protestant governor to replace his brother. He also added several Protestants to the council. In addition, the new governor, William Stone, promised a group of about 300 Virginia Puritans land, toleration, and full civil rights if they settled in Maryland. These Puritans received land on the Severn River, near the later settlement of Annapolis. The Assembly in 1649 passed an "Act Concerning Religion" which granted toleration to all Christian denominations. This was the first such legislation in the English-speaking world.

Toleration of religions other than their own, however, was not a Puritan trait. They took control of the colony in 1654, defeated the governor and his soldiers in a 1655 skirmish known as the Battle of the Severn, and held power until November 1657. Lord Baltimore regained control of Maryland and agreed to grant amnesty to his opponents. The act of toleration, which the Puritans had repealed, was restored.

The last serious threat to Baltimore's rule came in 1660. It was an uncertain affair known as Fendall's Rebellion, after the governor who was involved. Lord Baltimore termed the revolt the "pygmie rebellion," because it lasted so briefly.

TOBACCO

Tobacco required more effort to grow than any other Maryland crop. Workers were busy in the fields from early spring to late fall, and tobacco-related tasks filled their winter hours, as well.

Planters cleared land for their crops by cutting a groove around tree trunks, thereby killing the trees. The dead trees were left standing, but they produced no leaves that would keep sunlight from reaching the tobacco plants. In early spring, seeds saved from the previous year's crop were sown in a special bed, and by June the plants were large enough to be moved, on a damp day, to the cleared fields. Seedlings were planted four feet apart among the trees. Every day, workers hoed the fields to kill weeds and picked tobacco worms off the plants. When enough leaves had formed on the tobacco plants, workers pinched off the tops of the plants to keep them from flowering.

In the fall, when the tobacco was fully ripe, the entire plant was cut, carried to the tobacco house, and hung to dry for about six weeks. When the leaves had dried enough to prevent rotting but not enough to crumble, they were stripped from the stalk and packed in large barrels known as hogsheads. The hogsheads were then rolled to the waterfront to be loaded on the ships that would take them to England. During the winter, workers cleared new fields and prepared hogsheads for the next year's crop.

thermore, in the fighting, homes, livestock, outbuildings, and crops that colonists had worked long hours to accumulate had been destroyed.

Nevertheless, new counties were created throughout the period, so growth, as well as turmoil, was a part of the seventeenth century. The small planter living in Charles County or Somerset County was not likely to be concerned with challenges to Baltimore's rule. He was occupied with clearing a new field for a crop of tobacco or building a tobacco house to hold the crop. He worried about the weather or the price of tobacco.

The Tobacco Economy

By the time the Maryland settlement began, Virginians had already established tobacco as the money crop for the Chesapeake region. Both the climate and the soil were suitable, and there were European customers for the "stinking weed," as it was known. Planters around the Chesapeake concentrated on producing tobacco. They used the money they received for their crop to buy manufactured goods from Europe. In time, larger planters began to buy cloth, tools, and other items in quantity, which they then sold to their less wealthy neighbors. In return, they took the small planter's tobacco or gave him credit.

The ordinary planter, working by himself, could tend up to three acres of tobacco a year. In addition, he grew corn to feed himself and his household. He raised hogs and cattle for meat and milk and other dairy products, and for leather to make shoes and clothing. As time allowed, colonists planted apple orchards and grew vegetables and herbs. To move beyond subsistence, or the ability to satisfy basic needs, a planter needed more than just his own labor. If he married, he had the help of his wife, and of their children when they were old enough.

Bound Labor

To obtain greater profits from farming, the planter had to use bound, or unfree, labor. Initially, the bound workers were indentured servants. After completing their service, servants received freedom dues from their master—clothing, corn, and a few tools—and the right to claim 50 acres of land. Many servants eventually did become landowners, after paying ownership fees. The most successful brought the process full circle by acquiring servants of their own. Masters replaced former servants with new ones, and the population grew.

THE PLANTER'S WIFE

For most of the seventeenth century, planters' wives were immigrants who had survived seasoning and completed their terms as servants. Most of these women, therefore, married in their mid-twenties. Furthermore, because of high mortality in the Chesapeake region, only one in three marriages lasted even ten years. Most marriages produced three or four children. Of these children, one probably died as an infant and one or two more died before they became adults. Thus, the planter's wife might see only one of her children reach maturity.

Exposure to malaria made childbearing riskier for Chesapeake wives, as pregnant women were particularly vulnerable to malaria. Those who did survive childbearing were likely to survive their husbands as well, for wives were often much younger. Generally, widows with small children to feed and a tobacco crop to grow soon remarried.

In addition to raising the children, the planter's wife prepared the family food, which was a time-consuming task. For example, corn had to be ground into flour in a mortar or handmill before it could be baked as bread. She also washed the family's clothing and linens, and sometimes made the clothing, as well. In a large household, these jobs probably consumed most of her time, but she found time to raise vegetables in a kitchen garden, milk the cows, and make butter and cheese. Toward the end of the century, as tobacco earnings fell, wives did more spinning and weaving to make cloth for the family's clothing. In households without any laborers, wives undoubtedly provided valuable help in the fields, as well.

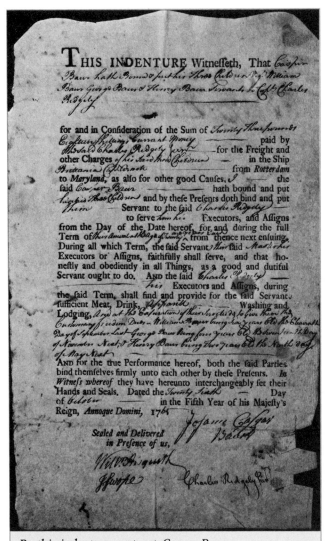

By this indenture contract, Casper Baur agreed to have his three children—William, age 6, George, age 4, and Henry, age 2— work as servants for Captain Charles Ridgely until their twentieth birthdays. In exchange, Ridgely provided free passage to the New World and food, clothing, lodging, and laundry.

Merchant-Planters

Men with enough wealth to import a large number of servants acquired more land and therefore harvested larger crops. Their large income allowed them to buy extra imported goods to sell to their neighbors. They also speculated in land, buying large lots that they resold when the price of land was higher.

As merchant-planters, they organized the colony's commercial agriculture and trade. Because of their wealth, they held prominent social positions in their neighborhoods and counties and took part in the government of the colony. If they lived long enough to marry and have children, they also contributed to the growth of the native-born elite that governed the colony in the eighteenth century.

Merchant-planters were also least hurt by a depression of the tobacco market in the 1680s. When tobacco prices began to fall, small planters increasingly lacked cash or credit to buy bound labor. At the same time, the supply of indentured servants dwindled. By the 1690s, slaves began to replace servants as the colony's bound labor force. However, only wealthy planters could afford to buy slaves, who cost more because they served for life.

Slaves and Other Africans

Although most of the manual labor in Maryland was performed by bound workers from Europe before 1690, a few Africans were living in the colony by that time. Most Africans, then and later, came involuntarily. Their legal status, however, was not clearly defined. Records are few, but there are examples of Africans who served as indentured servants. When they completed their term and received their freedom, some became landowners.

Some of the laws that affected the large number of slaves who came later were worked out during this early period. After the arrival of 13 Africans at St. Mary's City in 1642, such laws began to evolve. Colonial courts frequently decided that a slave who was baptised as a Christian could be freed. In order to prevent the loss of their slaves, the planters in the Maryland Assembly passed a law in 1664 which said that baptism should not affect a slave's status. Several years later, the Assembly officially encouraged masters to convert their slaves to Christianity.

One of the harshest aspects of the American system of slavery began in Maryland in 1663, when the Assembly ruled that all blacks brought into the colony should be slaves for life. The law specified that children of slaves should also serve as slaves for life. Only a few people were affected when these laws were first passed, as the first large-scale arrivals of African slaves occurred in the late 1690s.

Ethnic and Religious Groups

During the seventeenth century, the lure of tobacco-based wealth drew thousands of immigrants to the Maryland colony. These immigrants differed considerably in status. Some were wealthy landowners, and others were bound workers.

The people who came to Maryland had different ethnic backgrounds. Most slaves came from regions along the west coast of Africa, and some had lived in the West Indies. Almost all of the other immigrants were Europeans, most of them from the British Isles. A few Dutch, French, German, and Italian settlers arrived during the century. The dominant British element were the English. The Scotch-Irish, the second largest British element, began to settle on the Eastern Shore in the 1680s.

The colonists brought more religious than ethnic diversity to Maryland. For the first fifteen years, most of the settlers belonged to the Anglican and Roman Catholic faiths, and then Puritans came by way of Virginia in 1649. The Scotch-Irish were predominantly Presbyterians. Although they were persecuted in most other colonies, members of the Society of Friends, or Quakers, found asylum in Lord Baltimore's colony. In particular, Quakers formed an influential part of the community in Anne Arundel County and on the Eastern Shore.

A native-born population also developed in the seventeenth century. By about the end of the century, the majority of Maryland inhabitants had been born in the colony, and population growth depended on births rather than on immigration.

Effects on the Environment

The growing population, the spreading settlement, the continued clearing of land for crops, and the introduction of livestock had severe effects on the environment. The light soils of the bayside coastal plain washed away easily in heavy rains, particularly after they had been broken up for planting, and the runoff caused silting in streams and creeks. Silt killed marine life and blocked passage for larger ships. Tobacco crops used up important soil nutrients of lime and potash in 4 to 6 years time. Planters had to abandon fields for a period of 15 to 20 years to allow the soil to recover its fertility. In the meantime, other fields had to be cleared and planted. A planter had to own 20 acres of tobacco land for every worker on a plantation so that he could rest worn-out fields.

As settlers claimed more and more land in the colony, they made it harder for Indians to follow their traditional practice of combining hunting and agriculture for their livelihood. Settlers slaughtered fur-bearing animals (either for their skins or because they threatened livestock), constantly cleared woodland, and destroyed plants and animals that Indians relied on, so Indians became increasingly dependent on Europeans for food, clothing, utensils, and other goods.

In addition, Europeans introduced alcohol and smallpox to the New World; both were destructive. Smallpox, in particular, decimated the native population. Many smaller tribes simply moved away or disappeared as other tribes took in their remaining members. A few, such as the Piscataways, managed to coexist with the settlers during the seventeenth century. The Nanticokes and the Choptank asked for and received land in Dorchester County to use as reservations. Settling on reservations bought time for the two tribes, but it did not provide a permanent solution to their problems.

The Royal Period, 1689-1715

In 1689, a group of Maryland colonists succeeded where earlier settlers had failed. They were able to take control of the province from Charles Calvert, the third Lord Baltimore. For 25 years, Maryland was a royal rather than a proprietary colony, and as such it was administered directly by the Crown rather than by Lord Baltimore. The Calvert family regained the government of the province in 1715, only after Benedict Leonard Calvert, who had earlier converted to the Anglican faith, inherited the title Lord Baltimore from his father. The Calverts, however, continued to own the land and to collect quitrents throughout the royal period.

The Revolution of 1689

Two main sources of tension in the colony were behind the revolution of 1689. Like the causes of the earlier conflicts, the problems had mixed religious and political origins. First, Protestants resented Baltimore's practice of giving provincial offices to his kin

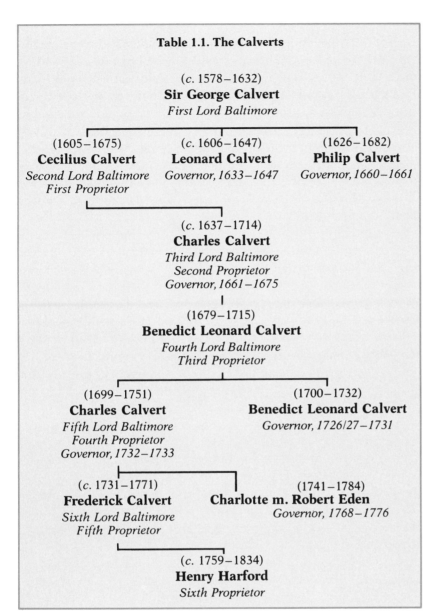

Table 1.1. The Calverts

(*c.* 1578–1632)
Sir George Calvert
First Lord Baltimore

(1605–1675)
Cecilius Calvert
Second Lord Baltimore
First Proprietor

(*c.* 1606–1647)
Leonard Calvert
Governor, 1633–1647

(1626–1682)
Philip Calvert
Governor, 1660–1661

(*c.* 1637–1714)
Charles Calvert
Third Lord Baltimore
Second Proprietor
Governor, 1661–1675

(1679–1715)
Benedict Leonard Calvert
Fourth Lord Baltimore
Third Proprietor

(1699–1751)
Charles Calvert
Fifth Lord Baltimore
Fourth Proprietor
Governor, 1732–1733

(1700–1732)
Benedict Leonard Calvert
Governor, 1726/27–1731

(*c.* 1731–1771)
Frederick Calvert
Sixth Lord Baltimore
Fifth Proprietor

(1741–1784)
Charlotte m. Robert Eden
Governor, 1768–1776

(*c.* 1759–1834)
Henry Harford
Sixth Proprietor

and Catholics. Second, Baltimore's policy of toleration aided Catholic and dissenting faiths more than the Anglican church, the official Church of England. Because it lacked government support, the Anglican church in Maryland had few ministers and places of worship.

Discontented colonists seized the opportunity given them by events in England. In 1689, Parliament replaced the Catholic king, James II, with his Protestant daughter, Mary, and her husband, William of Orange. The English called this peaceful change the

Glorious Revolution. The events in England gave those opposed to Lord Baltimore their chance. In July 1689, John Coode and other Protestant leaders on the lower Western Shore gathered a force of men. By the first of August they had taken control of the government at St. Mary's.

The colony's new leaders, known as the Protestant Association, asked the Crown to establish a Protestant government for Maryland. At the same time, the Association called a new General Assembly. During its session, the Assembly named civil and military officials for all counties. This government ruled the colony peacefully for the next two years, in a bloodless change of authority.

When the royal governor, Lionel Copley, arrived in 1692, a new Assembly was chosen. Use of standing committees made the Assembly a smaller, colonial version of Parliament. One of the main factors behind the successful revolt of the colonies from England in the next century was the long experience of self-government that the settlers obtained in their own colonial assemblies. Marylanders began that learning process in earnest with their "revolution in government."

Francis Nicholson, Royal Governor

Copley's death in 1693 brought Francis Nicholson to Maryland as the next royal governor. Nicholson strongly influenced the colony's development in several ways. One of his first actions was to propose moving the capital from St. Mary's, which was on the edge of the settled area. An act of 1694 made the more centrally located "Arundell Town" the new capital. Annapolis, as it was renamed in 1695, owes its distinctive plan of circles, squares, and radiating streets to a design by Nicholson.

Nicholson's concern for education also aided the colony. In response to his interest, the Assembly in 1696 passed an act founding King William's School in Annapolis. King William's School was the first Maryland school supported by public money. The school would instruct male students in Greek, Latin, writing, and other subjects to prepare them to enter the newly formed College of William and Mary in Virginia. Nicholson supported the venture with gifts of money and land.

The Establishment of the Anglican Church

Nicholson's efforts also benefited the Anglican church. An act of the Association Assembly had made the Anglican faith the official religion of the colony, but no action was taken to put the law into effect until Nicholson became governor. When he came to Maryland, the colony had only three qualified Anglican ministers; in contrast, Quakers met in one of seventeen weekly meetings, as their congregations are called, and eight priests cared for Catholic colonists.

Nicholson took several steps to make the Anglican church stronger. He offered to give money to each parish that built a house and provided land for a minister, and worked effectively with the bishop of London to find ministers for all of the colony's parishes. Finally, he succeeded in having a local supervisor appointed to oversee the church. Passage of a poll tax also aided the Anglican church. Forty pounds of tobacco were collected for each taxable person to pay the salaries of the parish ministers.

Thus, Catholics, Quakers, and other dissenters paid taxes to support the Anglican church, but they had to raise funds among themselves for their own meetings or churches. Furthermore, Quakers lost their right to sit in the Assembly. Catholics, facing the strongest discrimination, were forbidden to hold any public office and to celebrate mass in public.

War and the Tobacco Market

The years of royal rule were also years of international warfare that hurt the colony. England fought against France in King William's War from 1689 to 1697 and then Queen Anne's War from 1702 to 1713. Attacks on tobacco ships by French privateers disrupted the tobacco trade. Governor Nicholson obtained convoys of British warships to sail with the tobacco fleets, but trade continued to be limited by the fighting. Tobacco exports fell, and the supply of European imports dried up. Shortages forced many settlers to make their own cloth, shoes, and other items, or do without.

The colony experienced a short economic boom during the brief period between the two wars, as the European market for tobacco opened up again. During these years, large shipments of slaves began arriving. Slaves, who accounted for only 3,000 of the colony's people in 1697, totaled nearly 8,000, roughly 18 percent of Maryland's population, in 1710. The greater number of slaves accompanied the growth of a new group of planters. The great planters, who owned a dozen or more workers and vast tracts of land, began to emerge as a distinct group within the population.

Maryland in Transition

Maryland society at the end of the royal period reflected the changes that took place during the preceding century. Instead of an immigrant population of young men, there was a larger native-born population made up of family groups. Instead of a society with a very few wealthy men and a large number of small landowners or tenants, there was a broader variety of small, middling, and large planters. A labor force of permanently enslaved blacks began to replace short-term white servants. Large planters and the wealthiest of the middling group made up an elite that took an active part in both local and provincial government.

Even though the late seventeenth century was a time of political and economic difficulties, life improved in many ways. Families began to enjoy the benefits of the work done by their fathers and grandfathers, who had settled the colony. Colonists could now devote some of their income to expanding or rebuilding the family home, or filling it with better furnishings. The bare existence of the early years began to give way to a lifestyle with more comforts.

The royal period thus marked a pivotal era in the colony's history. In these years, the province went through a transformation from an experiment in colony building to an Anglo-American society firmly planted in the New World.

Colonial Politics

Throughout the royal period, members of the Calvert family worked in England to get their proprietorship restored. When the Calvert heirs converted to Protestantism, King George I was convinced to return Maryland to their authority. In 1715, Benedict Calvert, the fourth Lord Baltimore, became proprietor of Maryland. When he died eight weeks later, the title and the proprietorship passed to his teenage son, Charles, the fifth Lord Baltimore.

The changes that took place during the period of royal rule meant that the Calverts and their appointed governors faced a political situation that differed greatly from the situation their predecessors had faced two decades earlier. Religious discrimination was the law. The population was larger, and it was divided into identifiable social groups. Maryland's local leaders had grown in both wealth and political experience. They had effectively challenged the power of the later royal governors and were prepared to stand up to the proprietor for their own interests.

Leaders of the emerging Country party represented the colonists' views. The men who opposed the Country party consisted mainly of a small group around the governor, whom Lord Baltimore appointed. They included councillors and major provincial officeholders. Because these men owed their posts to Calvert, they were known as the Court party. Disputes between Court and Country parties did not occur continuously, but they did occur often during the years before the American Revolution.

Political Controversies

The proprietor and the Country party's delegates in the General Assembly fought in the 1720s and early 1730s on a number of issues. One of these centered on the claim made by the colonists that they enjoyed all the protections of English law. They claimed that they had the same rights as men living in England. Marylanders saw English law as protection against the power of Lord Baltimore and the officials he appointed.

A second dispute developed over the fees paid to colonial officials. Colonists, who paid the salaries, wanted to keep them as low as possible and to have their elected representatives in the Lower House determine what they would be. This also would increase the power of the elected representatives over the appointed officials.

The third disagreement centered on an economic issue. Tobacco had been used as money in colonial Maryland, but it was bulky to carry around. Also, it was difficult to make small payments with tobacco. The colonists wanted their government to print paper money and authorize its use in Maryland, but the proprietor had refused this request.

Disagreements between the two sides brought some sessions of the legislature to an early end. In other years, the governor avoided quarrelsome meetings by simply not calling the delegates into session. The Country party often turned to the printing press to aid its fight. In 1728 a pamphlet entitled "The Right of the Inhabitants of Maryland to the Benefit of English Laws" set forth the party's views on the issue of the laws. In it, Daniel Dulany the Elder presented one of the earliest arguments on a theme that reappeared later in the struggle for independence. He claimed that the American colonists did, in fact, enjoy all the rights of Englishmen.

Daniel Dulany the Elder came to Maryland as an indentured servant. By the time he died, he was one of the wealthiest and most powerful men in the colony.

Lord Baltimore's Visit

The contest between the two parties reached a settlement of sorts when Charles Calvert visited the colony in 1732. The colonists greeted him in Annapolis with a royal salute, bonfires, dancing, and toasts of rum. A glittering social season did not distract the proprietor from the main goals of his visit, however. First, he silenced his most able opponent by naming Daniel Dulany the Elder to three provincial offices. Second, he agreed to the passage of a bill allowing the colony to print paper money.

Thus, Lord Baltimore won over his main opponent and accepted one of the programs sought by the Country party. He then settled the remaining issues of concern to him on his own terms. One of these involved his own finances. Since 1717 the proprietor had collected a duty on tobacco in place of the rents that landowners owed, but in 1733 Baltimore changed the policy and began collecting rents through local agents. His rent revenue totaled far more than the tobacco duty ever had. In later years, the proprietor always rejected proposals by the Lower House to return to a version of the old system.

Charles Calvert also settled the dispute over the payment of colonial officials. He specified that the governor would be paid a salary that did not depend on a vote by the Assembly. Thus, Lord Baltimore took from the delegates a strong weapon—control of the governor's salary—that other colonial assemblies used in fights with their governors. Finally, Baltimore settled the question of officers' fees by issuing a new table of fees by proclamation. Early in the summer of 1733, having settled the disputes to his satisfaction, Lord Baltimore sailed for England.

Baltimore's settlement left the Country party without strong leaders and without major issues. For a time, the governor, the chief officials in Maryland, and Lord Baltimore's staff in England directed the colony's affairs. The English secretaries and advisors issued instructions, drew up positions, appointed men to patronage offices, and examined laws for threats to Baltimore's powers. Along with Lord Baltimore, they enjoyed the income from the proprietor's revenues and a share of the fees paid to provincial officials.

Not until 1738 did the Country party enjoy a rebirth of leadership and assertiveness. Dr. Charles Carroll, a leading Anglican landowner, merchant, and iron manufacturer, and a group of similar men were elected to the Assembly, and they were prepared to challenge Lord Baltimore. Brief and stormy sessions characterized the legislature in the 1740s as delegates again took up the issue of officials' fees. Neither Governor Samuel Ogle nor Governor William Bladen, who followed him, could calm the protests. With a century of settlement behind them, the colonists were no longer willing to accept the subordinate role that the Maryland charter allowed them.

The Tobacco Inspection Act

The dispute over fees became mixed up with an effort to raise the price of tobacco. This happened because officials were paid in tobacco. In 1730 Virginia had passed a tobacco inspection act that succeeded in raising the price paid for Virginia tobacco. A similar system set up in Maryland would allow officials to inspect all tobacco and burn any of inferior quality. The superior quality tobacco would then command a higher price in England. Although fewer pounds of tobacco would be sold, the total income would be greater.

Maryland's Assembly insisted on including a provision for lowering the amount of tobacco paid as fees to the colonial officials and to the Anglican clergymen. For a while the proprietor would not accept a law that adjusted the fees for the increased value of the tobacco, but repeated letters from Daniel Dulany finally convinced him to accept the compromise.

A Period of Expansion

Tobacco was still the major export and source of revenue for Maryland during the eighteenth century. During this period, however, the colony began to develop a more diversified economy. Wheat brought new prosperity to both farmers and shippers, local craftsmen began to make goods, merchants began to sell goods imported from England, and the growing population built towns that became centers of trade and culture.

Changes in the Tobacco Trade

The return of normal trade following peace in Europe in 1713 accounted in part for the improvement in the tobacco economy. In addition, buyers from countries other than England, particularly French buyers, became more and more important as customers for Chesapeake tobacco.

DR. CHARLES CARROLL: COLONIAL MERCHANT

Dr. Charles Carroll was born in Ireland around 1691 and immigrated to Maryland sometime after 1715. Carroll, a convert to the Anglican faith, settled in Annapolis and established his medical practice. Beginning in 1738 he served as a delegate to the General Assembly from Anne Arundel County and acted as one of the leaders of the Country party.

Carroll practiced medicine until the last decade of his life. However, soon after he arrived in the colony, he began to expand his activities beyond medicine by taking the profits from his medical practice and investing them in land and in trade. He shipped his tobacco and his neighbors' tobacco to merchants in London and Bristol. He also sent cargoes of lumber, barrel staves, grain, and other food items to the West Indies, southern Europe, and the Wine Islands. In return, Carroll received cargoes of sugar, molasses, and wine, which he then sold, or else he received a form of payment called bills of exchange, which he could use to buy goods in England.

Carroll invested in the ships that carried his cargoes and in the land that produced them. In addition, he was one of the five men who began the Baltimore Iron Works. While Carroll's land purchases included working plantations, his major holdings were more than 28,000 acres of undeveloped western land. As new settlers moved into the area, Carroll subdivided his property and sold it at a profit. When he died in 1755, Carroll left his son, Charles Carroll, Barrister of Baltimore, a "handsome estate," which he had built up over the years through the success of his diverse economic activities.

The Old Wye Grist Mill stands on the border between Talbot and Queen Anne's counties. A grain mill has stood on this site since 1664.

New marketing systems also aided the small planter. Agents working for English and Scottish merchants began to set up permanent stores in the colony in the 1730s. They bought the crops of small planters and sold imported goods in return, usually on long-term credit. Besides giving planters steadier prices, the new system also enabled them to use the merchants' credit to borrow money and expand their tobacco production.

A planter became wealthier using unpaid, rather than paid, workers, and so, as tobacco production increased, more and more planters acquired slaves. In 1720, only about one-quarter of all Maryland planters owned slaves, but by 1760, nearly one-half owned slaves. Most of the owners had no more than five slaves, but even five slaves could produce four times as much tobacco as a single planter could. Planters spent only a minimal amount to feed, clothe, and house their slaves. They kept for their own use most of the income earned by the crops and products that the slaves produced.

Agricultural Diversification

The shift to slave labor was one of the changes that took place in the eighteenth century. Another change was the greater diversity of economic life. Although tobacco continued to be the primary cash crop for the whole colony, cereal crops grew in importance. The value of the corn crop exceeded the value of tobacco on many estates. Planters used corn to feed their households and fatten livestock, and they traded it to the West Indies, where sugar planters bought it to feed slaves.

During the first half of the century, wheat began to replace tobacco as the main cash crop in some areas, particularly near Pennsylvania. By the middle of the century, southern European demand for wheat stimulated growth of the flour-milling industry in the Philadelphia area, and agents for the mills looked to Maryland for more wheat. As settlers moved into the Piedmont region, wheat became the major cash crop there, as well.

Planters could also diversify by producing barrel staves, planks, and other products from their timber. In the lower Eastern Shore counties of Dorchester, Somerset, and Worcester, which had larger areas of poor soil, marshland, and swamps than the upper Bay or Western Shore counties, settlers emphasized lumber products. Planters in every region enlarged their herds of livestock because they could sell salted beef and pork to the West Indies.

Nonagricultural Activity

Colonists also moved into nonagricultural activities. As early as 1715, investors built a profitable iron works at Principio Creek, in Cecil County. They took advantage of high-grade ore that was easy to mine, of forests, which supplied the charcoal used to process the ore, and of water routes for shipping the iron to markets. In 1731, five wealthy colonists set up the Baltimore Iron Works on the Patapsco River, in Baltimore County. This was the most successful of all the Maryland works and returned a handsome profit to its owners for many years.

Shipbuilding also made use of Maryland's natural resources. Somerset County was an early center of production and ships were built there throughout the century. As settlement and population grew more rapidly on the Western Shore, shipyards prospered on that side of the Bay, particularly in Anne Arundel County.

Craftsmen became more numerous in the colony, but there was never the variety found among the artisans in the more urban colonies to the north or in England. Carpenters and other woodworkers, shoemakers and tanners, tailors, and blacksmiths served their neighbors as craftsmen. Other men followed careers as members of the professions, chiefly as lawyers, physicians, or clergymen, and many were merchants.

Wealthy colonists also invested in vacant land. As settlement spread to frontier areas, landowners sold property to the newcomers. During the eighteenth century, areas around the Bay became more populated. Settlers also began to develop the Piedmont region. Colonists moving outward from Prince George's, Anne Arundel, and Baltimore counties joined large numbers of German settlers moving south from Pennsylvania.

The Development of Towns

The growth of a more diversified and prosperous economy led to the development of the first towns in the region. At first, the area was too thinly settled to allow towns to grow. Annapolis, which became the capital in 1694, grew only because it was the seat of government. It provided services and homes for members of the government and for colonists who were drawn to the capital by legislative sessions or government-related business.

The Maryland Assembly then "created" towns: Oxford in 1706, Chestertown in 1707, Joppa in 1724, and Port Tobacco and Baltimore Town in 1729, among them. Development of the towns, however, depended on more than legislative acts. Oxford, for example,

In 1752, Baltimore was a tiny town on the Patapsco River. Its 200 residents supported a church, a hotel, two taverns, a barber shop, a tobacco inspection house, and a brewery.

COLONIAL BALTIMORE

In the 1660s, settlers first claimed land in the area that is now Baltimore, and by the 1720s, the area's population was large enough to spur the creation of a town. The Assembly chose 60 acres of Carroll family land as the site of Baltimore Town in 1729. The site had a good harbor, rapid streams to provide water power for mills, a fertile backcountry, and forests to supply wood for fuel and buildings.

An earlier settlement, in the nearby Fells Point area, had three homes, several tobacco houses, an orchard, and a mill. A third settlement grew up at the mouth of Jones's Falls. Named Jones's Town, it was linked to Baltimore Town by a bridge over the stream. In 1745 Jones's Town became part of Baltimore Town, but Fells Point was not added until 1773.

In the 1750s Baltimore began to grow as a center for processing and exporting wheat. Wheat moved into town on a network of roads that extended into central and western Maryland and into Pennsylvania. Wagons brought grain to mills along Jones's and Gwynns's Falls, and ships carried flour from the mills, as well as wheat and baked ship's bread, to overseas markets. Baltimore also served as the port through which the area's iron works shipped iron to Britain.

At this time Germans began to enter Maryland through Baltimore rather than through Philadelphia. Refugees fleeing western settlements during the French and Indian War also swelled the town's population. During the decade, several new churches were built and a public wharf was constructed. By 1764 the town had grown to about 200 houses, and in 1768 the Assembly recognized Baltimore's growth by making it the county seat for Baltimore County.

became a thriving port for about forty years, but the town never drew many residents or craftsmen. Joppa and Port Tobacco languished, as well. Chestertown prospered because the upper Bay became a wheat-producing area. Baltimore Town grew only slowly for several decades but then, like Chestertown, its prosperity became linked with the grain trade and it grew rapidly.

Western Towns

Wheat stimulated town development more than tobacco did. For crops of equal value, wheat was bulkier than tobacco and required more processing before it left the colony, so wheat farmers needed wagons to move their grain and mills to grind it into flour. Landlocked western settlers also needed stores where they could buy needed supplies.

In Frederick County, Daniel Dulany the Elder, chief developer of the western area, arranged in 1747 for the survey of a town site near the Monocacy River. By offering good terms to artisans and tradesmen, he drew craftsmen and professional men to Frederick Town, which quickly became the center of western settlement.

Thirty miles farther west, another center grew up around the property of Jonathan Hager. Hager bought his first tract in the area in 1739; by the 1760s he owned 2,500 acres. In 1762, probably

This stone house built by Jonathan Hager is like many of the homes built by prosperous western settlers.

Fort Cumberland, built at the junction of Will's Creek and the North Fork of the Potomac River, is pictured here in 1755. Because of British restric-tions on western settlement, the town of Cumber-land was not laid out until after the Revolution.

THE FRENCH AND INDIAN WAR

While Englishmen settled colonies along the Atlantic Coast, Frenchmen built forts, missions, and trading posts in Canada and down the Mississippi River. French and English settlers competed for furs, for fish, and for control of the region between the Appalachian Mountains and the Mississippi. The French began building a series of forts in the Ohio River valley to control the direct route from Canada to Louisiana. Pennsylvania fur traders and Virginia land speculators with claims in the area opposed their plans, and fighting erupted in 1754 over a French fort at the head of the Ohio.

Maryland formed a company of riflemen to protect settlements from Frederick Town to Hager's Town. In February 1755, General Edward Braddock arrived from England to lead 2,000 men (British regulars and colonial volunteers) against the French. George Wash-ington accompanied him as an aide, while Maryland Governor Horatio Sharpe and Benjamin Franklin of Philadelphia organized the supply effort. Braddock's defeat in July at Fort Duquesne left Maryland's western settlements open to attacks by France's Indian allies, and refugees from these settlements fled as far east as Baltimore. The Maryland legislature was afraid the colony would be attacked, and it voted money for the war effort in 1754 and 1756. British troops continued to fight the French, and succeeded by capturing French forts and then by taking Quebec in 1759. Their efforts relieved pressure on western Maryland and shifted fighting away from the colony. When the war ended in 1763, France ceded to Britain all of its territory in North America except New Orleans, which went to Spain.

inspired by the success of Frederick Town, he laid out a town. Hager named it after his wife, Elizabeth, but local people called it Hager's Town.

In 1754, Carolina and Virginia troops built an outpost farther west, on the high land along the Potomac River. The next year General Edward Braddock strengthened the outpost and renamed it Fort Cumberland. Little effort was made to develop towns in this area, however. Indian raids during the French and Indian War and British opposition to land grants west of the Appalachians held back settlement of western Maryland. Furthermore, members of the Calvert family would not sell any of their western Maryland land until they had reserved the best for their own use.

Town Life

In the mid-eighteenth century, most Marylanders still lived on farms. By 1755 as many as 1,000 people may have lived in Annapolis, but the total town-dwelling population in the rest of Maryland was not more than 2,000. Thus, no more than 2 out of every 100 people in the colony lived in a town. Of these towns, only Annapolis offered some of the amenities available to residents of colonial cities like Philadelphia and Boston.

The 1750s were a "Golden Age" for Annapolis. For several decades it was the social and cultural center of the colony. It attracted lawyers and merchants, who made Annapolis their home, and members of the elite, who came to Annapolis for sessions of the legislature. The wealthy clientele was good for business, and the kind of craftsmen who were seldom, if ever, found elsewhere in the colony settled in Annapolis. They included watchmakers, hatters, wigmakers, saddlers, and silversmiths, as well as the most skilled cabinetmakers.

The colony's only newspaper, the *Maryland Gazette*, began to be published regularly in Annapolis in 1745. It printed news from abroad and from other colonies, provided a forum for debating public issues, ran notices of runaway servants and slaves, and advertised land and merchandise that was offered for sale. Traveling theater groups from England and the other colonies regularly visited Annapolis in the 1750s, performing material from Shakespeare to farces. Social clubs like the Tuesday Club, founded in 1745, brought together members of the elite, while horse races attracted enthusiasts from all social groups.

Outside of Annapolis, there were no newspapers or theaters and few clubs. Horse races were run in country towns, however, and were equally popular there. The neighborhood tavern, Sunday

SLAVE FAMILY LIFE

Slave women usually married in their late teens and formed a new household with their children. Mothers took their newborn children with them to the fields, where the infants lay on the ground while their mothers worked. Older children stayed at home, playing among themselves while women who were too old for field work looked after them.

Children began to work in the fields between the ages of 7 and 10, picking up stones or pulling worms off tobacco plants. Most children older than 10 years were trained as field workers. A few boys might be taught carpentry, smithing, or other skills, and some girls would be trained as cooks or other household servants.

Slavery both fragmented and extended black family life. Planters kept women and their small children together, but they often separated husbands and teenage children from the rest of the family. Small planters in particular often left a slave or two to their widows and divided the rest among their children. Slaves were also likely to be mortgaged or sold to cover debts. Although family members were frequently separated in this way, the distances involved were usually small. At night and on Sundays and holidays, slaves visited their family and kin on nearby plantations.

church services, and sessions of the county court all provided places for social gathering. A network of roads and paths, as well as many rivers and creeks, connected plantations to local centers like churches, stores, taverns, and the courthouse. Well-traveled main roads linked the colony's towns and also extended north and south to Pennsylvania, Virginia, and beyond.

Maryland Society at Midcentury

In 1764, *Gentleman's Magazine* of London printed a census taken of Maryland in 1755, when nearly 153,000 people lived in the colony. Marylanders occupied 15 counties in 1755. Older counties in the east were not full, and Frederick, Baltimore, and western Anne Arundel counties still held large stretches of vacant land.

All people belonged to several different groups made up of male and female; young and old; black and white; free and unfree; immigrant and native-born; rich, middling, and poor. People's rights, privileges, and ways of life varied with all these factors. Only the 15 percent of the population who were free white adult males enjoyed full legal rights. An even smaller group of property holders had the right to vote and hold office.

Slaves

In 1755 blacks comprised 28 percent of Maryland's population, while mulattoes (people of both black and white parentage) made up 2 percent. The proportion of blacks to whites varied from region to region, however. In prime tobacco-producing areas like Anne Arundel and the lower Western Shore counties, 40 to 50 percent of the population was black. This was because tobacco was a labor-intensive crop that required steady care from first planting to packing for market.

Wheat, however, needed less care. For one or two weeks, a wheat farmer needed extra help to harvest his crop, and he could hire free or slave labor for that brief period. So, in northern and western wheat-producing counties such as Frederick and Cecil, blacks made up just 13 or 14 percent of the population.

Slaves formed the broad group at the bottom of colonial society, and much of the wealth and privilege of those at the top of society was based on slave labor. Slaves enjoyed few legal rights. They

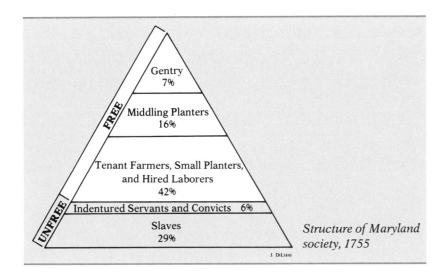

Gentry
7%

Middling Planters
16%

Tenant Farmers, Small Planters, and Hired Laborers
42%

Indentured Servants and Convicts 6%

Slaves
29%

FREE

UNFREE

Structure of Maryland society, 1755

J. DiLisio

were protected by law from extreme abuse, but they could not bring suit in court or testify on their own behalf except in petitions for freedom. Slaves could marry, but they could not sue to prevent the breakup of a marriage or a family. They were legally unable to own property, but in practice they did have the right to tend a patch of ground and raise poultry. They could sell chickens, eggs, and any crops they raised and use the proceeds as they wished.

On larger plantations, slaves lived in small cabins that were furnished with mattresses and blankets for sleeping, perhaps a crude homemade table and some stools, and a few utensils for cooking. On small plantations, the few slaves might live in a hut or in the kitchen loft. By mid-century, slaves had begun to develop broad kinship networks in their neighborhoods. Those who lived on plantations with 20 or more slaves generally lived with groups of kinfolk, while slaves on small plantations had relatives on nearby farms.

Free Blacks

Not all blacks were slaves. About 1 percent of all blacks and 40 percent of mulattoes were free. A few were descended from the earliest Africans who were brought to Maryland and Virginia before the laws of slavery were complete. Others had been granted their freedom.

It was common for free blacks to work as field hands or servants in the homes of wealthy whites. Other free blacks worked as craftsmen, and a few became independent farmers, owning land and raising crops in the same manner as white farmers did.

Servants and Hired Laborers

Servants made up the 8 percent of all white people who were not free in 1755. They may have been hired laborers, under indentures, or deported convicts. In 1717 Parliament had passed a law allowing convicted criminals to be sent to the colonies for sale as servants. Transported convicts—men, women, and children—accounted for one of every five servants.

Hired laborers became an increasingly large source of workers during the eighteenth century. Greater numbers of young men reached their teens and early twenties without inheriting land or the money to buy, or even rent, land of their own. By working as a hired hand for a neighboring planter or by doing odd jobs while helping with the family's crops, these young men could try to save the money they needed to become farmers of their own land.

Tenant Farmers and Small Planters

Tenant farmers and small landowners made up the next level of society. Together they accounted for more than one-half of free householders. Tenant farmers had an extra expense—their rent—that landowners did not have. In terms of living standards, however, the differences between tenants and small landowners were not great. Both were likely to be married and have several children. Most owned one or two horses, and nearly as many raised some cattle and a small herd of pigs. Nearly all grew tobacco, from which they earned between £5 and £10 a year. In addition, most raised crops of corn, and many cultivated wheat.

Families lived in simple one- or two-room houses that often had a loft for sleeping and storage and a separate kitchen. The farms had tobacco houses and perhaps a corn house, but no barns to shelter animals. Their houses were sparsely furnished, but these farmers lived more comfortably than their grandfathers or even fathers had.

Shoemaker David Prichard was a typical member of this group. Prichard was a servant in 1725, but by 1733 he was the head of his own household and had at least three children. Prichard owned no land, but he rented property on which he kept horses, cows, and hogs, and he grew tobacco and corn. The Prichards furnished their house with two beds, a pine table, a chest, a chest of drawers, and one arm chair and four side chairs. Mary Prichard prepared the family's meals in a kitchen equipped with iron and tin utensils, pewter dishes, and a small amount of earthenware. She also had tubs for washing clothes and linens, a box iron for pressing them,

The Le Comte House in Dorchester County, the oldest surviving colonial house in Maryland, is a typical middle-class home of the colonial period.

and a woolen wheel for spinning yarn. In addition to his shoemaking equipment, Prichard owned two plows and some basic carpentry tools, as well as a supply of leather and hides.

The Middling Group

A group known to the colonists as "middling" planters occupied the next level and comprised about one-quarter of the colony's freemen. Within this group, 70 percent owned land, with the average owner holding nearly 200 acres. The same percentage of middling planters owned slaves, usually between one and five. Nearly all of the middling planters raised cattle, horses, sheep, and hogs. Just as many raised tobacco, corn, and wheat.

Middling planters earned about twice as much as small planters. Similarly, middling planters enjoyed greater comforts in their homes. They were likely to have rebuilt or enlarged the family home so that it was now a full two stories with at least two rooms on each floor. In addition to a separate kitchen and tobacco and corn houses, there might be a smokehouse or henhouse or barn.

Noah Corner, a native-born carpenter and planter, was a member of the middling group. Corner and his family lived on a 250-acre plantation, where Corner raised tobacco, corn, wheat, and oats. Cattle, horses, sheep, and pigs foraged on the land. Corner did not own a slave, but he bought one servant during his career. He also took in an orphan, whom he agreed to train as a house carpenter.

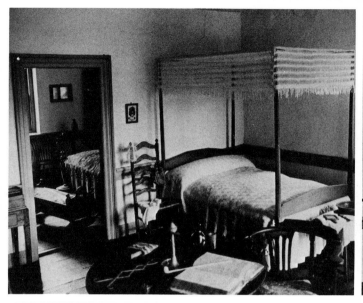

Left: *The large bedrooms and comfortable beds upstairs in the Hager house contrast sharply with the sleeping lofts found in smaller, cruder houses.* Right: *The well-crafted furniture and utensils in the Hager house indicate that Hager's family enjoyed more comforts than earlier colonial settlers did.*

Corner furnished his home with four beds with feather mattresses (the best mattresses available), a cot, three tables, three chests, eight chairs, and a walnut desk. An hour glass and a silver watch measured time, candlesticks held candles that provided light for reading, and a looking glass allowed Corner to adjust his brown wig. Rachel Corner prepared food for her family in a kitchen equipped with brass skillets and skimmers, two dozen glass bottles, flasks, iron and tinware, pewter dishes and serving pieces, and a tea kettle.

The Gentry

Above the middling group, at the top of the social pyramid, stood the gentry. These men owned the greatest share of the colony's wealth, organized its trade and other commercial activities, and filled its political and judicial offices. No more than 10 percent of the colony's householders were of the gentry, yet they owned nearly one-half of all patented land, nearly two-thirds of total moveable wealth, and nearly two-thirds of the colony's slaves. A scattering of craftsmen accumulated enough wealth to become members of this group. Most members of the elite, however, were merchants, planters, lawyers, and government officials.

The gulf between the gentry and the middling planter was far

wider than that between the middling and small planters. The small planter could vote and occasionally served as a juror; middling planters were constables and jurors. The gentry, however, served as justices and delegates. Small and middling planters earned a living from their crops and livestock and perhaps by a craft. The gentry combined planting (with the labor performed by slaves) with a profession, business, investments, office holding, or land speculation. They built large brick Georgian homes that have come to symbolize tidewater society and furnished them with many marks of wealth such as imported mahogany furniture, silver tea and coffee services, prints and pictures, including portraits of themselves and their families, and large collections of books.

Jeremiah Nicolls, a typical member of this group, was a merchant and planter in Talbot County who married the daughter of one of the county's richest and oldest families. Nicolls held the offices of justice and sheriff and acted as the Talbot agent for a London tobacco firm. Twenty-three slaves worked Nicolls's 500 acres, cared for his livestock, and ran his ferry across the Choptank River. Nicolls's mahogany tea table, backgammon table, violin, large library, wine cellar, lavish wardrobe, gold jewelry, silver tea and coffee services, and small carriage all marked him as a member of the colony's wealthy elite.

Despite differences in wealth and power, numerous strands wove the various groups of planters together. Kinship ties or a relationship of employer and employee or landlord and tenant linked some. Small and middling planters gave the elite their votes. In turn, the gentry used their power to hold down the costs of government, to enforce contracts and payment of debts, to prosecute those who stole from or assaulted members of the community, and to settle disputes over ownership of land. Members of the elite also helped middling and small planters by marketing their crops, extending them credit, or hiring out a slave when an extra hand was needed. In these ways, the groups worked together to foster a stable society and an ordered economy.

Men, Women, and Children

In the colony as a whole, there were as many free white men as there were free white women, but here again there were regional variations. In Frederick County, men made up 56 percent of the free white population, the highest percentage of any county. This imbalance reflected the frontier nature of Frederick's settlement, which drew young men who could not afford land in the older counties.

Planters continued to prefer adult males when they bought workers. As a result, 70 percent of servants were men. Planters could also choose to buy men when they were purchasing imported slaves, but by mid-century most slaves, like most whites, were native born. Blacks, therefore, like whites, were evenly divided between men and women.

Children 15 years or younger made up 52 percent of the free white population. This represented a great change from the seventeenth century, when most immigrants were adults and there were few children in the colony. Children also accounted for 52 percent of the total black population.

Tax-Exempt Groups

Two other groups were counted separately in the census because they did not pay taxes. Thirty-five clergymen lived in Maryland in 1755, serving Anglicans in all counties. Another 647 men were exempt from taxes because they were too poor to pay them. People needing assistance from the county had to appear at the November court and explain to the justices their reasons for seeking aid. Generally, those who needed help were either too old or too disabled by sickness or injury to earn a living.

The Original Marylanders

One final group composed part of the total population of the state, but the census figures did not include these people. Members of the Nanticoke and Choptank tribes continued to live on their reservations in the eighteenth century. A 1756 estimate placed the number of "domestic Indians" at about 140, the remnants of various tribes whose members had numbered at least 8,000 at the beginning of the seventeenth century.

As early as the 1740s Nanticoke Indians began moving north to join tribes in Pennsylvania, New York, and Canada. By the 1760s the colony sought to buy back the reservation land. A small group of Choptank Indians continued to live on their reservation, but by the end of the century they, too, had gone. The only Indians left in Maryland were scattered families who lived in remote areas, usually marshes or swamps.

The Colony Matures

In the course of 130 years of settlement, the men and women who crossed the Atlantic, and their descendants, cleared land, planted crops, raised livestock, built houses and churches, cultivated orchards, erected fences, cleared roads, and operated stores, taverns, and ferries. They took a landscape that they described as an endless forest and created a new society on it. Three thousand miles from Europe, they nevertheless were firmly linked to it through a vast trade network that stretched across the Atlantic. Although the colonists came from widely varied backgrounds, they were particularly connected to England by the shared institutions of government and political ideas.

In the 1760s British imperial needs clashed with the interests of the colonists, just as proprietary and colonial interests had clashed in earlier decades. Their English heritage and their colonial experience of self-government and economic development powerfully shaped the ways in which the colonists responded to the challenges of the 1760s. These same colonists shaped the nation's future in the American War for Independence in the 1770s.

MARYLAND		THE NATION AND THE WORLD
Mason and Dixon survey Maryland boundary with Delaware and Pennsylvania	1763– 1767	Treaty of Paris signed
Zachariah Hood, Maryland stamp collector, burned in effigy	1765	Stamp Act
	1767	Townshend Acts
Robert Eden sworn as governor of Maryland	1769	
Governor Eden issues Fee Proclamation	1770	Boston Massacre
Frederick Calvert, sixth Lord Baltimore, dies; son Henry Harford becomes proprietor of Maryland	1771	
Cornerstone laid for new State House in Annapolis	1772	
Caroline and Harford counties formed	1773	Tea Act Boston Tea Party
First convention meets in Annapolis *Peggy Stewart* burned in Annapolis harbor	1774	First Continental Congress meets
	1775	Battles of Lexington and Concord George Washington becomes commander in chief of American army
Governor Eden leaves Maryland Montgomery and Washington counties formed First Maryland Constitution adopted Continental Congress meets in Baltimore	1776	Declaration of Independence signed
First General Assembly elected under new constitution meets in Annapolis Thomas Johnson takes office as first state governor	1777	
Maryland signs Articles of Confederation	1781	Articles of Confederation adopted British surrender at Yorktown, Virginia
Washington College established at Chestertown	1782	
Importation of slaves into Maryland for sale prohibited U.S. Congress meets at State House in Annapolis	1783	Treaty of Paris signed, affirms American independence George Washington resigns his military commission
	1784	Treaty of Paris ratified by Congress
St. John's College established at Annapolis	1785	
Annapolis Convention calls for a convention at Philadelphia	1786	
	1787	Constitutional Convention held in Philadelphia
Maryland Convention ratifies U.S. Constitution	1788	U.S. Constitution ratified by the nine states necessary for adoption
	1789	George Washington inaugurated as U.S. president French Revolution begins

CHAPTER 2

The Revolutionary War Era, 1763–1789

In early February 1763 Maryland's Governor Horatio Sharpe announced that a peace treaty between Britain and France had been signed in Paris, ending the French and Indian War. Marylanders, like other Americans, were happy to be colonists of the most powerful nation in the world. Just 13 years later, however, Britain and America were at war with each other. Representatives to the Second Continental Congress pledged their lives, fortunes, and sacred honor—and that of 2½ million fellow Americans—to fight for independence from England.

Marylanders supported independence for reasons that differed somewhat from the reasons other colonists gave for supporting the cause. From its founding, Maryland had been a bit different. In some ways it was like the northern colonies, and in other ways it was like the colonies to the south.

Once they declared independence, Marylanders faced a whole new set of problems, because when they declared independence, they broke ties to both Britain and the Calvert family, the proprietors of the colony. For the first time Marylanders were on their own. They would have to turn to the people in the other newly declared states. For better or for worse, the 13 colonies had become the United States, and these former colonists of Britain had become Americans.

New British Policies

By the 1760s political power in Maryland was concentrated in the hands of just a few people. At the very top stood the proprietor

The Maryland Gazette *denounced the Stamp Act. The skull and crossbones, symbol of mortal danger, appeared in the October 10, 1765, issue.*

in England and his officials in the colony. In the counties, the gentry led local politics. The well-educated and at least moderately wealthy gentry often owned large plantations. In Annapolis, Baltimore, and other towns, lawyers and merchants were the local gentry. Below them were most of the population: the tradesmen, small planters, farmers, tenants, servants, free blacks, and slaves. Many of these people, and all women, were not permitted to take any part in politics.

After winning a large amount of new land in the French and Indian War, Britain expected the Americans to pay at least part of the costs for protecting the new territory. Britain levied a number of new taxes, which angered the colonists. In the 1760s and 1770s members of the gentry became leaders in protesting these new taxes.

The Sugar Act

To raise more money from the colonies, Lord George Grenville, the British official in charge of finances, came up with a plan known as the Sugar Act of 1764. Prior to the Sugar Act, molasses was often smuggled into the colonies because people wanted to avoid paying the tax on it. Grenville hoped that a lower tax would encourage more people to pay, and thus increase British revenues. Maryland was not affected much by the Sugar Act, because not many Marylanders were involved in the West Indian molasses trade. On the other hand, New Englanders used large quantities of molasses to make rum and were thought to smuggle a great deal of it.

The Stamp Act

New Englanders were already complaining that their liberties were being threatened by the Sugar Act. Marylanders were also soon to feel the pressure of the new British laws. In 1765, Grenville proposed another revenue bill that affected every American colony. The Stamp Act required colonists to purchase tax stamps, which were to be attached to all legal and commercial documents, newspapers, playing cards, dice, and licenses. The law mostly affected those who held political power: the wealthy planters, lawyers, and merchants.

Zachariah Hood, Stamp Collector

In Maryland, anger against the hated Stamp Act focused on Zachariah Hood, an Annapolis merchant. He accepted the position of stamp collector for Maryland while on a business trip to England, and the *Maryland Gazette* announced his appointment. The newspaper quoted Hood as saying that if the colonists had to be taxed, it would best be done by a native son.

Marylanders did not agree with Hood's statement, nor did they believe that colonists should be taxed unless they agreed to be taxed. Twenty-four-year-old Samuel Chase assembled a "considerable number of people, assertors of British American privileges," in Annapolis on August 26, 1765. They made an effigy of Hood and hanged and burned his stuffed likeness on a gallows. A few days later, just after Hood arrived back in Maryland, a mob of more than 300 people tore down his Annapolis warehouse. The terrified Hood fled to New York.

Others rose up against the Stamp Act. Some political leaders asked Governor Sharpe to call a special session of the Assembly to discuss the Stamp Act. Some saw the Stamp Act as a threat to Lord Baltimore's rights. All agreed that the Maryland charter forbade taxing Maryland citizens without the approval of their representatives. The British Parliament, in passing the Stamp Act, had directly violated this provision.

The governor called the Assembly on September 23, 1765, and members discussed no business except the Stamp Act. They chose three people to attend the Stamp Act Congress, which was to be held in New York that October. They ordered these delegates to support the idea that the colonists could not be taxed without representation. Then the Assembly passed eight resolutions of its own which asserted the rights of Marylanders under the Maryland charter and the British constitution.

Daniel Dulany the Younger argued against the Stamp Act. On other issues, however, he was a leading supporter of the proprietor.

Dulany's "Considerations"

The next chapter in the protest against the Stamp Act came from an unexpected source. Daniel Dulany the Younger was the son of Daniel Dulany the Elder and was as conservative and well connected as any person in the province. He wrote a stinging attack on the Stamp Act entitled "Considerations on the Propriety of Imposing Taxes in the British Colonies." A brilliant lawyer, Dulany was a strong supporter of the proprietor. His reputation and his argument against the Stamp Act did a great deal to win the support of conservatives in the fight against the act.

Governor Sharpe realized that the people of Maryland would not stand for stamps in the colony. When the first shipment of stamps arrived in the Annapolis harbor in late October 1765, he asked the ship's captain to keep them on board his vessel. Because there were

The use of tax stamps such as these was strongly resisted by the American colonists.

no stamps and no stamp collector, all business in Maryland ports and courts stopped on November 1, 1765. This date was called "Dooms-Day" by the editor of the *Maryland Gazette*, who promptly stopped publishing his newspaper.

The nearly complete shutdown of the colony did not continue for long, however. The justices in Frederick County soon resumed business, even though they had no stamps to make their papers valid. Yet Marylanders supported their actions. As the winter wore on, groups who called themselves the Sons of Liberty forced the county courts throughout Maryland, and the offices in the capital, to open.

The Stamp Act Is Repealed

Business at all levels of government had nearly returned to normal by the spring of 1766. Then, on April 10, 1766, the *Maryland Gazette* announced Parliament's repeal of the Stamp Act. The news was received with joy in Maryland.

Thoughtful politicians pointed out the lessons taught by the Stamp Act, however. They realized that the king and Parliament might interfere in their lives and government, and they warned that the colonists' rights under the proprietor and the Maryland charter were fragile. The fight against the Stamp Act gave some younger men, such as Samuel Chase and William Paca, who organized the Annapolis Sons of Liberty, an opportunity to become leaders. The Baltimore Sons of Liberty included not only wealthy merchants like William Lux, but also ordinary tradesmen. The protest had given them all experience in organizing resistance to authority. This experience would be valuable sooner than they expected in struggles against both the proprietor and Parliament.

Religion and Taxes

With the Stamp Act threat behind them, Maryland political leaders turned their attention to matters at home. Throughout the eighteenth century, the proprietor was of more concern to Marylanders than the king and Parliament. A loosely organized group called the Country party or Popular party fought what it considered unreasonable acts by the proprietor and his officials. The Popular party was strong because it had support in the elected Lower House of the Assembly. The governor and his council (which also made up the Upper House of the Assembly) were all appointed by

Anne Catherine Green

Mary Katherine Goddard

ANNE CATHERINE GREEN AND MARY KATHERINE GODDARD: PRINTERS

Politics in colonial Maryland was a male affair. When a man wanted to express his views in the pages of the local newspaper, however, he often had dealings with women. From 1767 until her death in 1775, Anne Catherine Green published the *Maryland Gazette* in Annapolis. In 1774, William Goddard started a rival newspaper in Baltimore, the *Maryland Journal and the Baltimore Advertiser*, and one year later his sister Mary Katherine Goddard took over the paper. She published it all through the War for Independence.

Anne Catherine Green began printing the *Maryland Gazette* after her husband, Jonas Green, died in 1767. Jonas Green had been the public printer, meaning that he did all of the printing work required by the Maryland government. The mother of fourteen, six of whom were still alive, Anne Green finished the printing work her husband had underway at the time of his death. She was then appointed public printer by the General Assembly.

Mary Katherine Goddard gained her experience in the printing business because her brother would never stay in one place long enough to finish what he had started. After her physician father died, Mary Goddard and her mother helped her brother start printing businesses in Providence, Rhode Island, and Philadelphia. In 1773 William settled in Baltimore and began publishing a newspaper there. As usual, however, he soon became interested in other projects and left the business. After settling the family's affairs in Philadelphia, Mary Katherine Goddard moved south to take over operation of the Baltimore press.

Anne Catherine Green and Mary Katherine Goddard kept Marylanders informed in the important years before and during the War for Independence. They must have faced prejudice and discrimination often. But the hundreds of pages of newsprint they filled, and the dozens of books and pamphlets they published and sold, show how well both women did their jobs.

Top, *the seal of the Calvert family.* Bottom, *the Maryland state seal used during the colonial period. The motto translates "grow and multiply."*

the proprietor. In exchange for Lord Baltimore's favors, the governor and the council members were careful to see that the colony was governed according to the proprietor's wishes.

The Proprietor's Churchmen

One of Lord Baltimore's rights was appointing clergymen to parishes of Maryland's Anglican church. These ministers were supported by a tax levied on white males and all slaves who lived in a parish, whether they attended the Anglican church or not. The tax, called a poll tax or head tax, was paid in tobacco, and in large parishes the large amount of tobacco collected could be sold for a handsome income.

Members of the Popular party objected to the high cost of supporting these clergymen, and they did not like the ministers' close connections with the proprietor. When the Reverend Bennett Allen arrived in late 1766, the colony's popular leaders found a focus for their disgust.

The Reverend Allen was very proud of his close connections with Frederick, the sixth Lord Baltimore. He claimed that Lord Baltimore had promised him the richest parish in the province, and when he found that the richest parish already had a clergyman, he demanded that the governor give him two parishes. Allen never achieved this goal, but his struggle to get two parishes to satisfy his greed caused nearly everyone to turn against him.

Allen also drank to excess. He told Samuel Chew, a prominent Anne Arundel County merchant, that the large income of one church he had been offered would barely keep him in liquor. He fought in public and behaved in a cowardly way by backing out of a duel he had arranged. Most dangerous of all, he attacked the powerful Dulanys in nasty letters that were published in the *Maryland Gazette*.

When Governor Sharpe appointed him to All Saints' Parish in Frederick County, the Reverend Allen finally got to lead the richest parish in the colony. Allen's bad behavior in Annapolis was well known to the people of Frederick, and because he knew he would not be welcome in the new parish, Allen secretly slipped into the church. He read his induction ceremony before only two people.

During services the following Sunday, members of the congregation tried to pull Allen out of the pulpit, but Allen escaped unharmed and made his way to Philadelphia, eventually returning to England. Allen's feud with the powerful in Maryland did not end there, however. In 1782 Allen killed Lloyd Dulany, half-brother of Daniel Dulany, in a duel in London. During his brief stay in Maryland, the Reverend Bennett Allen clearly showed the problems that could arise when the proprietor appointed the clergy of the Anglican church. Many Marylanders, particularly members of other churches, objected to the use of their tax money to support such appointees of the proprietor.

The Townshend Acts

While Marylanders were busy with the Bennett Allen affair, the British government pushed through Parliament another series of measures to raise money from the colonies. Charles Townshend, appointed head of the treasury in 1766, approved of Grenville's idea of taxing the colonies, but he adopted an approach he believed the colonists would find acceptable.

In protesting the Stamp Act, the colonists had argued that there was a difference between internal and external taxes. They admitted that Parliament had a right to collect duties, or "external" taxes, on goods imported into the colonies. They insisted, however, that direct, or "internal," taxes on goods produced and used within the colonies could only be passed by the colonists' own representatives. Townshend did not consider this difference between internal and external taxes important. He was willing to take the Americans at their word, however, and he imposed an export duty, or "external" tax, on tea, paper, glass, and painters' colors.

The Townshend taxes were most troublesome to colonies like New York and Massachusetts, because they imported many goods from England. The discontent in the northern colonies did not spread to Maryland until 1768. Then the issue came to a head only because of the continuous conflict between the Lower House of the Assembly and the proprietor's representatives.

Opposition to the Townshend Acts

The controversy in Maryland was sparked by a letter from the Massachusetts House of Representatives which argued that the Townshend Acts were illegal. Governor Sharpe ordered delegates in the Maryland Assembly to ignore the letter, but the Lower House, desiring to show Sharpe that he could not tell elected representatives when or how to act, wrote a letter to the governor saying they had a right to tell the king of their concerns. Sharpe responded by adjourning the Assembly. Before leaving, however, members of the Lower House sent a letter to the king declaring that they agreed with Massachusetts.

Sir Robert Eden, the last colonial governor of Maryland, faced protests during his entire administration.

Nonimportation

In August 1768 Boston merchants agreed to stop importing goods from England. They hoped this would cripple British commerce and force a repeal of the Townshend Acts. By March 1769, Baltimore merchants signed an agreement to stop importing British goods, and Anne Arundel County followed in May. By June almost all Maryland counties had formed associations to see that British goods were not imported.

Even though Maryland was slow in opposing the Townshend Acts, its citizens never weakened once public feeling was raised against the tax. A new governor, Robert Eden, arrived in early June 1769. He tried to head off problems by announcing shortly after his arrival that Parliament intended to repeal all of the duties except the one on tea. But Maryland merchants and planters stood firm.

The plan not to import goods broke down in 1770. Most of the Townshend Acts were repealed in April of that year. Merchants in parts of Massachusetts, New York City, and Philadelphia started trading again. Baltimore merchants had to begin trading in order to stay in business. Even so, it had become clear that the Americans could put considerable pressure on England by refusing to trade, which cost England a great deal of money. The importance of the Townshend Acts in Maryland, in fact, was that the protest had demonstrated to merchants their power and their ability to join together to oppose British policies effectively.

Tobacco and Tea

No longer having to deal with English taxes, Maryland political leaders directed their attention to problems at home. This time they debated the Tobacco Inspection Act, initiating a controversy that moved Marylanders closer to revolution. The Tobacco Inspection Act of 1747 had set up inspection guidelines so that only tobacco of good quality was exported from the colony. The proprietor stood to benefit, because when his fees were paid in good tobacco, they were worth more. The Assembly had passed the bill only after the proprietor agreed to limit the amount of money or tobacco that clergymen and other proprietary officeholders could collect from the people.

In this drawing, hogsheads of tobacco are being loaded for shipment. The Tobacco Inspection Act was designed to keep up the quality—and the price—of this major export.

The Tobacco Inspection Act

The Maryland colonists were used to quarreling with the proprietor. They had fought to limit the proprietor's rights for many years. In 1770, with the Tobacco Inspection Act of 1747 due to end, the tension was especially high. Everyone agreed that a new Tobacco Inspection Act was necessary, because tobacco prices would drop if poor quality tobacco was exported along with the good, and Maryland depended on tobacco. Marylanders also knew that Virginia, Maryland's chief competitor in the tobacco trade, had a strong inspection system. The situation was urgent, but the Upper and Lower houses of the Assembly failed to agree on a new act.

Both the Tobacco Inspection Act and the fee schedule ended on October 20, 1770. The Lower House of the Assembly warned public officials and clergymen not to accept any more fees. William Stewart, clerk of the Land Office, was arrested for ignoring the warning. Governor Eden dismissed the Assembly, freed Stewart, and then, on November 26, 1770, issued his famous Fee Proclamation.

The Fee Proclamation

Eden's Fee Proclamation disregarded the Assembly's discussion. The governor allowed all officers and clergymen who had received fees for performing official duties to continue to accept the fees. After Eden issued his proclamation, the lines of battle were drawn. The Lower House, which spoke for the people, demanded its repeal. In response, the governor and the council, who spoke for the

Governor Eden's Fee Proclamation.

proprietor, blamed the Lower House for refusing to pass a new tobacco inspection law.

Arguments over the Fee Bill raged on for three years. During 1773 Charles Carroll of Carrollton and Daniel Dulany began a long newspaper debate on the question. Carroll wrote under the pen name "First Citizen," and Dulany signed his writings "Antilon." Carroll argued that the fees, like the Stamp Act and the Townshend Acts, were nothing more than taxation without representation. His reasoning won many friends for the Popular party, and because of his position on the issue he became one of the leaders of the antiproprietary movement.

People made their opposition to the Fee Bill known through carefully planned street demonstrations that brought together ordinary citizens and leaders of the Popular party. After the election for new Maryland Assembly delegates in May 1773, voters walked in solemn procession to bury Governor Eden's hated Fee Proclamation under the public gallows. William Paca and Matthias Hammond, two Popular party leaders who had just won the election, led the protest.

The Fee Bill controversy ended later in 1773, when the Assembly passed a new Tobacco Inspection Act that had no fee bill. Both sides won. The Assembly got its list of fees separated from the Tobacco Inspection Act, so inspection of tobacco would no longer mean support for the proprietor's officials. And Eden's Fee Proclamation remained in effect, so the proprietor's officials continued to receive their money. The problem of the clergy's salaries would be settled separately. The amount of the poll tax was kept the same, but taxpayers could pay in either money or tobacco. No sooner had the problem of fees been solved than the colony's attention was again directed to the wider world. This time tea became the symbol of British oppression.

The Tea Act

In May 1773 Parliament passed the Tea Act, which enabled the East India Company to undersell all other companies in the American colonies. The East India Company's monopoly of the tea trade angered the colonists. They were afraid that Parliament's claim that it could grant such privileges would be extended to other kinds of trade, crippling colonial businesses. Massachusetts was first to react against the Tea Act. In that colony's most famous act of protest, the Boston Tea Party of December 1773, Bostonians dumped a cargo of tea into Boston's harbor.

The Port Act

Just as Maryland Popular leaders began to be concerned about the Tea Act, word came that Parliament had passed the Boston Port Act, the first of the so-called Intolerable Acts. This law punished Boston for dumping the East India Company's tea into the harbor. It completely closed the port of Boston and allowed the port to reopen only if Boston paid for the lost tea.

Boston depended on its port. With the port closed, citizens could not get many of the things they needed. The town sent letters to all the other colonies asking for help and support. In response, colonies from all sections of the country hurried to send clothing, food, and other goods toward Boston. A convention of delegates from 12 of the 13 colonies met in Philadelphia in 1774 to discuss what further action to take.

Revolutionary Governments

The Philadelphia Convention became known as the First Continental Congress. Its members wrote the king asking for relief and voted to stop all trade to and from England. The formation of the Continental Congress was a large step toward independence from Britain. In 1774 liberty and rights were the delegates' main concern. Many of the delegates were willing to move toward independence if Britain did not answer the colonies' demands.

PHILADELPHIA.

In CONGRESS, Thursday, September 22, 1774.

RESOLVED,

THAT the Congress request the Merchants and Others, in the several Colonies, not to send to Great Britain any Orders for Goods, and to direct the execution of all Orders already sent, to be delayed or suspended, until the sense of the Congress, on the means to be taken for the preservation of the Liberties of *America,* is made public.

An Extract from the Minutes,
CHARLES THOMSON, *Sec.*

Printed by *W.* and *T. BRADFORD.*

The First Maryland Convention

Organized opposition to British policies reached a new high with the Continental Congress. In Maryland the same thing was happening, with even more dramatic results. Immediately after receiving the letter from Boston about the closing of the port, political leaders in Annapolis called for action by all the counties of Maryland. Within days, a convention of delegates met in Annapolis, even though Maryland law did not allow such a meeting. This meeting was extralegal, or outside the law, but no one in authority tried to stop it.

In Annapolis on June 22, 1774, the 92 delegates elected a chairman, Matthew Tilghman, and conducted business as if they constituted a legal assembly. They condemned the Boston Port Act and decided to send aid to Boston's citizens. They also voted to send delegates to the Congress scheduled to meet in Philadelphia. The decisions of the first Maryland Convention were called "resolves" instead of laws, but they had the force of law. Local political organizations in the counties and towns, called Committees of Observation and Committees of Correspondence, publicized and enforced the resolves.

Encouraged by the results of this convention, Marylanders called for others in November and December of 1774. By the fourth convention, held in April 1775, these extralegal meetings of delegates had taken over all law-making power in Maryland. The fifth convention, in August 1775, agreed to appoint a Council of Safety to govern between sessions of the convention. Governor Eden remained in the colony until June 1776, but he did not dare to interfere with the new government created by the convention.

A New Government Emerges

The new system of government formed in Maryland was made up of the Conventions, the Councils of Safety, and the local Committees of Observation and Correspondence. This extralegal government did much to quiet dissatisfaction in the colony. While it began as a protest against specific British actions, this unofficial government quickly *became* the government. Eden simply stepped aside, keeping his title as governor though he did not act as one.

The longstanding tension between the Popular party and the proprietor's officials was largely solved in this way. Eden could not prevent the Popular party from taking control of the government, and their political successes convinced most Maryland leaders that the greatest threat to their liberties had been removed. Popular leaders now controlled the government. No longer would Marylanders be at the mercy of the proprietor or his colonial officials.

Now that they controlled the government, Maryland political leaders saw little need for cutting ties to the king. As a result, from 1774 until almost the moment the vote for independence was taken in Philadelphia in 1776, Marylanders worked hard to remain loyal subjects of the king.

The Burning of the *Peggy Stewart*

That Governor Eden and other proprietary officials were powerless to stand in the way of the Popular party is demonstrated by an event that happened shortly after the first convention met. On October 15, 1774, the brig *Peggy Stewart* arrived at the port of An-

napolis. The ship was owned by Anthony Stewart, an Annapolis merchant who had named the brig for his daughter. Aboard ship were more than 2,300 pounds of tea that had been ordered by an Annapolis company.

Before Stewart could land the goods, the tea was discovered and news of it spread. Despite Stewart's published apology, people gathered to decide the fate of the *Peggy Stewart* and the tea. Neither the governor nor any of his officials stepped forward to protect Stewart or his property. Stewart offered to burn all the tea, and some Marylanders even voted to spare Stewart's ship. But a few were furious that a merchant would try to bring in tea from Britain, and they demanded extreme action.

Afraid for his family's safety, Stewart boarded his ship and ordered his crew to run the *Peggy Stewart* aground in full sight of Annapolis. There he set fire to his ship. The blazing ship must have convinced everyone that true political power in Maryland lay with Maryland's popular leaders, who had become a government with an effective means of enforcing its will.

The Association of Freemen

In July 1775, the fifth Maryland Convention resolved to form an "Association of Freemen of Maryland." It asked signers of a pledge to promise to maintain "good order and the public peace, to support the civil power in the due execution of laws . . . and to defend, with [their] utmost power, all persons from every species of outrage to themselves or their property."

Copies of the association pledge went to all parts of Maryland. Every adult male was ordered to sign, and those who refused were to be reported to Annapolis. The association thus served two purposes: it provided a list of men eligible for military service, and it identified those who refused to sign as persons whose loyalty to the extralegal government could not be trusted.

Opposition to Independence

Although the extralegal government was strengthened through the Association of Freemen, the Maryland Convention still would not support independence from Britain. In December 1775, and again as late as May 1776, the convention instructed its delegates in the Continental Congress not to vote for independence. Marylanders believed it was still possible to get along with Britain. The convention's resolution of May 21, 1776, stated its firm belief that

The burning of the Peggy Stewart *was the climax of Maryland's protest over tea. While anchored in the Annapolis harbor, the ship was actually burned by its owner, Anthony Stewart, who feared for the safety of his home and family.*

once the misunderstandings about the colonists' rights and liberties were worked out, Maryland could happily remain a British colony.

Maryland's strong resistance to independence frustrated and annoyed many members of the Continental Congress. John Adams of Massachusetts wrote a friend that nearly every state except Maryland was ready to support independence. Maryland, Adams continued, "is so eccentric a Colony—sometimes so hot, sometimes so cold; now so high, then so low—that I know not what to say about it or to expect from it."

War Approaches

Maryland political leaders wanted no part of anything that would lead to a permanent break with England. Yet, in opposing independence, Marylanders were hoping against hope. The American colonies were actually at war with England, although neither side had declared hostilities. The number of British troops in America increased monthly. Marylanders knew of the outbreaks of violence against British soldiers in Massachusetts, and they were aware of British vessels entering the Chesapeake Bay. In March 1776, the Maryland Convention's warship *Defence* captured the British ship *Otter* and several other enemy vessels in Maryland waters. In June 1776, Maryland agreed for the first time to send more than 2,000 men out of the colony to join the Continental army in fighting British troops.

In June 1776, Governor Robert Eden finally was forced to leave Maryland. Both Eden and the Council of Safety decided that Eden could no longer serve a useful purpose in the colony. The convention's letter to Eden asking him to leave ended by expressing the wish that he would return to govern the colony when peace returned.

The Virginia Resolution

Against this background of events the Maryland Council of Safety called another meeting of the convention in June 1776. The main business before the convention was the Virginia Resolution that had been introduced in Congress on June 7, 1776. The resolution stated: "These United Colonies are, and of right ought to be, free and independent States, that they are absolved from all allegiance to the British Crown, and that all political connection between them and the State of Great Britain is and ought to be totally dissolved." This separation was what so many Marylanders had dreaded, and the Maryland Convention again tried to postpone a decision on independence.

The convention adopted a resolution on June 21 asking Congress to put off consideration of the Virginia Resolution. Maryland's political leaders asked Congress to allow the colony's delegates to return to Annapolis to meet with them. Congress flatly refused.

At the same time, Samuel Chase, Charles Carroll of Carrollton, Matthew Tilghman, Thomas Johnson, and others concluded that Maryland had no choice but to join the other colonies in declaring independence. They wrote to political leaders all over Maryland urging them to support separation from Britain. The result, on the surface at least, was a remarkable change of heart. On June 28, the Maryland Convention unanimously adopted a resolution freeing its delegates in Congress to support independence.

In truth, Maryland's beliefs had not changed overnight. Most Maryland politicians simply recognized that the struggle for compromise had failed and that Maryland could not afford to stand alone against the other colonies. It was clear that the vote in Congress would be cast for independence. Maryland, for better or worse, must succeed or fail with the rest.

Independence

The new instructions from the Maryland Convention arrived in Philadelphia on July 1, 1776. The delegates to the Continental Congress were just entering the great debate over independence. Only three members of the Maryland delegation were present in Congress: William Paca, Thomas Stone, and John Rogers. These three Marylanders, along with other members of Congress, debated the Virginia Resolution for nine hours on July 1. The following day, they joined the other delegates in declaring the colonies free and independent states. Two days later these same three Marylanders approved the language of the Declaration of Independence, which explained to the world why the colonists had declared themselves independent.

Two facts about the decision to declare independence and Maryland's part in it are of interest. First, independence was actually voted on July 2, not July 4. Second, four Marylanders, not three, are remembered as signers of the Declaration of Independence. Congress decided that an official parchment copy of the declaration should be prepared and signed by all the delegates, but nearly

Charles Carroll of Carrollton

William Paca

MARYLAND'S SIGNERS OF THE DECLARATION OF INDEPENDENCE

Maryland's four signers of the Declaration of Independence—Charles Carroll of Carrollton, William Paca, Samuel Chase, and Thomas Stone—were all leaders of the Popular party in the years before the Revolution.

The wealthiest of the four was Charles Carroll of Carrollton. Born in Annapolis in 1737, Carroll was the only child of one of Maryland's richest landowners, Charles Carroll of Annapolis. He received a fine education in France and a law degree in England before returning to Maryland at the time of the Stamp Act. Just one thing stood in the way of a brilliant and successful career for Carroll: he was Catholic. At that time Catholics could not vote, hold public office, or worship openly in Maryland.

The young Carroll nevertheless took an active part in the protests against the policies of the proprietor and Parliament during the 1760s. He gained fame in 1773 writing as "First Citizen" in the newspaper debate with Daniel Dulany over Eden's Fee Proclamation. When the government of Maryland was taken over by the Maryland Convention, the rules against the election of Catholics were set aside. Carroll attended the convention and was elected as a delegate to the Continental Congress in 1776.

Charles Carroll of Carrollton had a long and honorable career. He served in the Maryland Senate from

1776 to 1800 and as a U.S. senator from 1789 to 1792. During his long life, Carroll made a large fortune through planting, leasing land, and investing in iron manufacturing and other projects. He is best remembered today, however, for two things that he had no control over: he was the only Catholic signer of the Declaration of Independence, and he lived longer than any other signer. Charles Carroll of Carrollton died on November 14, 1832, at age 95.

William Paca was born on October 31, 1740, in the area of Baltimore County that would later become Harford County. He was the second son of a well-to-do and politically active planter. Paca was given a good education by his father so that he could make his fortune by practicing law. But Paca found a surer way to wealth, influence, and power. Shortly after finishing his legal studies, Paca married Mary Chew, one of the richest women in Maryland.

Paca used his wife's wealth to build a great brick mansion in Annapolis, but politics was his first love. He quickly became a leader of the Popular party in Annapolis. After independence, he served in both houses of the General Assembly and served three terms as governor. For the last ten years of his life, Paca served as a federal judge for the district of Maryland. He died at

Samuel Chase

Thomas Stone

his estate on Wye Island in Queen Anne's County on October 13, 1799.

Samuel Chase has been called the "stormy patriot." He was a gifted speaker who could raise a mob in the streets as quickly as he could sway a jury in the courtroom. Chase was born near Princess Anne in Somerset County on April 17, 1741. His father, an Anglican minister, was not well-to-do, but he gave his son a fine education and sent him to Annapolis to study law. Chase spent much of his life trying to gain the wealth and status denied him by his humble birth. He was often in or near bankruptcy.

Chase's long and outstanding public career was crowned by his appointment to the U.S. Supreme Court in 1796. A strong Federalist, Chase was accused of using his position on the bench to make political remarks. Because judges are not to argue for either side of any question, he was impeached by the U.S. House of Representatives in 1804. Following a dramatic trial in the U.S. Senate, Chase was found innocent on March 1, 1805. He remained on the Supreme Court until his death on June 19, 1811.

Chase was a man who had intense friends and violent enemies. Even his enemies, however, agreed that he made many valuable contributions to his state and

the nation. One man who knew him said that as disagreeable as most people thought Chase was, he was "the mover of almost every thing this state has to boast of—Strange, inconsistent man!"

Thomas Stone was born in 1743 in Charles County. He was well educated and, like his fellow signers, he trained as a lawyer. Unlike them, he decided to pursue his career in far-off Frederick Town in Frederick County. He was, therefore, away from the center of politics during the 1760s, but in 1771 he moved back to Charles County, and in 1774 his political career began with his election to the first Maryland Convention. After independence, Stone served in both houses of the General Assembly and as a delegate to the Constitutional Convention.

Stone's life ended tragically. His wife's health began to fail in 1776, after she received a smallpox vaccination. Margaret Stone suffered from rheumatism for the next eleven years, and then died suddenly on June 1, 1787. Stone was crushed by the loss of his wife. He resigned from public office and, on the advice of his doctors, planned a sea voyage to recover from his grief. But he died in Alexandria, Virginia, on October 5, 1787, while waiting for the ship that was to take him on the voyage.

The Second Continental Congress assembled in Philadelphia and voted on July 2, 1776, to declare independence from England. Marylanders William Paca, Thomas Stone, and John Rogers were present that day.

a month passed before this copy was ready, and by then, Maryland had elected new delegates to the Continental Congress. John Rogers was not returned as a delegate. On August 2, 1776, when members of Congress signed the parchment copy of the Declaration of Independence, the Marylanders present were Charles Carroll of Carrollton, Samuel Chase, Thomas Stone, and William Paca. Of the four, only Stone and Paca had actually voted for independence on July 2.

A "Declaration of the Delegates of Maryland"

On July 6, two days before news of the Declaration of Independence reached Annapolis from Philadelphia, the Maryland Convention issued "A Declaration of the Delegates of Maryland." This declaration explained why the convention had allowed their delegates in Congress to vote for independence. The declaration was almost apologetic. It said that "no ambitious views, no desire of independence induced the people of Maryland to form a union with the other colonies." All Marylanders had asked for was freedom from taxation by Parliament and the right to regulate the local affairs of the colony through their own General Assembly.

Even after they voted for independence, the Maryland delegates believed it was necessary to explain why they had desired, if circumstances had permitted, to remain British colonists. Maryland political leaders were always willing to fight for greater rights for themselves against the proprietor or Parliament if it would result in more freedom to govern as they saw fit. Independence, however, was something most of them were forced to accept only after they had tried long and hard to remain loyal citizens of Britain. For the men who directed Maryland politics, independence became an unfortunate necessity.

Maryland's Reasons for Caution

Marylanders were not hesitant to support independence because they were unpatriotic or unconcerned about protecting the liberties of the colony's citizens. Instead, their hesitancy resulted from the caution of those individuals who controlled Maryland politics before the Revolution.

The leaders had good reason to be cautious. Too much could be lost, not only in lives, but also in valued commercial and cultural ties. Under the circumstances, Marylanders were probably right to seek a compromise that would preserve their rights to be governed under the Maryland charter. No sensible person would think that the 13 separate and poorly organized states could successfully wage war against Britain. After all, Britain had the greatest land and sea force in the world and had defeated a great European power in the French and Indian War just a few years before. The risks were so great that caution was the best course. Both Maryland politics and Maryland politicians were by nature extremely cautious.

Maryland and the War for Independence

Once Maryland joined the struggle for independence, no one could question its loyalty or the energy of its leaders. Problems were plentiful, as they were in other states. Supplies of all types were scarce. Many of Maryland's men left their homes and jobs to join the fighting, while other Marylanders concentrated their energies on producing food and equipment for the American armies.

WILLIAM PACA: HOW DID *HE* PRONOUNCE HIS NAME?

A Baltimore native will pronounce William Paca's name with a short *a* (*Pack-uh*) as surely as he will call his own town "Bawlmer." But in Annapolis, where Paca built a beautiful brick mansion, residents insist his name should be pronounced *Pay-kuh*, with a long *a*. Which pronunciation is correct? How did William Paca pronounce his own name? This is one puzzle the historian can solve.

During the winter of 1770 a new social club, called the Hominy Club, was formed in Annapolis. Members included leading citizens in the community, and William Paca was invited to join. Part of the fun of the club was putting all communications to and from club members in the form of verse.

On March 21, 1771, two nonmembers asked to attend a meeting. In response to the request, club members responded in rhyme. John Clapham, secretary of the club, wrote,

> If any man gainsay, on his Pate I will rap him,
> By virtue of my commission, Secretary John Clapham.

Clapham was followed by William Eddis, who wrote,

> I fully assent to what above said is,
> And am your most obedient Will. Eddis.

If Paca had pronounced the first syllable of his name with a short *a*, the way Paca Street is pronounced today in Baltimore, he might have written

> And so do I, tho' I fear we may lack a
> Spare glass of wine, but no more from Will Paca.

Instead, Paca selected a word with a long *a* to rhyme with his name:

> And so do I, tho' I cannot but think we take a
> Rash Step in so doing, but no more from Will Paca.

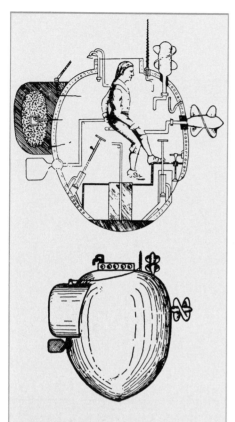

A sidelight to the battle of New York was the exploit of the world's first combat submarine, named the Turtle, *built by David Bushnell of Saybrook, Connecticut. The top diagram shows the position of the operator of the* Turtle. *The submarine had enough air to support life for a half hour; a bottle of phosphorus was used to illuminate the compass and water gauge—water was admitted into the bottom to submerge the submarine and then pumped out for surfacing. On September 6, 1776, the* Turtle *approached the flagship of the British fleet. However, the copper-sheathed hull of the H.M.S.* Eagle *was too tough for the bomb carried by the submarine to be attached securely. The subsequent explosion did no damage either to the ship or to the* Turtle's *operator, an army sergeant named Ezra Lee, but it did give the British Admiral Howe an unwelcome scare.*

The Battle of Long Island

Americans had been at war with Britain for more than a year by August 1776. Major battles had been fought around Boston, in Canada near Montreal and Quebec, and at Charleston, South Carolina. The American invasion of Canada had failed, but at Boston and Charleston, the Americans had forced the British to withdraw.

Since 1775, General William Howe, commander of the British forces in America, had planned an attack on New York. He believed that by capturing the port city and driving up the Hudson River valley, he could divide the colonies. General Washington believed New York had to be held at all cost, and he spent the summer fortifying the city as well as Brooklyn Heights, across the East River. By August 1776 Howe was ready to make his move.

On August 23 and 24, General Howe landed 20,000 men on Long Island. He knew that the Americans had only 10,000 men defending Brooklyn Heights. On the morning of August 27, the British and their German mercenaries, or hired professional soldiers, quickly surrounded the American troops on three sides. Faced by an overwhelmingly superior force, most of the Americans panicked and ran. The entire army would have been lost if it had not been for the heroic stand taken by the Maryland Continentals.

Once the British closed in behind the American line, the Americans had two choices: surrender or retreat to Brooklyn Heights. But the way to Brooklyn Heights was blocked by Gowanus Creek and a large marsh. Major Mordecai Gist led about 250 Marylanders in an attack on the British right wing, which was commanded by Lord Cornwallis. Greatly outnumbered, Gist and his men charged the British line again and again. Each time they suffered terrible losses, but they held the British long enough to allow the rest of the American army to reach safety. Then Gist ordered his men to retreat. Surrounded by the enemy, the men separated and tried to reach safety. Only Major Gist and nine others escaped.

The toll in dead and wounded at the Battle of Long Island amounted to over 1,000, and 256 of the casualties were Marylanders. Howe did not follow up on his advantage. Washington was able to regroup his army across the East River in Manhattan. The Americans lost an important battle on Long Island, but thanks to the brave Marylanders the army remained to fight again.

Kip's Bay

An account of the Battle of Kip's Bay, which took place only one month after the Battle of Long Island, fully demonstrates the bravery of the Maryland troops at Long Island.

On September 15 General Howe began landing his troops at Kip's Bay on Manhattan Island. Judging the defense of Manhattan to be impossible, General Washington ordered a retreat from the city. During the retreat, an entire brigade of New England troops ran away from about 50 British soldiers. Outraged, Washington rode into the mass of fleeing men and ordered them to regroup and fight, but nothing could stop their panic. One eyewitness recorded that Washington exclaimed, "Are these the men with which I am to defend America?"

Harlem Heights

The very next day, September 16, 1776, the difference between the New England and Maryland troops became more sharply fo-

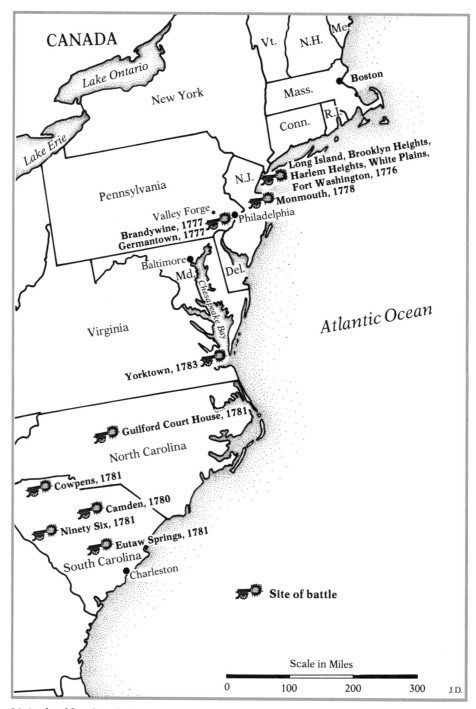

CANADA

Lake Ontario

Lake Erie

New York

Pennsylvania

Vt.　N.H.　Me.

Mass.　Boston

Conn.　R.I.

N.J.

Long Island, Brooklyn Heights,
Harlem Heights, White Plains,
Fort Washington, 1776
Monmouth, 1778

Valley Forge
Brandywine, 1777
Germantown, 1777

Philadelphia

Baltimore

Md.

Del.

Chesapeake Bay

Virginia

Atlantic Ocean

Yorktown, 1783

Guilford Court House, 1781

North Carolina

Cowpens, 1781

Camden, 1780

Ninety Six, 1781

Eutaw Springs, 1781

South Carolina

Charleston

Site of battle

Scale in Miles

0　　100　　200　　300

J.D.

*Major land battles of the American Revolution involving Maryland troops,
1775–1783*

cused. The British launched an attack on the American position at Harlem Heights, the last remaining American position on Manhattan Island. General Washington personally commanded the defense of the heights. After fighting back three British charges, he ordered up reinforcements, which consisted largely of Maryland troops. In his report to Congress, Washington wrote that the Marylanders "charged the enemy with great spirit, and drove them from the wood into the plain."

The Battle of Harlem Heights was little more than a skirmish. But because of the Maryland soldiers, the Americans routed the British for the first time since the colonies had declared independence. This had a tremendous effect on the spirits of the American army. Washington himself honored the Marylanders in a special way on the evening of the Battle of Harlem Heights. The password and countersign for the Continental army were to be *Bell* and *Maryland*. The password was in honor of General Rezin Beall (pronounced *bell*), commander of four units of the Maryland Flying Camp which took part in the victory at Harlem Heights.

Maryland's troops were among the best soldiers who fought in the Revolution. These troops represented the whole range of Maryland's people. The officers, selected by the government, tended to be from the gentry, while the private soldiers came from the very large class of common people. Many soldiers were farmers. Some were artisans. Free black men and some slaves served in the Maryland militia. German-speaking immigrants fought alongside their English-speaking neighbors. This combination of officers and soldiers created an effective fighting force in the War for Independence.

The Maryland Home Front

No battles were fought on Maryland soil, but there was always the threat of British invasion. The British did enter the Chesapeake Bay on several occasions. Maryland, in fact, was a major highway of both American and British troops. Both armies used the Chesapeake Bay as a direct route for transporting thousands of troops north and south, and both British and American troops caused local suffering as they passed through Maryland. They looted farms, stole fence rails for firewood, and made dinners of farm animals. Cecil County, at the northern end of the Bay, suffered more than other areas from this looting.

This 1788 illustration shows wheat being harvested in Maryland by a new method. Rather than having one worker perform all of the tasks involved in harvesting wheat, each worker was assigned to a specific task—cutting, filling bags, or loading bags onto wagons, for example. This division of labor was said to increase productivity 160 percent.

Financial Problems

The cost of financing the war also hurt many Marylanders. Inflation, in particular, was a problem. The Maryland revolutionary government printed paper money to use in purchasing supplies for the army. Many people feared that the government would not back up the paper money with gold or silver and that it would therefore be worthless. Since people doubted the money's worth, they asked for higher and higher amounts of it to pay for goods and services. In this way inflation increased throughout the years of fighting.

Prices rose during the war, but many goods were hard to find at any price, which also made the lives of Marylanders more difficult. As food, cloth, shoes, and other goods were sold to the army, civilians could not always buy what they wanted. Most of the items imported from England before the war, such as furniture, tools, clothing, and even sewing needles, were no longer available. With so much being spent on the war effort, many peacetime projects had to be put aside. Baltimore, for example, had to wait to pave its streets. Its citizens had to put up with dusty roads in summer and deep mud in winter until the war was over.

Wartime Economic Expansion

The war caused hardships, but the revolutionary period also brought growth to Maryland's economy. Wheat replaced tobacco as Maryland's main crop. The state justly earned the title of the "Breadbasket of the Revolution." In addition, Maryland iron foundries supplied cannon and shot. Saltworks, where sea water was boiled or evaporated to get salt, eased the shortage of salt, an important item that had been imported prior to the war.

Merchants and shippers in ports like Baltimore and Annapolis prospered, especially from the grain trade. Some of them bought large amounts of land on the frontier, and others bought town lots with their profits and held them for resale in peacetime. Others invested their profits in the building of more ships. In Baltimore, especially, the shipbuilding industry boomed. Shipbuilding, trade, and manufacturing especially helped Baltimore during the war. By the end of the period, it had become the largest city in Maryland and the third largest city in the United States.

The War on the Water

Maryland's shipping industry was very important to the American cause. It provided ships for both trade and battle. Baltimore shipyards equipped the *Wasp* and the *Hornet*, two of the first ships in the American navy.

Many Maryland captains became privateers, ship captains who were licensed by the government to capture enemy ships and the cargoes they carried. A risky adventure, privateering brought wealth and glory to some men, like Joshua Barney, and ruin or death to others. Locally, Maryland ship pilots, both black and white, patrolled the state's rivers and the Chesapeake Bay. Their great knowledge of Maryland's waterways served the nation well during the Revolution.

Loyalists

Not everyone agreed on independence. Indeed, some Marylanders believed that life would be better if they remained under British rule. Colonists who believed this were called loyalists. People had different reasons for becoming loyalists. Men who worked for the proprietor or the king had their jobs and incomes at stake. Some people did not like the way Maryland's extralegal revolutionary government tried to force everyone to join the protest.

Many people, especially in the Eastern Shore counties of Caroline, Dorchester, Somerset, and Worcester, did not like the leaders of Maryland's independence movement. They believed the merchants and gentry did not care about their rights and problems. On several occasions troops had to subdue Eastern Shore loyalists who rebelled against the authority of the revolutionary government.

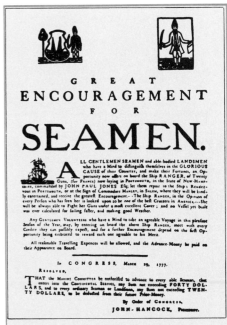

Posters like this one were used to recruit men to serve on ships.

Maryland's slaves had a particularly strong reason to join the British side. Virginia's governor, Lord Dunmore, got permission to offer slaves a place in the British army. Freedom would be the reward for their service. Although some northern states matched this offer, Maryland and states farther south never did. Maryland's leaders were fighting for freedom from British control, not for slaves to be free from slavery. Knowing this, many slaves from Maryland and Virginia escaped from their owners and fled to the British army. Some did receive their freedom and were transported to British territory in the West Indies and Canada after the war.

The New State Government

Independence ended the authority of Maryland's proprietary government. After July 1776 Maryland, like all the states, had to form a new government. The states wrote new constitutions to spell out what powers their governments would have and who would vote for their officials. During the war, all the states were ruled by legislatures set up by these constitutions. The first Maryland Constitution was written by members of the ninth convention who gathered in Annapolis in August 1776. The constitution was one of the most conservative documents adopted by any of the newly declared free and independent states.

Despite the Revolution raging about them, Maryland political leaders felt strongly that politics in Maryland should not become revolutionary. They wanted to ensure that they, not the lower classes, would govern. Samuel Chase, William Paca, Matthew Tilghman, George Plater, Charles Carroll, Barrister, Charles Carroll of Carrollton, and Robert Goldsborough, all leaders of the Popular party, were chosen by the ninth convention to draft a bill of rights and a constitution for the new state. These men worked to keep the government as stable as possible. At a time when many people wanted reform as well as independence, they fought to do away with democratic tendencies wherever they could.

Maryland's Conservative Constitution of 1776

Conservatives were pleased with the state constitution of 1776. Fearing the consequences if the lower classes got power, the writers of the constitution kept government in the hands of men with property. Fearing the consequences if the people pouring into the western section of the state were given an equal voice in government, they made the county the basic unit of representation. This measure ignored the democratic ideal of "one man one vote." Fearing the consequences if an evil man got control of the government, they made the office of governor weak. Fearing a misuse of power by the directly elected General Assembly, they created a system where members of the Senate would be indirectly elected to lessen the chances of abuse. Many of their fears made sense in terms of the problems and threats of the war years, but after the crises of war passed, people began to ask whether a more democratic government might be better for the citizens of Maryland.

The Maryland Constitution limited the role of ordinary people in the government in several ways. In order to vote for sheriff or delegates to the General Assembly, a person had to be male, at least 21 years of age, and own property. The same property ownership requirements held for the men who selected the state Senate electors. These property requirements meant that many poor people and recent immigrants could not vote.

People with enough property to vote were often more conservative than their poorer neighbors. They had more to lose, so they were opposed to higher taxes and other government actions that would take from them what they owned. Voting itself was viva voce. That is, the voter would announce his vote out loud, and the clerk would enter the vote next to the voter's name in a poll book.

Officeholders had to meet even higher qualifications than voters. The more important an office was, the higher the requirements were in terms of amount of property owned, age, and length of time a person had lived in the state. This guaranteed that no poor person, or recent immigrant—no matter how wealthy—could hold an important office.

The General Assembly was organized to represent counties, not voters. Each county could elect four delegates, and the cities of Annapolis and Baltimore elected two delegates each. This meant that the smallest county had as much power in the legislature as the largest. The people in the vast western portion of the state could get a larger voice in the General Assembly only if new counties were created, but new counties could only be created by the General Assembly. The counties already represented in the assembly did not want to lessen their power by adding delegates from new counties to the legislature.

State seal of Maryland, designed in 1794 by Charles Willson Peale.

Thomas Johnson, Jr., became the first governor of the state of Maryland in 1777.

Regionalism

The new state constitution gave power to the counties. It also recognized the two major regions of the state, the Western Shore and the Eastern Shore. The Upper House of the Assembly, called the Senate, was made up of 15 members, 9 of whom were to come from the Western Shore, and the remaining 6 from the Eastern Shore. In addition, there were two sets of state offices. The offices serving the Western Shore were in Annapolis, and the offices for the Eastern Shore were located in Easton. This Western Shore–Eastern Shore division became an important political issue as the state grew after the Revolution.

Fear of the Abuse of Power

Maryland's first constitution was written to reduce the possibility of an abuse of power, either by the people or by the government. Conservatives saw to it that most people could not vote or hold office. They also tried to prevent any single branch of government from becoming too powerful. They sought to achieve these goals through indirect elections and through a General Assembly in which legislative power was balanced between the Lower House, called the House of Delegates, and the Senate. The Lower House was elected directly by the people, and the Senate was indirectly chosen, through electors.

In an indirect election, the voters do not directly select the person who is to hold an office. In one type of indirect election, the voters choose electors who meet and select the person who is to hold the office in government. By not allowing the voters to choose the actual officeholders, conservatives believed an unqualified person was less likely to win election. But indirect elections can also result in the selection of officeholders who are not popular with the voters. In addition, people elected indirectly do not owe their jobs to the voters, so they can feel free to vote for policies not favored by the general population.

Under the first Maryland Constitution, the state Senate was indirectly elected. Every five years voters chose electors who in turn elected the men who would serve in the Upper House of the General Assembly. The governor was also indirectly elected, but not by electors. Instead, the constitution provided that the governor be elected by a joint ballot of both houses of the General Assembly. Many local government officials were not elected at all. They were appointed by the governor and his council.

The kitchen and dining area of cabinetmaker Joseph Neall's 1795 cottage in Easton has been re-created by the Talbot County Historical Society. The Neall family spent many hours by the warm fireplace in this room.

The elaborate dining room of the Hammond-Harwood House in Annapolis contrasts with the more typical Neall cottage. During the revolutionary period, many wealthy people did not want to risk their status and lifestyle by sharing political power through a more democratic system.

Attempts to Make Government More Democratic

Some delegates to the ninth convention wanted to make Maryland government more democratic. Although many delegates sided against them, they won some points. The growing importance of western Maryland was recognized by the creation of two new counties, Washington and Montgomery. The new delegates from western Maryland would make the Lower House of the General Assembly more representative. The new constitution also ended state support for the Church of England. The hated poll tax, which had been used to support the Anglican clergy, was also ended.

The new constitution guaranteed freedom of religion for all Christians. This provision had special importance for Maryland Catholics. The colony had been founded by a Catholic Lord Baltimore as a shelter for Catholics persecuted in England, but Maryland Catholics had not been allowed to vote, to hold public office, or to worship openly since the revolution of 1689. Now Catholics could once again participate in all areas of public life. Jews could not vote under the new constitution, but the state's small Jewish community was able to worship without government interference.

Under the new constitution, a few more Maryland men were qualified to vote, because the amount of property a man had to own in order to vote was reduced. Still, this was far from the demands made by some, that all men in the army have a right to vote. It was even farther from the ideal of others, that all white men be able to vote. Maryland was, however, one of the few states that did not specifically prohibit free blacks from voting. A few who met the property requirement did vote in the state until early in the nineteenth century.

A Conservative Victory in the First Constitution

In the end, the first Maryland Constitution was a carefully written and a very conservative document. It ensured continued control by those who had authority in the counties and in the Lower House of the General Assembly before independence. A few steps were taken in the direction of increasing the number of people who could participate in politics, but even these few steps were viewed with suspicion by men who, just months before, had led in the movement to declare independence from Britain. The leaders of the Popular party—Charles Carroll of Carrollton, William Paca, Samuel Chase, and others—succeeded in stopping or slowing the movement toward a more democratic government.

The End of the War for Independence

Despite the conservative views of the men who wrote Maryland's first constitution, the war involved more people in government than ever before. Most Marylanders were unable to vote, but they could serve in the army or help protect the Chesapeake Bay. Men and women, both black and white, slave and free, joined together to build local defenses wherever a British invasion threatened. People who stayed at home grew additional bushels of wheat or an extra hog or cow to feed the troops. Thousands of citizens came forward with what they could spare for the war effort. Some of the state's political leaders might continue to hate and fear them, but without the hard work and sacrifices of the common people, the war could not have been won.

Victory in the War for Independence took years to achieve. Washington and his ragtag army suffered terribly. They suffered more because of poor clothing, shoes, and supplies than because of defeat at the hands of the British. Then, in 1778, France joined the war on the side of the Americans. France was not as interested in the United States winning as it was determined to see its old enemy, England, lose. Still, the French, with their large fleet of ships and well-trained soldiers and sailors, greatly improved the Americans' chances of winning the war.

Victory at Yorktown

Finally, in October 1781, good luck and bad weather combined to trap the main part of the British army at Yorktown, Virginia. Troops from the north raced across Maryland on foot and down the Chesapeake Bay by boat to reinforce Washington's army. After the British commander, Lord Cornwallis, ordered his troops to leave the town by water, a severe storm scattered his vessels and left him and his men stranded. The British had heavily fortified the town, but the Americans slowly closed the noose. The French fleet, under Admiral de Grasse, blocked the Chesapeake Bay, and, unable to escape, Lord Cornwallis had no choice but to surrender. On October 17 Cornwallis asked for terms. Two days later, while British fifes and drums played a "melancholy tune," the British soldiers marched out of Yorktown and stacked their weapons as the victorious Americans and French looked on.

BE IT REMEMBERED!

THAT on the 17th of October, 1781, Lieutenant-General Earl CORNWALLIS, with above Five thousand British Troops, surrendered themselves Prisoners of War to his Excellency Gen. GEORGE WASHINGTON, Commander in Chief of the allied Forces of France and America.

LAUS DEO!

GLORIOUS NEWS.

PROVIDĒCE, October 25, 1781.

Three o'Clock, P. M.

THIS MOMENT an EXPRESS arrived at his Honour the Deputy-Governor's, from Col. Christopher Olney, Commandant on Rhode-Island, announcing the important Intelligence of the Surrender of Lord Cornwallis and his Army, an Account of which was printed This Morning at Newport, and is as follows, viz.

Newport, October 25, 1781.

YESTERDAY afternoon arrived in this Harbour Capt. Lovett, of the Schooner Adventure, from York-River, in Chesapeak-Bay (which he left the 20th Instant) and brought us the glorious News of the Surrender of Lord CORNWALLIS and his Army Prisoners of War to the allied Army, under the Command of our illustrious General, and the French Fleet, under the Command of his Excellency the Count de GRASSE.

A Cessation of Arms took Place on Thursday the 18th Instant, in Consequence of Proposals from Lord Cornwallis for a Capitulation. His Lordship proposed a Cessation of Twenty-four Hours, but Two only were granted by His Excellency General WASHINGTON. The Articles were completed the same Day, and the next Day the allied Army took Possession of York-Town.

By this glorious Conquest, NINE THOUSAND of the Enemy, including Seamen, fell into our Hands, with an immense Quantity of Warlike Stores, a forty Gun Ship, a Frigate, an armed Vessel, and about One Hundred Sail of Transports.

PRINTED BY EDWARD E. POWARS, in STATE-STREET.

Messengers and printed flyers were used to spread the word of the British surrender at Yorktown, Virginia.

John Shaw, an Annapolis cabinet-maker, made two American flags for the meeting of the U.S. Congress.

Congress Comes to Annapolis

After Lord Cornwallis and the British army surrendered at York-town, the war ended for all practical purposes. Serious peace nego-tiations began in France in the spring of 1782, but delegates there found that drafting an acceptable treaty was difficult.

While awaiting a final peace, Congress was trying to decide on a permanent home. Philadelphia had served as the home for Con-gress since 1774, except when that city was threatened by the Brit-ish or occupied by the enemy. But neither the Continental Congress nor the body known as the United States in Congress Assembled, which replaced it, had a permanent home.

Nearly every state wanted the honor and offered land for a capi-tal city. The discussion became especially heated in the summer of 1783, when Congress was again forced to leave Philadelphia, this time because it was threatened by a mob of unpaid soldiers. Once again forced to select a place to meet, members of Congress struck a compromise: until a permanent site could be selected, Congress would alternate every six months between Trenton, New Jersey, and Annapolis, Maryland.

Marylanders hoped their state would be chosen as the perma-nent home for Congress. Congress had met in Maryland before, from December 20, 1776, to February 27, 1777, at Henry Fite's house on Market (now Baltimore) Street in Baltimore. In 1783 Congress accepted an invitation from Maryland officials to meet in the nearly completed State House in Annapolis. The first congressional session in the State House at Annapolis was scheduled for November 26, 1783.

The weeks before Congress arrived were frantic for the state's officials. Construction of the State House had begun 11 years earlier, in April 1772, when Governor Robert Eden laid the cornerstone. But building materials were often hard to find during the war, so work on the State House had been slow. Much remained to be done to get it ready for Congress. Governor William Paca gathered work crews to complete the rooms and obtain furniture for Congress's use. He also commissioned the Annapolis cabinetmaker John Shaw to make two huge American flags. The completed flags measured nearly 10 feet wide by 23 feet long. The first of these so-called Shaw flags was hoisted in honor of the president of the Congress, Thomas Mifflin, who arrived in Annapolis on December 3, 1783.

Other congressional delegates arrived more slowly, and not until December 13 were enough states represented to hold the first session. Under the Articles of Confederation, which governed the actions of Congress, each state had only one vote, and for a state to be

The Congress of the United States met in the State House in Annapolis from December 1783 to June 1784. The Treaty of Paris, which formally ended the revolutionary war, was signed in the old Senate chamber in the State House.

A Front View of the State-House &c. at ANNAPOLIS the Capital of MARYLAND.

WHO WAS THE FIRST PRESIDENT OF THE UNITED STATES?

John Hanson

George Washington is not the correct answer! The first president of the United States was a Marylander, John Hanson. Hanson was born in Charles County and later lived in Frederick County.

The story of how John Hanson became the first president of the United States reveals something about an often forgotten period of American history. Shortly after independence was declared, the Continental Congress drafted a formal plan to bind the 13 states together. No one wanted a strong central government. Instead, it was decided that each state would govern itself but would also cooperate with the other states. This plan was called a confederation.

Congress worked nearly two years on a plan of government. Finally, in November 1777, the Articles of Confederation were sent to the states for approval. Maryland refused. Before it would approve the plan, Maryland demanded that every state give up its claim to western lands. Virginia claimed lands as far west as the Mississippi River and did not want to give up that land, but Maryland would not budge. Finally, in January 1781, Virginia gave up its land claims. Maryland signed the Articles of Confederation on February 27 of that year. By stubbornly refusing to sign the articles until the western lands question had been settled, Maryland guided all future development of the United States. Congress finally approved the articles at noon on March 1, 1781.

John Hanson was elected first president of the United States in Congress Assembled, the official name of the confederation government, on November 5, 1781. Hanson suffered from poor health and complained of the "irksome" nature of the "form and ceremonies" required as president. He served his full one-year term, however, and then he returned to Maryland, where he died the following year.

able to cast its one vote, two delegates from that state had to be present. Congress could meet with a majority (seven) of the states represented, but votes on treaties required the presence of nine states.

The most important business before Congress that December was approving the treaty to end the war. The treaty was called the Treaty of Paris, because British and American negotiators had drafted the document in a town outside Paris, France. A copy had been delivered to Thomas Mifflin on November 22. Time was of the essence, because the treaty had to be ratified, or approved, and returned to Paris within six months, by March 3, 1784. Travel by ship between America and Europe was slow, especially during winter, so Congress could not afford to delay ratifying the treaty. But the members could not legally act until nine states were present.

Washington Resigns

Meanwhile, Congress was not without something to do, even with only seven states in attendance. On December 20 Congress received a letter from General George Washington in which the general asked to come before Congress to resign his military commission. He had been commander in chief since May 1775. His steady command of the army during the long war years had won him the respect of everyone, and some people even talked of making him king of the new United States. But Congress and Washington opposed such schemes, for they were determined that elected legislative bodies, not the military, would govern the new United States. The details of Washington's resignation ceremony were planned by Congress to emphasize this idea.

General Washington and his aides arrived at the State House at midday on December 23, 1783. The gallery at the back of the chamber and the balcony above were packed with spectators. One of those present to witness the solemn ceremony was the former governor Robert Eden, now titled Sir Robert Eden, first baron of Maryland. Another was the former proprietor Henry Harford. Harford had come to Maryland to apply for repayment for the losses he incurred when the state took over his property during the war.

When Washington entered the room, he faced the members of Congress and bowed, removing his hat as a gesture of respect. The members of Congress removed their hats briefly to recognize the general's presence, but they did not return his bow. In this way

General George Washington came before the Congress to resign his commission as commander in chief on December 23, 1783. The ceremony emphasized the authority of the civilian government over the military.

they symbolically showed their superiority, as representatives of an elected government, over the military.

In a brief but moving speech, Washington thanked Congress for the confidence it had shown in him during the long years of warfare. He then handed his commission as commander in chief to President Mifflin, who thanked Washington for his services to the country and accepted his resignation.

Washington was officially a private citizen once more. The members of Congress showed their respect for the former commander in chief by tipping their hats to him. After greeting the members of Congress and the spectators who had attended the ceremony, Washington departed for his home at Mount Vernon in Virginia. For the first time in eight years, Washington would spend Christmas Day with his wife and family in his own home.

The Treaty of Paris Is Ratified

By the end of December, there were still not enough states represented in Congress to ratify the Treaty of Paris. Finally, on January 14, 1784, representatives from Connecticut arrived in Annapolis. The same day, Richard Beresford of South Carolina, who had left his sickbed in Philadelphia to attend Congress, completed that state's delegation. Connecticut, Massachusetts, Rhode Island, Pennsylvania, Delaware, Virginia, North Carolina, South Carolina, and Maryland made up the nine states necessary for ratification. The vote was taken immediately, and the delegates from these states unanimously approved the Treaty of Paris ending the War for Independence.

Only six weeks remained for the ratified document to reach France. Congress sent three copies on different ships, hoping that one would arrive in time, but none did. Colonel Josiah Harmar, on board a French vessel, arrived in Paris first, at the end of March—three weeks too late.

Although the treaty did not arrive in France in time, the British did not complain. In fact, unknown to the Americans, the British did not ratify their copy until April 9, 1784, nearly five weeks after the deadline. The ratified copies of the Treaty of Paris were exchanged at Passy, France, on May 12, 1784. The war was officially over. The United States was recognized as an equal in the community of world nations.

Washington's resignation ceremony underscored the superiority of the civil authority over the military. The hasty ratification vote approving the Treaty of Paris officially defined the independent status, rights, and borders of the new United States. These events ended the War for Independence. But they were also the beginning for the United States. Maryland and the other states could now get on with the business of shaping a new nation out of 13 colonies. Each of the new states faced the challenge of independence differently, but they all realized that they would have to work both separately and together as never before if American independence was to succeed.

The War's Effects in Maryland

In Maryland the conservative nature of the political leaders and the state's constitution ensured a measure of stability, but the long and costly war brought changes in the political landscape. Baltimore, for example, grew rapidly during the war. Unlike Philadelphia, New York, or Charleston, the port of Baltimore was never occupied by the British during the War for Independence. Baltimore had been an important shipping point for grain, flour, bread, pickled beef, and other goods in the 10 years before the Revolution, and during the war it became even more important. When independence was declared in 1776, Baltimore's population was about 5,600. By war's end in 1784, 12,000 people lived there. Baltimore had become the largest and most active town in Maryland by far. As its fortunes increased, so did those of the state as a whole.

New Opportunities

The war brought about important changes and opened up new opportunities for people in Maryland. Fortunes were made by some merchants who supplied and transported goods for the army. Other people were able to buy land.

Property belonging to those who remained loyal to Britain was taken and sold by the state to raise funds to support the state's war effort. The largest of these estates belonged to Henry Harford, the illegitimate son of the last Lord Baltimore and the proprietor of Maryland at the time independence was declared. Most people who bought loyalist land already had large estates, but some people who had not formerly owned property were able for the first time to become landowners by purchasing property at the sales.

The war also made a difference for Maryland soldiers. Except for those who had come to Maryland as indentured servants, most of the men who became soldiers had never been more than a day's

EDUCATION OF THE REVOLUTIONARY GENERATION

Nowhere was the difference between classes in colonial Maryland more clear than in education. Poor Maryland children did not go to school at all. If the mother or father knew how to read, write, and do arithmetic, they taught their children during the off season, when work in the fields was impossible. Many poor people only learned how to sign their names, however, and others not even that.

Education for the sons and daughters of the wealthy was a very different matter. Whether they attended a neighborhood school or were privately tutored at home, boys received an English education. This meant that Latin and religion were very important. Boys began their study with a simple ABC book or hornbook with the letters of the alphabet and the Lord's Prayer printed on it. As soon as he had learned the letters, a boy was given a Latin grammar. For hours each day, several months of the year, he worked on his Latin lessons. Once a boy had learned Latin, he also was expected to learn at least a little Greek. Arithmetic, geography, and frequent study of Scriptures rounded out the course of study.

Girls from well-to-do families were not expected to study foreign languages as part of their schooling. After learning to read, write, and do simple arithmetic, girls spent most of their time learning useful arts and the social graces. Music, dancing, and fancy sewing were required parts of a girl's education.

Some girls felt that they should learn the same things as boys. Eliza Custis, stepgranddaughter of George Washington and great-granddaughter of Charles Calvert, the fifth Lord Baltimore, complained that her stepfather had told her tutor that she was "an extraordinary child & would if a *Boy*, make a Brilliant figure." Eliza did not see that her sex made a difference. "I told them to teach me what they pleased, & observed to them I thought it hard [unfortunate] they could not teach me Greek & Latin because I was a girl. They laughed & said women ought not to know those things, & mending, writing, Arithmetic, & Music was all I could be permitted to acquire. I thought of this often, with deep regret."

journey from home. When these men enlisted in the army they were marched hundreds of miles from Maryland. They were able to see other parts of the country and to meet people like themselves from other states. Many of the common soldiers in Maryland came from the lowest social and economic class, and most of them faced a life as tenants or sharecroppers working other men's land. Traveling with the revolutionary war army helped break the ties to home that had prevented many of them from moving on in search of greater opportunity.

Opening of the West

American victory in the war also removed British restrictions on settling in the west. The whole country was opened up for the taking. As a result, the years after the war saw a great westward movement of Maryland tenants and their families. The war thus provided a safety valve for Maryland's population. The poor in Maryland had few opportunities, even after the Revolution, but now they were able to move on in the hope of improving their fortunes elsewhere.

Black Marylanders

The war also had some benefits for black Marylanders. From at least 1777, Maryland blacks assisted in the American war effort. At least two blacks, Negro Tom, a slave, and a man called Black Yankee, worked on the *Defence*, Maryland's first warship.

Maryland blacks, both slave and free, worked at many jobs during the Revolution, but until late in the war they were not allowed to enlist in the army. By 1780 recruits were in such short supply that the law prohibiting blacks from enlisting was changed. A person's race was usually not recorded in the state's military records, but some blacks are known to have enlisted once they were legally able to do so. Five of the 308 men recruited in the spring of 1782 by General William Smallwood were black. Other blacks worked on the boats that patrolled the Chesapeake Bay to defend the shoreline from British attack. For some blacks, then, the war provided freedom of movement and a chance to serve their country that they did not have before independence.

Opposition to both slavery and racial discrimination grew during the war. Free blacks who met the same property qualifications as whites were allowed to vote under the terms of the first state constitution. In 1783 the General Assembly made it illegal to import slaves into Maryland for sale.

Most important in the long run for Maryland blacks was the increase in the number of manumissions during and after the war. A manumission took place when a master voluntarily freed a slave. Religion was the main cause for the increase in manumissions, as Quakers in 1777 and Methodists in 1780 prohibited their members from owning slaves. In Maryland, hundreds of slaves received their freedom because their Methodist or Quaker owners became convinced that slaveholding was wrong. Blacks freed during and after the revolutionary war formed the basis of a community that continued to grow and develop in the nineteenth century.

The Perils and Promise of Independence

Too much can be made of the changes that occurred in Maryland because of the Revolution. When peace finally came in 1784, eight long years after the struggle for independence had begun, most

LIBERTY AND JUSTICE FOR ALL . . . EXCEPT SLAVES

The Declaration of Independence said that "all men are created equal" and promised "liberty and justice for all." American victory in the War for Indepedence encouraged the growing number of Americans who were against slavery. They hoped that the new United States would give "liberty and justice" to slaves.

The reasons slavery should be ended were listed by "Vox Africanorum," the "Voice of Africans," in the *Maryland Gazette* on May 15, 1783. The writer pointed out that Britain's "unjust and wicked attempts to forge chains to enslave America" had led Americans to respond "WE WILL BE FREE." Now that victory was won, the author asked how Americans could tolerate "fellow creatures groaning under the chains of slavery and oppression."

Everyone desires freedom and has a right to it, "Vox Africanorum" argued. To deny freedom to blacks because of the color of their skin made no sense. Greed alone enabled whites to keep blacks in slavery. "Vox Africanorum" concluded: "Ye fathers of your country; friends of liberty and of mankind, behold our chains! Lend an ear to the voice of oppression. To you we look up for justice—deny it not—it is our right."

Eighty-one years would pass before slavery was finally abolished in Maryland. Slavery was continued only by denying the promises of the Declaration of Independence to a large and growing number of black Marylanders. Whites said blacks were not able to exercise the rights of free men and women. Vox Africanorum, and countless Maryland blacks, knew that was a lie.

Maryland blacks were still slaves, and opportunity was still beyond the grasp of the majority of the large number of poor whites in the state. Women, regardless of their class, had few legal rights, and no women could vote. The government was still firmly in the control of men who were against widespread democracy. Evolution, not revolution, would characterize Maryland society and politics in the years following independence.

But independence did break the ties that had bound Marylanders to the Crown and the proprietor, and the War for Independence disrupted much more. Revolution leaves little unchanged or unchallenged. Never again could things be exactly as they had been before. The Declaration of Independence said, whether Maryland political leaders liked it or not, that everyone was created equal. It pledged Americans to fight for God-given rights and liberties that could be denied to no one.

The years of warfare showed that the old political order would have to change. In truth, greater political participation and freedom for all Marylanders remained many years in the future. But when the War for Independence ended, few could deny that changes in that direction had already begun. Freedom was more than a word.

Peacetime Problems

To participants, the political conflicts of the 1780s were as important as the Revolution itself. The struggle between people who believed that political power should remain in the hands of men of property and people who favored more democracy continued. Economic problems served to increase the differences between these two groups, and an economic depression after the war made matters worse.

The Government in Debt

As the war dragged on, Maryland's government ran low on funds. The government had so little money, in fact, that often it could not pay the salaries of the soldiers. Nor could it pay the people who provided the army with food, weapons, and other supplies. Instead of paying what it owed, the government issued IOUs. These remained unpaid when peace finally came.

One reason the government had no money was that many people could not pay their taxes. Men who were not paid for grain or wagons that they supplied to the army were in turn unable to pay their taxes. Merchants whose trade with England was cut off could not pay their taxes. Soldiers often were exempted from paying taxes as an inducement to enlist. People could not pay their taxes, so the government could not pay its bills.

People in Debt

The shortage of money affected the people of Maryland as well as the government. When the government failed to pay its debts, the men it owed could not pay their rent, their debts to local merchants, or their taxes. Poor people were not alone in suffering from a lack of money. Even people who had been rich before the war had trouble paying their bills.

One attempt to solve the money problem only made things worse. Maryland sold loyalists' land to raise cash to pay for the war effort, but the purchasers often could not keep up their payments. Some lost their land. Others owed money to the government for many years.

Other problems made the shortage of money much worse. Europe produced large crops of grain in the mid-1780s, which drove down the price paid to Americans for their wheat. Also, the winter of 1784–85 was so cold that Baltimore's harbor was blocked by ice until March, and merchants could not trade. The spring thaw brought heavy floods that destroyed farms and killed farm animals. There seemed to be no end to the economic hardship.

The Search for Relief

Many people who owed money thought the problems could be solved if the state issued new paper money. The state could pay its debts with the paper bills, and the people who received those payments could then pay *their* bills. Leaders like Samuel Chase of Annapolis and Charles Ridgely of Baltimore County supported the paper money bill, claiming it would make Maryland prosperous again. Both Chase and Ridgely, however, would also benefit from the bill. They had bought land put up for sale by the government and they still owed payment.

The House of Delegates supported bills to issue paper money to help people who owed money. The more conservative Senate, however, rejected all these bills. By summer 1786 the problem had become so great that debtors rioted in Charles and Harford counties. Still the House and the Senate could not agree on legislation.

The debtor crisis began to ease by 1787, when good prices for tobacco brought new money into the economy. The political effects, however, remained. Debtors blamed conservatives, who held power in the government, for their suffering. Conservatives saw the violent protests and the storming of courthouses during the crisis as signs of what could happen if they lost control of the Maryland government.

Toward a New National Government

What kind of national government would be best for the new country? This question required an answer in the years following the Revolution. Some leaders were concerned that the national government under the Articles of Confederation had been unable to solve the problems of the 1780s and to get the states to work together. They wanted a more powerful central government that would ensure law and order and protect private property. Those who thought the government under the Articles of Confederation needed to be changed called a meeting in Annapolis to discuss the matter.

The Annapolis Convention

For four days in September 1786, the Annapolis Convention discussed the need to improve trade among the states. Only five states sent representatives to the convention. Maryland did not attend, because the State Senate felt that the issue of trade between states should be handled by Congress. The men who wanted a stronger central government were under the leadership of Alexander Hamilton of New York. They wanted the states to meet in a new convention in Philadelphia the following May to change the Articles of Confederation to make the central government stronger. The delegates to the Annapolis Convention agreed to call for a convention to meet in Philadelphia to work toward that goal.

The Philadelphia Convention and the Constitution

The convention met in Philadelphia between May and September of 1787. Maryland sent five delegates: Luther Martin, John Francis Mercer, Daniel Carroll, James McHenry, and Daniel of St. Thomas Jenifer. Two of the state's most influential political leaders, Samuel Chase and Charles Carroll of Carrollton, chose to remain at home.

Instead of revising the Articles of Confederation, the men who met in Philadelphia wrote a completely new Constitution providing for a new federal government that would have the power to raise money from taxes, declare war, and regulate trade. The Articles of Confederation made the states equal partners with the central government, but the new Constitution took away many of the states' powers and created a strong national government that could make the states do what it chose. The Philadelphia Convention offered this new Constitution for the states' approval on September 17, 1787.

The debate over the Constitution divided people into two groups. The Federalists favored ratification, or approval. Maryland's Federalists were led by Charles Carroll of Carrollton and others who believed that the nation needed a strong government to ensure prosperity and guarantee law and order. The Anti-Federalists, who were against the Constitution, argued that the new government would be too strong. They wanted to defeat the Constitution or to change it by adding amendments. Samuel Chase, Luther Martin, and William Paca led this Anti-Federalist movement in Maryland. They offered amendments to the Constitution that would have given the states more power and protected the rights of citizens against actions of the federal government.

Despite the concerns of the Anti-Federalists, the state of Maryland overwhelmingly approved the new Constitution, without amendment, on April 28, 1788. Maryland was the seventh state to ratify the U.S. Constitution. Men like Paca and Chase continued to work for amendments to the Constitution that would protect the rights of the states and individuals. Their efforts succeeded when the first ten amendments to the Constitution, known as the Bill of Rights, were adopted in 1791. The Bill of Rights guaranteed freedom of speech, assembly, and worship, freedom of the press, and the right to trial by jury.

The New Federal City

Ratification of the Constitution brought renewed interest in a capital for the national government. Many cities, including Baltimore and Annapolis, offered to be the nation's permanent capital. Some people argued that Congress should choose a small town like Annapolis, because the government might be attacked by mobs in a large city. Others argued that only places like New York City and Philadelphia were large enough to provide the services and buildings required by Congress. Other politicians felt that the capital ought to be located somewhere near the center of the country, because travel was often difficult and always long.

Rivalry within Maryland

Maryland leaders favored several locations bordered by the Susquehanna River on the north and the Potomac River on the south. Some suggested building a new city on the Susquehanna or locating Congress in an existing city, such as Baltimore, Annapolis, or Georgetown. In May 1783 the Maryland legislature proposed to move the state's capital to Baltimore and to make Annapolis the site of the nation's capital. It offered to give the national government the State House and the governor's mansion, and it promised to build 13 hotels to house the state delegations. This offer was not accepted.

Some politicians favored a site on the Potomac River. The Potomac was the gateway to the Ohio valley, and there were plans to build a canal to improve navigation on the river. Georgetown was frequently mentioned as an ideal location. Furthermore, a Potomac River site would lie closer to the South, and therefore be more centrally located, than other cities that had been proposed. These arguments were convincing, and in 1790 it was decided to locate the federal district along the Potomac.

Washington, D.C.

The new federal city was built on land donated by Maryland. It was located south of Georgetown, Maryland, and across the Potomac River from Alexandria, Virginia. President George Washington appointed Andrew Ellicott of Maryland to survey the city. Planners expected enough money to be earned from the sale of land in the district to pay for the buildings needed by the new federal government, but they were disappointed.

The capital today is very different from the way it was when Congress first met there in 1800. Then the grand avenues were but broad dirt streets, the buildings inadequate, and the social life dull. Improvements were so slow that when the capital was burned during the War of 1812, some felt it ought to be abandoned rather than rebuilt. It would take many years, with continued support from the Maryland government, for Washington to become a real city.

The End of an Era

The years from 1763 to 1789 were years of conflict and great change. Although they were reluctant to break off from England, Marylanders strongly supported the war for independence with soldiers and supplies. Independence brought with it new problems. For one thing, neither the government nor the people could easily pay their war debts.

Independence also brought about new political relationships. Although they cooperated easily during the Revolution, the states found it difficult to work together in peacetime. The central government under the Articles of Confederation was too weak to force the new states to work out their problems. A stronger, central, national government was formed by the adoption of the present Constitution of the United States.

Maryland and the nation faced many challenges and dangers during these years. Independence had been won on the battlefield. State and federal constitutions had to guarantee that government would serve the needs of the people. Independence was an experiment that had not been tried before. The experiment succeeded because Marylanders and all Americans believed that freedom, and the new nation, were too precious to lose. In the decades ahead, Maryland experienced the growing pains of a new state in a new nation.

MARYLAND		THE NATION AND THE WORLD
Allegany County formed	1789	U.S. Constitution signed
	1793–1815	War between Britain and France
	1794	Whiskey Rebellion Embargo
	1800	Congress meets in Washington, D.C.
	1801	Thomas Jefferson becomes president
Property requirements for voting abolished	1803	
Medical College of Maryland established	1807	*Chesapeake* Affair Embargo
Anti-Federalist violence in Baltimore	1812	War of 1812
Defense of Baltimore	1814	Washington, D.C., burned by British troops
Bethel African Methodist Episcopal Church formed in Baltimore	1816	
	1817	Construction of Erie Canal begun
Religious test for voting and office holding removed	1826	
Construction of C & O Canal and B & O Railroad begun	1828	
Cross-Cut Canal opened	1829	Andrew Jackson becomes president
	1831	Nat Turner rebellion
	1833	Bank of United States crisis
	1835	Chief Justice John Marshall dies
Eight Million Dollar Act	1836	Roger B. Taney appointed chief justice
Reform Act Carroll County formed	1837	
C & O Canal reaches Cumberland	1850	
New Maryland Constitution adopted Howard County formed	1851	

CHAPTER 3

Maryland in the New Nation, 1789–1850

A sense of national unity followed the ratification of the Constitution in 1788 and the adoption of the Bill of Rights in 1791. Earlier opponents of the Constitution, like Marylanders Samuel Chase and Luther Martin, joined the Federalists in supporting the document. The apparent unity did not last, however, and the years 1789 to 1850 witnessed conflicts over many different issues.

A new party, the Republicans, rose to challenge the Federalists. The nation once again fought the British, in the War of 1812. Not all Americans thought this was a wise war. Disagreements between the country's three major geographical sections grew also, as the East, the South, and the West all wanted federal policies that would benefit their people.

During these years, cities began to grow large and to industrialize. Immigrants from abroad swelled their populations and increased their ethnic, racial, and religious variety. Ordinary working people demanded and won a more democratic society. Slavery stood out as the nation's least democratic feature: more than any other single issue, it divided Americans by 1850.

The Political System Matures

The new national administration, led by President George Washington, wanted to create a strong government, as the authors of the Constitution had intended. The president also wanted his administration to be nonpartisan, without parties that opposed each other while representing different interest groups. Washington

THE WHISKEY REBELLION

The Whiskey Rebellion occurred in the western parts of Pennsylvania and the adjacent areas of Maryland during the summer of 1794. Most of the disturbances were in Pennsylvania. But "Whiskey Boys" (farmers protesting the federal government's collection of an excise tax on whiskey) were active in both Hagerstown and Westminster.

The farmers believed that the tax was unfair. They distilled whiskey from grain because it was easier to transport to market than bulk grain, and it brought a nice profit. In addition, like tobacco during the colonial period, whiskey was a medium of exchange in frontier areas where money was scarce.

President Washington and Alexander Hamilton believed the rebellion ought to be subdued forcefully to demonstrate the strength of the federal government. They mobilized militia units from the surrounding states. General Samuel Smith led a Maryland unit in a march to protect the federal arsenal in Frederick and into Pennsylvania to help defeat the rebels there.

The Whiskey Rebellion was put down. Hamilton arrested the ringleaders, and order was restored. Many people, including the farmers of western Maryland and Pennsylvania, continued to object to Alexander Hamilton's economic policies, and they turned to political activity to bring about change.

hoped that all Americans would unite in a common program for the good of the country.

The nation still faced many economic problems that had developed during the Revolution. In the 1790s Secretary of the Treasury Alexander Hamilton put together a program that he hoped would establish a strong national economy. He wanted the federal government to assume, or take over, all the debts of the individual states. He proposed creating a federal Bank of the United States. He also believed that the United States should rebuild good relations with Great Britain, so that trade could be resumed.

Not everyone agreed with these Federalist policies. Men like Thomas Jefferson believed that Hamilton's proposals gave the federal government too much power and that under Hamilton's system, the rich would gain and the ordinary people would be neglected. The opponents of Hamilton's policies came to be known as the Republican party.

Early Parties in Maryland

Although men of wealth continued to dominate the state's political leadership, more Marylanders became politically active in the 1780s and 1790s, so leaders had to pay more attention to voters. Politicians sought out groups of potential voters at militia musters, Methodist meetings, civic events, and barbecues. They used party newspapers to attract and organize active support.

Politics became less of a local affair. The new federal election system, which often placed more than one county in a congressional election district, encouraged politicians to look beyond county boundaries for support and alliances. State leaders visited all the counties, making appeals for support on the local level.

As the Federalist and Republican parties became organized, Marylanders chose sides. The Eastern Shore and southern Maryland emerged as early strongholds of Federalism. Baltimore City, which had supported the Constitution, threw its support increasingly to the Republican party. The upper Western Shore was divided by the early rivalries, but it tended to support the Republican party.

The Federalists

There was a vital two-party competition in Maryland between 1790 and 1820. Federalists portrayed themselves as heroes of the Revolution and as the saviors of the nation in 1788. They claimed to be protectors of an ordered and religious society. As men of property and standing, they saw themselves as society's natural leaders, much as President Washington himself.

Federalists drew leaders from Maryland's elite. Charles Carroll of Carrollton and Colonel John Eager Howard were men of great wealth and influence. Others who had achieved recognition in the war effort, such as General Otho H. Williams and James McHenry, were prominent in the party. When Robert Goodloe Harper moved to Baltimore from South Carolina and married into the Carroll family, he was readily accepted as a political leader.

The Republicans

Republicans were far less radical than the Federalists portrayed them. They, too, supported the Revolution and the Constitution, but they had reservations about the administration's domestic and foreign policies. They were suspicious about British policies and more friendly toward the French. Republicans had a stronger belief in democratic government. Maryland Republicans saw strength in the state's underlying social and religious diversity, and therefore they wanted to allow more people to take part in government.

Republican leaders, like their Federalist counterparts, were men of wealth, experience, and wide social connections. Many, like Samuel Smith of Baltimore, were former Federalists who left the party in the 1790s in protest against Alexander Hamilton's policies. Other leaders emerged from the broader community. Members of the Shriver family, which had extensive connections with Maryland Germans, were party leaders in Frederick County.

General Samuel Smith, a Baltimore Republican, led the state in war and peace. He organized the defense of Baltimore during the War of 1812, and he served as a U.S. congressman, a U.S. senator, and, later, as mayor of Baltimore.

The Election of 1800

When Thomas Jefferson was elected president in 1800, the Federalists were devastated. The party in power had to turn the presidency over to the leader of the opposition. Federalists feared that the Republicans would put the government into the hands of the masses, whom they called a "mob." They feared that people like the debtors who had closed courts in the 1780s would lead dissatisfied citizens in attacks on private property. While Republicans gloated and conservatives cursed their fate, Federalist James McHenry observed: "Public men, you will observe, are changed and changing. Whether there will be a *total* revolution in measures also, time must disclose."

Republican Reform

The national Republican victory was repeated in Maryland. For the next several years Maryland Republicans worked in the General Assembly on an ambitious reform program. They wanted to do away with property requirements for voting and office holding, to abolish religious qualifications, and to have direct elections for governor, the Senate, and certain local offices. But their success was limited by the fact that Federalists still controlled the state Senate.

By 1803 Republicans did abolish the property requirements for voting and replaced viva-voce voting with the ballot. They also reformed the court system and were able generally to lower property requirements for office holding. But their efforts to replace indirect elections with direct elections failed, and the restriction that only Christians could hold public office would remain in effect until 1826.

Republicans hoped to achieve more, but their hope were dashed as Presidents Thomas Jefferson and James Madison became increasingly embroiled in foreign policy problems. Many of the Republican-backed reforms would be addressed again during the Jacksonian era. For now, the War of 1812 was on the horizon.

The War of 1812

The origins of the War of 1812 lay in America's need for foreign commerce. After independence, treaties regulated American relations with the British Empire, but many Americans believed that these treaties were biased against the United States. The problems worsened when war erupted between Britain and France, causing American trade to become a victim of European politics.

Americans claimed the right of neutrals to trade with all sides, especially the European New World colonies, where American produce brought high prices. The warring nations felt differently. The British tried to blockade European ports to prevent goods from reaching France. France argued that anyone trading with Britain was its enemy. America was caught in the middle.

The British also insulted America's pride. Because they had difficulty manning their fleet, the British followed a policy called impressment. Ships of the Royal Navy stopped American ships at sea, removed sailors, and pressed them into service with the British fleet. They claimed that these men were British citizens, but often that was not true. Americans were outraged at this practice. One Baltimore newspaper called Britain "the merciless marauder of the seas."

An Early Skirmish and the Embargoes

In 1807 the naval frigate *Chesapeake* was attacked at the mouth of the Chesapeake Bay, just off the Virginia coast, by the British ship *Leopard*. After a short battle, the *Chesapeake* was forced to surrender. Three of its crew were killed, 18 injured. The British boarded and impressed 4 sailors.

The federal government faced a dilemma. If diplomacy failed to protect American rights, the United States could either stop trading with Europe or go to war to defend those rights. The government tried the first alternative by declaring an embargo on trade in 1794 and again in 1807.

The embargoes kept American ships off the sea, but they also stopped all commerce. Merchants lost money and mariners lost their jobs. Because trade was the primary source of federal revenue, the embargoes also dried up the treasury as America prepared for defense.

The United States Declares War

This state of affairs plagued three presidential administrations. John Adams, Thomas Jefferson, and James Madison each tried to steer clear of war. The Federalist party favored Britain and argued that Jefferson and Madison were puppets of the French. The Republican party argued that British policies were unfair and that America should follow a neutral course.

In the end, a neutral position became impossible because the British pushed the Americans too far. President Madison issued the formal declaration of war in June 1812. Many Americans saw this war as a second War for Independence.

Some Americans also saw the War of 1812 in terms of opportunity. Some hoped to liberate Canada from British rule. They also wanted to remove British troops from the West, where they had remained illegally after the Revolution. Some Americans believed all this was possible because Britain was involved in a prolonged European war. Others worried that America could not win a war with such far-reaching goals.

The Bitterness of Party Spirit

Maryland partisans took strong positions. The Republicans, under the leadership of the popular U.S. Senator Samuel Smith of Baltimore, stood firmly behind Madison and the decision to fight. Republicans believed that some Federalists, known as "Blue Lights," were sending information to the Royal Navy by signal lamps.

The Federalists, the dominant party in state government, were divided. Moderate Federalists were led by Frederick lawyer Roger B. Taney and represented the views of many merchants. They initially opposed Madison's foreign policy, but stood with the nation after the declaration of war. A more radical group of Federalists was headed by Robert G. Harper and Alexander C. Hanson. These men persisted in their outspoken criticism of Madison even after the war began. Such bitter party spirit led angry mobs to clash in Baltimore in 1812.

America's Private Navy

Much of the significant action of the War of 1812 took place at sea. Because America maintained only a small navy, the national government licensed privateers, as it had during the War for Independence. Baltimore merchants, frustrated by the British blockade, saw privateering as a way to regain lost profits. They outfitted fast ships and instructed their captains to capture British merchant ships. Prizes were returned to port, condemned by special courts, and sold. Prize ships and their cargoes produced quick profits.

Maryland made a major contribution to the naval war. The Baltimore clippers, slim and light sailing vessels, were the fastest ships on the sea and easy to handle. Baltimore sent out more privateers than any other American port, so many that England called Baltimore a "nest of pirates."

Baltimore privateers were daring and dashing. Captain Thomas Boyle was an especially heroic figure. During the war he captured between 30 and 60 ships. In addition, while commanding the sleek *Chasseur* in the English Channel in 1814, he had the effrontery to declare a blockade of the British coast. Try as it might, the British navy could not capture the elusive Captain Boyle.

Changing Tides

The tide of war had shifted against America by 1813. The Canadians resisted invasion by the American army and treated the Ameri-

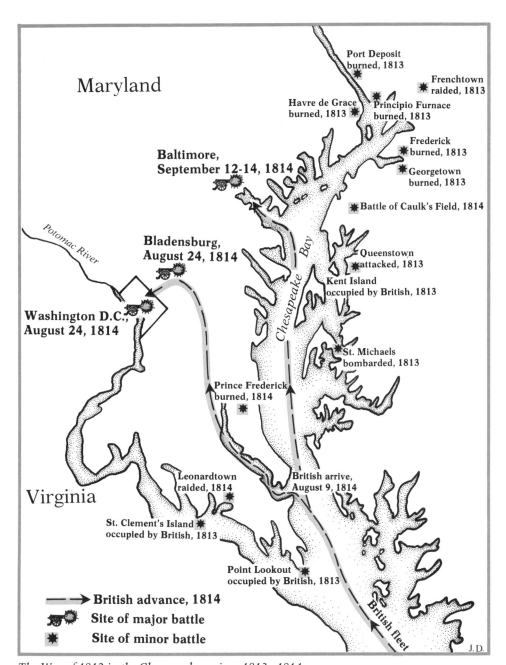

Maryland

Port Deposit
burned, 1813

Frenchtown
raided, 1813

Havre de Grace
burned, 1813

Principio Furnace
burned, 1813

Frederick
burned, 1813

Georgetown
burned, 1813

**Baltimore,
September 12-14, 1814**

Battle of Caulk's Field, 1814

Potomac River

**Bladensburg,
August 24, 1814**

Queenstown
attacked, 1813

Kent Island
occupied by British, 1813

**Washington D.C.,
August 24, 1814**

Chesapeake Bay

St. Michaels
bombarded, 1813

Prince Frederick
burned, 1814

Virginia

Leonardtown
raided, 1814

British arrive,
August 9, 1814

St. Clement's Island
occupied by British, 1813

Point Lookout
occupied by British, 1813

British fleet

J.D.

→ British advance, 1814

Site of major battle

Site of minor battle

The War of 1812 in the Chesapeake region, 1813–1814

In the spring of 1813, a British fleet sailed up the Chesapeake Bay, stopping along the way to burn and loot several towns. This painting is of the burning of Havre de Grace on June 1, 1813.

cans more like enemies than liberators. Despite occasional successes, defeats outnumbered victories on land and on sea. By 1813 a British blockade all but closed the Chesapeake Bay, and ships of the British fleet roamed the Chesapeake at will. The British burned and looted Havre de Grace and Frenchtown, and attacked St. Michaels as well as isolated farms around the Bay.

The British decided to attack the American capital. Rather than attack up the Potomac River, they chose to follow the Patuxent and send the army overland from Upper Marlboro in August of 1814. Their purpose was to humiliate the national government and loot the warehouses in Georgetown and Alexandria for prize money.

The Bladensburg Races

The American defense of Washington, D.C., was as confused as it was ineffective. Under the command of Brigadier General William Winder, the nephew of Maryland's Governor Levin Winder, a rag-tag army assembled at Bladensburg. Although it outnumbered the British force, it was composed of poorly equipped and poorly trained militia. When the British attacked, some units stood their ground, but most fled as the disciplined British veterans advanced. So many Americans ran away that newspapers called the encounter the "Bladensburg Races."

The British victory at Bladensburg opened the gates to the national capital and threatened Baltimore. The pride of Baltimore's militia straggled back toward the city in confusion. Commodore Joshua Barney, whose naval gunners had stood their ground against the British attack, lay severely wounded on the battlefield. General Winder was in disgrace.

As the British troops occupied and burned Washington, optimists hoped that the fleet would depart without doing further damage. Baltimore City leaders believed otherwise. They knew that the British had a grudge to settle. Baltimore's reputation as a Republican city, as a friend of the French, and as a haven for privateers irritated the British sorely. As a London paper put it: "There is not a spot in the whole United States where an infliction of British vengeance will be more entitled to our applause than . . . Baltimore."

The Defense of Baltimore

The defense of Baltimore was one of the few bright moments in the War of 1812. It was immortalized in the poem written by Francis Scott Key, a lawyer from Frederick, soon after he witnessed the bombardment of Fort McHenry. The words in his poem were set to music and gained instant popularity. "The Star Spangled Banner" became the national anthem by an act of Congress in 1931.

Baltimore's defense was better planned and executed than the defense of the national capital. Baltimoreans worked together under Samuel Smith, the ranking militia general from the city, in a frantic effort to meet the British attack. Militiamen, free blacks, slaves, boys, and old men dug fortifications. Women and girls prepared food and rolled bandages. Mary Young Pickersgill sewed a huge American flag, which flew from Fort McHenry to greet the British.

The defenders correctly anticipated the British strategy of at-

Commodore Joshua Barney

COMMODORE JOSHUA BARNEY: NAVAL HERO

Commodore Joshua Barney had a distinguished career as an American naval officer during the War for Independence, as a French officer during France's war with Britain, as captain of the privateer *Rosie,* and as commander of the naval flotilla defending Washington, D.C., during the War of 1812.

Barney's abilities as a sea captain were recognized while he was a young man. He received his first command in 1774, at age 15, when his captain died and he led the successful completion of the voyage. During the revolutionary war, he dis-

tinguished himself as captain of the *Hyder-Ally* in combat with the British ship *General Monk* off Cape May. Between 1796 and 1802 he commanded ships for the French Republic.

During the War of 1812, Commodore Barney commanded a flotilla of armed barges and other ships on the Chesapeake Bay. These vessels were forced up the Patuxent River by superior British forces, and their crews escaped with their guns after burning their boats.

Barney's force formed the core of the artillery at Bladensburg. As the militia units scattered, Barney's sail-

ors and marines held fast until the superior British forces overran his position. Gravely wounded, Barney fell into British hands. The British treated Commodore Barney with great respect and consideration. General Ross and Admiral Cockburn paroled him immediately and saw that he received medical attention.

Barney received a commemorative sword from the citizens of Washington, D.C., and he was later appointed naval officer of Baltimore. He died in Pittsburgh in 1818.

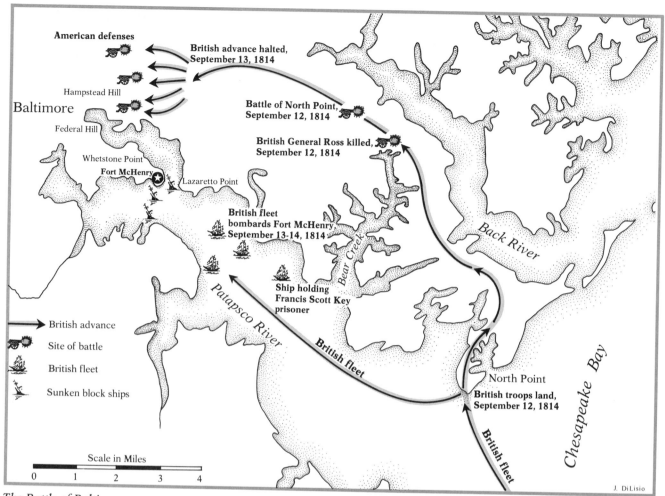

American defenses

British advance halted, September 13, 1814

Hampstead Hill

Baltimore

Federal Hill

Whetstone Point

Fort McHenry

Lazaretto Point

Battle of North Point, September 12, 1814

British General Ross killed, September 12, 1814

British fleet bombards Fort McHenry, September 13-14, 1814

Bear Creek

Back River

Ship holding Francis Scott Key prisoner

Patapsco River

British fleet

North Point

British troops land, September 12, 1814

British fleet

Chesapeake Bay

➤ British advance

Site of battle

British fleet

Sunken block ships

Scale in Miles
0   1   2   3   4

J. DiLisio

The Battle of Baltimore, September 12–14, 1814

tacking the city by water and overland. Fort McHenry, which had been built in 1798 but had never been tested in battle before, blocked access to the city by water. North Point was the most probable landing site for the army. Therefore, the defenders constructed an elaborate defensive works at Hampstead Hill, now the site of Patterson Park in Baltimore, on the outskirts of the city. They planned to meet the British attack farther out on North Point.

The British planned a coordinated attack on Baltimore. Under the command of Major General Robert Ross, the able and aggressive victor at Washington, the army landed at North Point on September 12, 1814. The fleet moved up the Patapsco River to take up positions to bombard Fort McHenry. When the British and the Americans clashed at North Point, both sides suffered losses, and then the defenders fell back to their fortified positions.

Above, left: *Seamstress Mary Pickersgill, working with her mother and her daughter in a Baltimore brewery, made the flag that flew over Fort McHenry and inspired Francis Scott Key to write "The Star-Spangled Banner."*
Above, right: *Francis Scott Key, born in the part of Frederick County that became Carroll County, was practicing law in Georgetown at the time of the War of 1812. He witnessed the bombardment of Fort McHenry from a* British ship he had boarded in order to secure the release of a civilian prisoner. What he saw inspired him to write the poem that became the national anthem in 1931.
Below: *An artist observed the British bombardment of Fort McHenry from Federal Hill. General Samuel Smith coordinated the successful defense of Baltimore.*

The American positions were stronger than the British had expected them to be. The bombardment of Fort McHenry, which began on the morning of the thirteenth, convinced the naval commander that he could not conquer the fort, and therefore attack the city directly, without sustaining significant losses. Among the British commanders, General Ross had been the most willing to take risks. When he was killed by a sniper on September 12, the British command fell to a less daring colonel. This new commander believed that an attack on Hampstead Hill would be very costly.

Victory and Peace

Under the cloak of the night bombardment so vividly remembered by Francis Scott Key, the British army withdrew. They reboarded their ships on September 14, and the fleet sailed away. The successful defense of Baltimore was one of several victories that restored American pride by the end of the war.

In September 1814, the British invasion from Canada was stopped by American forces in upstate New York. The British attack on New Orleans, in which the British used many of the ships and men who had attacked Baltimore, was thrown back in January 1815. The Battle of New Orleans was actually fought after the peace treaty was signed, but communications were so slow that neither side knew it.

Peace had come to the United States and, in 1815, to Britain and France, as well. This meant that Americans would be able to channel their energies to domestic concerns. By this time the political problems and conflicts of the earlier period had become less important.

The Federalist party's failure to support the war made many people view the party as unpatriotic, and it gradually withered away. The Republicans dominated state politics by 1820. New problems and new conflicts faced a young generation of Republican leaders coming into power after the War of 1812. The return of peace marked the end of an era.

The Regions of Maryland

During the years following the War of 1812, the nation turned inward. Marylanders, and most Americans, concentrated on American problems and building their new nation. Across the nation, this was a period of movement and growth. Explorers, then pioneers, then settlers, moved westward, developing more and more of the nation's open spaces. Cities grew in the East and along the river valleys of the Middle West. Immigrants crossed the Atlantic in great numbers and added their labor to the efforts of native-born Americans.

Maryland changed greatly during the first half of the nineteenth century. Its population grew from 319,728 at the first federal census, in 1790, to 583,034 in 1850. Some of this growth was caused by natural increase, some by migration from other states, and some by European immigration.

New people brought changes in the social structure. Marylanders pressed for political change, especially for a more democratic government than had been provided by the state constitution of 1776. More people and new technology brought major economic changes, also. Each of Maryland's vastly different regions experienced the changes in its own way.

The Eastern Shore

The Eastern Shore remained overwhelmingly rural and agricultural. Because the region was served by so many navigable rivers that reached far inland, goods continued to be transported easily by water. No extensive road system was built in this region in the first half of the nineteenth century.

Even before the Revolution, farmers had begun to abandon tobacco for wheat. The decline of the old-style tobacco economy brought social change, as well. In the early part of the nineteenth century, some Eastern Shore farmers left their old homes for the new and fertile soil of western counties like Harford and Frederick.

Another result of the new economy was that fewer farmers relied on slave labor. Some landowners, recognizing that less labor was needed to grow wheat, freed their slaves. They believed that it was cheaper to pay seasonal wages to free workers than to support slaves. Other people on the Eastern Shore freed their slaves for moral and religious reasons.

A large free black community grew up during this period. In 1790, only 9 percent of the area's blacks were free; by 1850, 49 percent of them were. On the Eastern Shore, which did not attract large numbers of European immigrants, there was a continuous demand for free black labor.

Eastern Shore towns had to adjust to Baltimore City's increasing commercial dominance. Former tobacco towns, such as Oxford, fell into decline from disuse. Other towns benefited from the ex-

Table 3.1. Maryland's Population by Region, 1790 and 1850

	Eastern Shore[a]		Southern Maryland[b]		Western Maryland[c]		Baltimore City	
	1790	1850	1790	1850	1790	1850	1790	1850
Total population	107,639	128,504	106,754	109,308	91,832	176,168	13,503	169,054
Total white population	65,141	77,737	55,893	50,396	75,685	149,144	11,925	140,666
Total slave population	38,591	25,997	48,711	47,785	14,479	13,640	1,255	2,946
Total free black population	3,907	24,770	2,150	11,127	1,668	13,384	323	25,442

[a]**Eastern Shore counties:** Cecil, Dorchester, Kent, Queen Anne's, Somerset, Talbot, Worcester.

[b]**Southern Maryland counties:** Anne Arundel, Calvert, Charles, Montgomery, Prince George's, St. Mary's.

[c]**Western Maryland counties:** Allegany, Baltimore, Carroll, Frederick, Harford, Washington.

pansion of commerce. St. Michaels expanded its boat-building and boat repair activities. Prosperity, however, depended on many factors. As trees were cut and not replaced, and other shipbuilding centers emerged on the Western Shore, hard times returned.

New pressures affected existing towns differently. Towns that grew around courthouses continued to be vital in county affairs. Easton, in Talbot County, prospered as Maryland's unofficial second capital. As the administrative center for the state's Eastern Shore offices, Easton developed newspapers, banks, and stores, making it an important commercial town.

Eastern Shore watermen participated actively in Chesapeake commerce. They carried agricultural goods and oysters to Baltimore markets. In Philadelphia the demand for Chesapeake oysters increased after 1829, when the Chesapeake and Delaware Canal opened, cutting across the Delmarva Peninsula. After 1829 Eastern Shore farmers, if they wished, could send their produce by boat up the Chesapeake Bay, over to the Delaware River, and on to Philadelphia.

Southern Maryland

Southern Maryland, like the Eastern Shore, was a predominantly agricultural area. Composed of Anne Arundel, Calvert, Charles, Prince George's and St. Mary's counties, this region remained the center of Maryland's tobacco production. It continued to rely on slave labor to cultivate the soil.

Population changes in southern Maryland illustrate the problems of tobacco cultivation in the nineteenth century. The area attracted few European immigrants, and its white population actually declined between 1790 and 1850. A number of people moved west.

The black population grew, but unlike on the Eastern Shore, the free black component remained relatively small. Free blacks were 4 percent of the total black population in 1790 and 19 percent in 1850. Where the slave population generally shrank between 1790 and 1850 in other regions of Maryland, it remained constant in southern Maryland.

Slavery and tobacco continued to be very important to the economic well-being of southern Maryland. Farmers on the Eastern Shore feared that slavery was a dying institution and that tobacco depleted the soil. But southern Maryland agriculturists believed that their livelihood and prosperity were tied to both slavery and tobacco. Some branched out to produce market goods for sale in Washington, D.C., or in Baltimore, but most followed the traditional pattern.

Like the Eastern Shore, southern Maryland had only a few large towns and roads. The abundance of navigable rivers met most of the transportation needs. Commercial goods continued to be exchanged for agricultural commodities from ships. There was little need for cities to develop as centers for commerce.

People in southern Maryland recognized the advantages of having the new federal city on the Potomac River. Not only did it generate demand for market produce, it also stimulated interest in improving the navigation of the Potomac into the Ohio valley. Such improvement would benefit the region as a whole.

Western Maryland

The rural upper and far western portion of the Western Shore was the area that absorbed much of the population growth that took place in western Maryland. This growth was the product of migration from other sections of Maryland and other states, as well as continued European immigration. The white population almost doubled. Slavery existed in western Maryland, but the number of slaves declined, while the free black population grew.

In the 1790s much of far western Maryland was part of the American frontier. It was a wild, unsettled area whose inhabitants

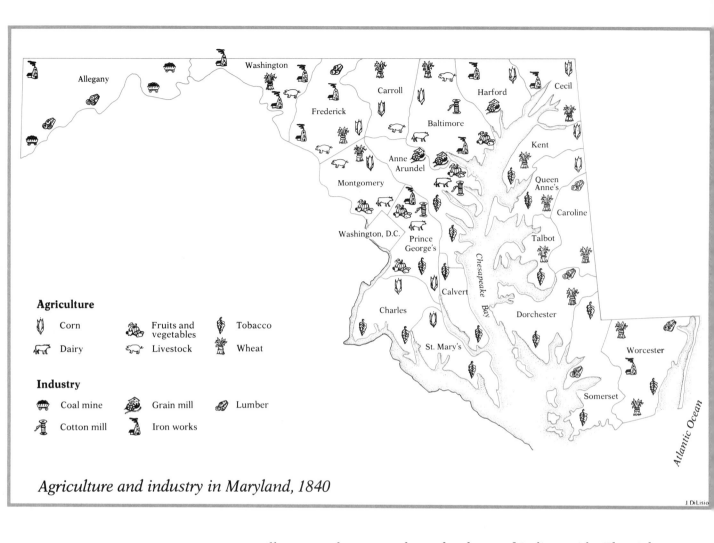

Agriculture and industry in Maryland, 1840

still expressed concern about the threat of Indian raids. The rich land produced a wealth of crops, however, and as settlement pushed westward, the threat of Indians subsided and the population grew. Several larger counties were divided to create new ones. Allegany County was created in 1789, Carroll County in 1837, and Howard County in 1851. This gave people in the developing region more convenient local government and greater representation in the state legislature.

Compared to other regions of the state, western Maryland was a complex cultural mixture. The people of the Eastern Shore and southern Maryland were primarily of British stock, with strong Catholic or Anglican religious roots. Western Marylanders were British, Scotch-Irish, and Germans. They represented a rich religious and cultural variety, especially in Carroll, Frederick, and Washington counties.

In the early period, many Germans preferred the German language and traditions. They maintained strong connections with German areas in western Pennsylvania and resisted assimilation into American culture. Indeed, the back pages of newspapers published in Frederick and Hagerstown reported the news in German. Official state documents were also available in the German language.

Farmers in western Maryland grew cereal crops. These crops, especially wheat, were in great demand. The rich soil, combined with the new use of deep plowing and crop rotation, increased yields, but there was a problem. Unlike the Eastern Shore or south-

Gruber's German Almanac, *published in Hagerstown, circulated widely among the German population of Frederick and Washington counties. This 1814 cover was identical to the cover of the first issue, which was published in 1797.*

OELLA AND OTHER FACTORY TOWNS

Oella is a picturesque factory town on the outskirts of Ellicott City. The Union Manufacturing Company built a cotton mill there in 1810 to take advantage of the abundant water power provided by the Patapsco River. By 1825 the town had more than 70 stone and brick buildings—mostly houses, with a company store, a schoolhouse, and a church—and a population of 700. W. J. Dickey & Sons bought the property in 1887 and operated a woolen factory there until 1972.

Other factory towns developed along fast-moving waterways during the early nineteenth century. On the outskirts of Baltimore, Dickeyville grew along the Gwinn's Falls, Hampden-Woodberry developed as an industrial site along Jones Falls, and Avalon grew as a factory town along the Patapsco River. In Howard County, Savage developed along the Little Patuxent River.

These mill villages and factory towns reflected the economic and social changes taking place during the Industrial Revolution. The factory system required new types of organization and work discipline. The towns also showed the continuing importance of water power in an age when steam power dominated many industries.

ern Maryland, which had an abundance of navigable rivers, western Maryland was mostly landlocked. Unless they lived close to the Potomac or the Susquehanna River, farmers in western Maryland needed a system of roads to get their grain to the mills and markets economically. Roads and turnpikes could be built in any direction. Western Marylanders supported all efforts to improve the transportation system.

The prosperous farms and their growing population supported regional towns. Frederick quickly became a booming place in the West where young men went to make their fortunes. Roger B. Taney, a young lawyer from Calvert County and future chief justice of the United States, moved there in 1801. He found a busy manufacturing center of 3,000 people. Iron and glass works, wagon makers, breweries, and potteries turned out goods for local farmers and for people passing through on their way west. Shoe, hat, and textile factories made clothing for the area. Merchants and bankers serving the community were glad to see the young lawyer who had left southern Maryland, and his practice grew rapidly.

Baltimore City

The development of Baltimore as a major commercial and urban center was a significant departure from Maryland's colonial past. Until the revolutionary era, Annapolis had been the colony's most important city, the center of government, and the main port. Although Baltimore was laid out as a city in 1729, it grew very slowly.

Tobacco v. Wheat

The original city planners wanted Baltimore to serve as a tobacco port, but it never became a tobacco port during the colonial period. In the 1750s, however, merchants began to ship grain in increasing quantities to Europe, and Baltimore was ideally located to collect, process, and ship grain from the surrounding counties. It also attracted the wheat trade from the Susquehanna River valley. Other towns near the mouth of the river, such as Havre de Grace in Harford County or Charlestown in Cecil County, competed for this trade. But Baltimore's growing commercial domination overcame the influence of these other towns.

Baltimore's success as a grain center concerned residents of other cities. Philadelphia merchants, for example, wanted to monopolize

---

ROGER B. TANEY: CHIEF JUSTICE

Roger B. Taney had a long and exciting career. Born in Calvert County in 1777, Taney studied law and was sent to the Maryland General Assembly in 1799 as a Federalist. Defeated in the following year, he moved to Frederick, where he married the sister of another young lawyer, Francis Scott Key. Taney was recognized for his legal talent in Frederick, and he continued to be active as a moderate Federalist. He was elected to the Maryland senate for a five-year term in 1816.

Taney moved to Baltimore in 1823. There he became an early supporter of Andrew Jackson. Jackson as president appointed him attorney general of the United States in 1831. He became a close advisor of the president, who appointed him secretary of the treasury in 1833.

As secretary of the treasury, Taney oversaw the removal of the federal deposits from the Second Bank of the United States. This policy was so controversial that Jackson's enemies blocked Taney's regular appointment as secretary of the treasury and his nomination the following year as associate justice of the Supreme Court. By the time Chief Justice John Marshall died, the composition in the senate had changed, and Taney's appointment as chief justice was ratified in 1836.

Taney served as chief justice of the Supreme Court from 1836 until his death in 1864. During this time the Court handed down many important decisions, but none was more far reaching than *Dred*

Roger Brooke Taney

Scott v. *Sandford* in 1857. In this decision, Taney argued that slaves were not citizens and therefore could not sue in federal court. He also held that Congress did not have the power to exclude slavery from the territories. The Court agreed with Taney and made its decision against Scott. By this decision, the Supreme Court questioned the authority of Congress to resolve the problem of the expansion of slavery.

By 1847, Baltimore had grown into a large and successful commercial city. This view is from Federal Hill.

the rich wheat-growing region in the interior counties of Pennsylvania and Maryland. These merchants complained about Baltimore's competitive advantages as early as the 1760s. As treacherous as the Susquehanna River could be, it was still less expensive to float produce by water than it was to haul it by wagon to Philadelphia. Baltimore would maintain this advantage until the Chesapeake and Delaware Canal was cut across the Delmarva Peninsula, connecting the Chesapeake Bay with the Delaware River. Trade could then flow down the Chesapeake Bay to Baltimore or across the Delmarva Peninsula and up the Delaware to Philadelphia.

The Influence of the Revolutionary Era

Baltimore was transformed into a thriving commercial city during the revolutionary era. Shipbuilding became a major money-making industry. Baltimore enjoyed the natural advantage of its location and was a relatively ice-free port in the winter. The British occupation of other American ports, notably Philadelphia and New York City, enhanced Baltimore's trade. Its major rival on the Chesapeake Bay was Norfolk, Virginia, and that city was burned by the British in 1776.

Baltimore merchants were active during the war. They supplied the American army and, when France joined the American cause, they supplied the French army and navy. This established a strong affinity between the city and the French nation. The most important development of the period, however, was Baltimore's involvement with the West Indies trade.

The West Indies

The West Indian islands in the Caribbean had been settled earlier as European colonies and quickly specialized in sugar production. Businessmen and farmers found that it was more profitable to grow only sugar and to import foodstuffs and other supplies. The islands quickly became dependent on outside sources.

During peacetime the European powers jealously regulated trade with their islands, to the home countries' advantage. War disrupted normal trade patterns. It created great opportunities for profit by enterprising merchants. During the American War for Independence and the conflict between the British and the French in the 1790s, Baltimore merchants aggressively expanded their trade into the West Indies. This stimulated Baltimore's commercial development even more, and enhanced its domination of the Chesapeake grain trade.

The New Urban Society

Compared to the rural sections of Maryland, Baltimore's commercial society appeared to be new and unstable. An individual's place in rural society was determined by family and the status acquired by ownership of land and, in some cases, slaves. The city seemed to be inhabited by strangers.

Monument Square, at the intersection of Calvert and Lexington streets in Baltimore, was a fashionable part of the commercial city in 1848. Maximilian Godefroy designed the Battle Monument, which commemorates the 1814 Battle of Baltimore.

THE ARTISAN SYSTEM

In the artisan system, children were apprenticed by their parents to work in the shops of master craftsmen to learn a trade. Apprentices lived and worked in the artisan's household until after they completed their training, when they became journeymen and worked for wages. Journeymen hoped to become master artisans and open their own shops.

The artisan system was an essential component of preindustrial society, as well as a source of stability and pride. It was based on the idea that success would follow ability and hard work in the gradual stages from apprentice to journeyman to master artisan. Artisans following the same craft often lived in the same neighborhood and marched together in civic celebrations.

In the nineteenth century the artisan system declined as emphasis centered on increased production rather than on quality workmanship. Costs were cut through speed and efficiency, and machines were introduced into more and more crafts to increase production. Machine-made goods cost less to manufacture and thus could be bought by more people.

Baltimore's elite was actually a combination of the old and new. Members of old and established families, like the Howards and the Carrolls, owned property in the city and influenced its affairs. But many of the affluent merchants were originally of modest means and undistinguished social backgrounds. Some were connected to German settlements or to Scotch-Irish Presbyterian families in western Maryland. Others were from Quaker families who had come to Baltimore from Philadelphia. Still others had immigrated from Europe.

These merchants often built trade networks linking Baltimore with the rural areas and with other cities. Many of these networks were built on family relationships. Merchants like the Scotch-Irish immigrant Alexander Brown believed that ties of blood were stronger than a common economic interest between people who were not related. The family was a strong institution in business.

Merchants were also actively involved in Baltimore's political and civic culture during the Revolution. Thereafter, they were active as political, civic, and religious leaders.

Artisans and Workers

Baltimore commerce drew men with varied skills. There were mariners and shipbuilders, who lived primarily in Fells Point. Artisans were needed to build houses and warehouses, to make and repair wagons, to craft barrels and furniture, to make clothing and shoes, to print newspapers, and to butcher animals for food. At the core of the new urban society was the artisan system.

There was also a great need for unskilled workers in the city. These men loaded and unloaded ships, hauled goods from the docks to the warehouses, and did general manual work. Because it was growing so fast, the city was home to many men who were willing to do unskilled labor.

The Urban Black Experience

Compared to that in other major cities, the black experience in Baltimore was unusual. Unlike in southern cities, where slavery flourished and slaves were the skilled artisans, slavery did not prosper in Baltimore City. Some slaves did work in the city, like Frederick Douglass, who was sent from Talbot County to work in the shipyards in Fells Point. However, Baltimore did not have many slaves.

Baltimore acted as a magnet for free blacks from throughout the state. By 1850, more than one-third of the free black population in Maryland resided in the city. It is easy to understand why free blacks preferred living in the city. Because there were so many people, it was easier for them to avoid the social restrictions found in rural areas. They also hoped, even if they worked mostly as un- skilled laborers, that the city would provide greater economic opportunity.

The Commercial Economy

Baltimore's commercial success generated pressures for other developments. During the 1790s the legislature chartered new banks and insurance companies to handle the complexity of in- creased trade. Baltimore became the financial center for the state. When the federal government created the Bank of the United States, it located one branch office in Baltimore.

Such activity attracted new people to the city. In 1790 Baltimore contained 4 percent of the state's population; in 1850 it contained 29 percent.

The Urban-Rural Conflict

Baltimore's rapid and unprecedented growth as an economic and population center created tensions within the state. In areas of the Eastern Shore and southern Maryland, which were losing pop- ulation or which saw themselves in decline, Baltimore's growth was a threat. Those who feared losing influence in the state legis- lature fought to keep the influence they had. Even in areas that were growing, such as western Maryland, there was concern that Baltimore might become too powerful.

Baltimore boosters feared that the city might lose its competitive advantage. They argued that commerce alone was not enough to assure prosperity, that new forms of transportation were needed to connect the city with western Maryland. These projects required legislation and money from the General Assembly, but the assem- bly was controlled by rural interests.

Some boosters feared that Baltimore's prominence might be short lived. As rapidly as the city prospered, so it might also fall into decline. Other Maryland cities, Georgetown, and the new fed- eral city sought transportation legislation to push into western Maryland to reap the profits of the grain trade. And there was al- ways Philadelphia to challenge Baltimore's prominence in trade.

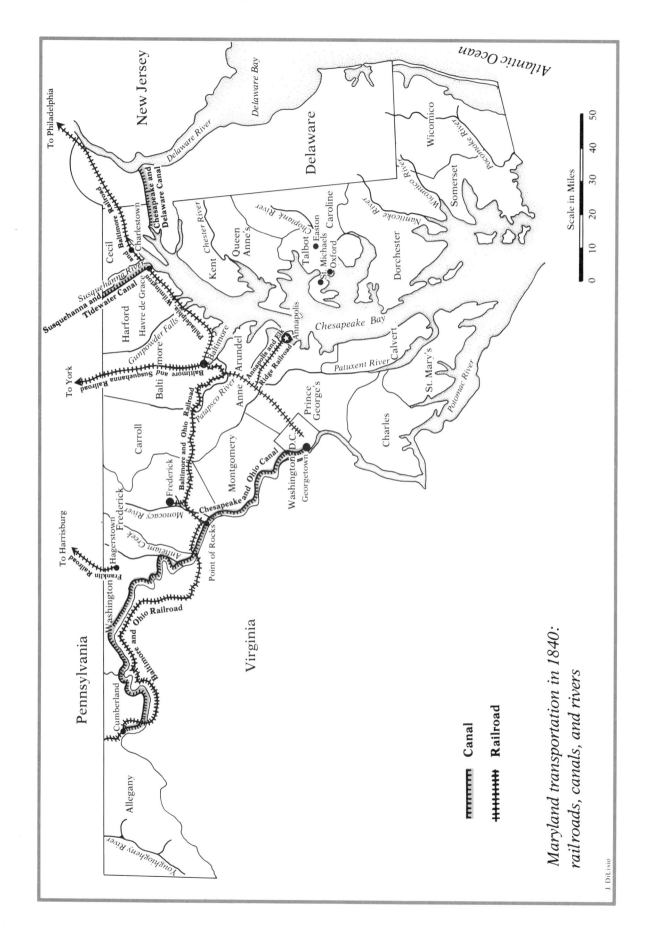

Maryland transportation in 1840: railroads, canals, and rivers

Canal

Railroad

Scale in Miles

0 10 20 30 40 50

Atlantic Ocean

New Jersey

Delaware

Delaware Bay

Delaware River

Wicomico

Pocomoke River

Somerset

Nanticoke River

Wicomico River

Dorchester

Caroline

Choptank River

Chester River

Kent

Queen Anne's

Talbot

Easton

St. Michaels

Oxford

Chesapeake Bay

To Philadelphia

Baltimore Railroad

Chesapeake and Delaware Canal

Charlestown

Cecil

Susquehanna River

Susquehanna and Tidewater Canal

Philadelphia Wilmington

Harford

Havre de Grace

Gunpowder Falls

To York

Baltimore and Susquehanna Railroad

Baltimore

Baltimore and Ohio Railroad

Patapsco River

Anne Arundel

Annapolis and Elk Ridge Railroad

Annapolis

Patuxent River

Calvert

St. Mary's

Potomac River

Charles

Prince George's

Washington D.C.

Georgetown

Chesapeake and Ohio Canal

Montgomery

Frederick

Monocacy River

Chesapeake and Ohio Canal

Point of Rocks

Anne Arundel

Carroll

Frederick

To Harrisburg

Franklin Railroad

Hagerstown

Washington and

Baltimore and Ohio Railroad

Antietam Creek

Pennsylvania

Virginia

Cumberland

Allegany

Youghiogheny River

J. DiLisio

The Promise of the Future: Internal Improvements

Marylanders hoped they could improve both the regional and the statewide economy by building internal improvements like roads and canals. The best natural route from the Atlantic seaboard to the Ohio valley cut across Maryland. Ambitious plans were made to build roads and canals, and even to experiment with the new technology of railroads.

To pay for such ventures, the legislature often authorized lotteries. The proceeds helped build roads, canals, monuments, and public buildings. But the difficulties and costs of constructing internal improvements were far greater than anyone imagined. Furthermore, when the Erie Canal, which connected the Great Lakes with the Hudson River, opened in 1825, it seemed to steal away Maryland's advantage to the benefit of New York City.

Roads and Turnpikes

The public road system was notoriously bad, and many roads had ruts and holes several feet deep. Few people wanted to pay higher taxes to build and maintain an adequate road system. Legislators did not want to support bills that would improve roads but raise taxes, so the state chartered private turnpike companies that promised to build all-weather, hard-surfaced roads if they could charge tolls. Private toll roads radiated out from Baltimore into western Maryland and Pennsylvania in the early nineteenth century.

The federal government was also building the National Road from Cumberland, Maryland, to Wheeling, Virginia. This encouraged private companies to build roads to Cumberland and to con-

The Waterloo Inn was the first stop on the stagecoach route from Washington to Baltimore. It was located in Howard County on what is today U.S. Route 1.

The C & O Canal never reached its final destination, the Ohio valley, but it did stretch from Georgetown to Cumberland. Using a system of locks it allowed boat traffic on the Potomac River to bypass waterfalls along the route.

tinue the National Road to Baltimore. It also stimulated developers to think of ways of attracting federal sponsorship of internal improvement projects.

Roads and turnpikes still had disadvantages. Hauling agricultural produce over them by wagon was expensive and slow, no matter how well constructed the roadways were. Turnpike travel from Cumberland to Baltimore took seven days. Good roads were necessary, but there had to be a more economical transportation system.

Canals

Maryland developers recognized the potential of improving the navigation of the Potomac and Susquehanna rivers. During the 1780s Virginia and Maryland interests chartered the Potomac Company, and a group of Baltimore merchants formed the Susquehanna Canal Company. Both projects ran into construction and cost difficulties. In addition, the Pennsylvania legislature refused to improve the Susquehanna above the Mason-Dixon line unless Maryland agreed to allow a canal through the Delmarva Peninsula.

The effectiveness of the British blockade during the War of 1812 stimulated renewed interest in canals. The Potomac Canal Company was reorganized as the Chesapeake and Ohio Canal Company in 1827. Backed with federal, state, and local stock subscriptions, the company began work on July 4, 1828, on an ambitious project to build the canal to the Ohio valley.

Industries grew up along the route of the B&O Railroad. The Avalon Nail and Iron Works, shown here in 1857, was located 10 miles west of Baltimore. The two-family houses in the foreground were provided for workers, and the "commons area" was for cattle and livestock.

Planners underestimated the difficulty and expense of the project. Plagued by construction, labor, and financial problems, the C & O Canal finally reached Cumberland in 1850. Despite the fact that it did not reach its final destination, the C & O Canal was used heavily for more than 70 years to transport produce and coal along the Potomac River.

Canal building on the Susquehanna was tied to the construction of a canal through the Delmarva Peninsula. Work on these projects was delayed because of regional rivalry between Maryland and Pennsylvania interests, and between sections within Maryland. The Cross-Cut Canal, as it was called, was completed in 1829, and the Susquehanna and Tidewater Canal opened in 1840.

Railroads

A group of enterprising Baltimore merchants recognized the potential of a new transportation technology being developed in Britain. Led by Philip E. Thomas and George Brown, these men petitioned the Maryland General Assembly in 1827 to charter the Baltimore and Ohio Railroad. Construction of the B & O began on the same day the C & O Canal was begun, July 4, 1828.

Initial construction of the B & O went quickly, and by May 1830 the first section was opened to Ellicott Mills. In the summer of 1830 cynics applauded when a horse defeated the steam engine *Tom Thumb* in a race. Supporters of the railroad persisted, however, and by December 1831 the line was built to Frederick. By

April 1832 it was completed to Point of Rocks on the Potomac River. Construction was then delayed by a lengthy legal controversy with the C & O Canal Company over the right-of-way at Point of Rocks. A national economic decline in the late 1830s also hurt the railroad's progress. The B & O reached Cumberland in 1842 and was completed to Wheeling, Virginia, in 1853.

The success of the B & O railroad assured that Baltimore City would continue to dominate Maryland commerce. As the B & O was being built, other railroads were chartered to connect Baltimore with Port Deposit on the Susquehanna, with Washington, D.C., and with Pennsylvania.

The railroads opened up new possibilities for all areas of the state. They carried coal from the mines around Cumberland. Because of the railroad, Laurel became a small manufacturing center serving southern Maryland, especially Prince George's County. It had a cotton mill large enough to employ 500 persons, a woolen mill, and a machine shop.

Regionalism

The persisting pressures of regionalism were apparent in the fight over internal improvements. Men interested in Baltimore's future did not want to use state money to benefit Potomac interests, and the Potomac and Eastern Shore groups saw no advantage in helping Baltimore. Ultimately, all of the improvement projects needed state support, and there arose, in the end, a spirit of compromise. In 1836 the state passed the Eight Million Dollar Act, which gave support to the C & O Canal, the B & O Railroad, several Western Shore railroads, and the construction of a railroad on the Eastern Shore.

The Decline of Slavery

Slavery gradually declined in Maryland for several reasons. Eastern Shore farmers were producing less tobacco, so fewer of them needed slave labor. Grain, vegetable, and dairy farmers simply did not use slave labor in the way tobacco planters had.

In the rapidly growing western section of the state, most farmers owned small farms, large enough to support a family but not large enough to yield money to buy slaves. Most of these farmers had never wanted to own slaves. As Baltimore concentrated on trade and crafts, slavery became less useful there, also.

Slavery declined in Maryland, then, partly for economic reasons. But in the postrevolutionary morality, many Marylanders believed that slavery was wrong. They opposed slavery on moral grounds.

Abolitionists

On the question of slavery, Marylanders represented the national divisions. In the early nineteenth century, most wealthy and influential men in Maryland owned slaves. At the same time, antislavery advocates called abolitionists worked to end the practice of slaveholding.

Following the Revolution, some Marylanders recognized the discrepancy between the institution of slavery and the words of the Declaration of Independence and the Bill of Rights. They believed that slavery went against the principles of liberty and equality they considered essentially American. Also, most Quakers and many Methodists who had owned slaves freed, or manumitted, them at this time because members of these religions were opposed to slavery.

Late in the eighteenth century, the Maryland Society for Promoting the Abolition of Slavery was established. Quakers like Elisha Tyson made up a large part of the membership of this and similar local societies, but many prominent people who were not Quakers also joined. They tried unsuccessfully to get the General Assembly to abolish slavery, as legislatures in states farther north had done.

During the 1820s an abolitionist of national renown, Benjamin Lundy, published the nation's only exclusively antislavery newspaper, *The Genius of Universal Emancipation*, in Baltimore. William

This nineteenth-century St. Mary's County building probably served as slave quarters. While slavery declined in other parts of the state, it continued to play a major role in southern Maryland's tobacco-based economy.

Lloyd Garrison, another prominent abolitionist, was Lundy's co-editor. After Lundy wrote a series of articles exposing the practices of a local slave trader, Lundy was attacked and beaten on the street. The judge in the case set Lundy's attacker free because he believed the attack had been provoked by the articles.

Free Blacks in Maryland

Despite strong opposition to abolitionism, the state's free black population grew. Legally freed slaves joined free black communities in Baltimore, on the Eastern Shore, and in other areas across the state.

In reality, free blacks were not slaves, but they were not entirely free, either. Many free blacks who were married to slaves stayed in the area to work for wages. On the Eastern Shore, which did not attract large numbers of European immigrants, there was a continuous demand for free black labor.

All free blacks found that being freed from slavery did not give them rights equal to those of whites. Free blacks, like slaves, could not testify against whites in court, and most did not have the right to vote. Free black men who met the property requirement could vote under the provisions of the state constitution of 1776. As free blacks increased in number, however, this right was gradually restricted until 1810, when all blacks were prohibited from voting.

Black churches and ministers played an important role in the free black communities. Church groups often organized benevolent societies, which provided sickness and death insurance. Many churches opened schools where children and adults alike could study. Although most of these emphasized basic reading, writing, and arithmetic, at least one black school in Baltimore offered a higher curriculum, including French and Latin, during the early 1800s.

The Maryland Colonization Society

The goals of the Maryland Colonization Society illustrate the complexity of the problems of free blacks living in a slave state. The society, founded in 1817, encouraged free blacks to emigrate to Liberia, in western Africa. It promised them that they would have a freer life there than in a slave society. Slave owners were concerned about the influence of the growing number of free blacks, so they did not oppose the society's plans.

Most free blacks, however, had little interest in leaving their homes in Maryland to go to a continent they had never seen. In 1833, 19 free blacks did sail from Baltimore on the brig *Ann* to

FREDERICK DOUGLASS: ABOLITIONIST

Frederick Douglass was an outstanding abolitionist spokesman in the 1840s and a defender of black rights during Reconstruction. Born into slavery in 1817, Douglass spent his early years working in the fields of Talbot County on the plantation of Edward Lloyd V. At nine he was sent to Baltimore City to be a companion to the son of relatives of the Lloyd family.

Frederick Douglass lived in Baltimore twice, the first time between 1826 and 1833. During the first two years he was primarily a companion to a boy his own age in the Auld household. The boy's mother taught Frederick the alphabet in violation of the custom of keeping slaves ignorant. When the son went to school, Frederick went to work in the shipyard doing odd jobs. He eventually became a caulker.

Young Frederick learned firsthand of the increasing racial tension after the Nat Turner rebellion in 1831. White workers went out of their way to abuse free black laborers. Frederick learned of the abolitionists during this time, too. He returned to St. Michaels in 1833.

Douglass's experience for the next three years was anything but pleasant. Identified as being too independent, he was sent to be broken by Edward Covey in 1834. Covey did not break Frederick's spirit, but he caused him great pain. After that experience, Douglass worked as a field hand.

Frederick Douglass returned to Fells Point in Baltimore in 1836 and worked again as a caulker. He lived on his own and enjoyed more independence, but racial tensions were greater. In 1838 he escaped from slavery by disguising himself as a sailor and taking the train to Philadelphia. His bold plan worked, and, as a free man, he became a leading abolitionist during the pre–Civil War years. He dedicated the rest of his life to working for black rights, and he died in 1895.

---

settle a small colony in Liberia which grew slowly over the next several decades.

The Nat Turner Insurrection

After 1832 the Maryland General Assembly passed a series of bills designed to control the free black communities. The stimulus was the Nat Turner rebellion in Virginia, in which a slave led others in a bloody uprising in 1831. Although there was no uprising in Maryland, this incident provoked a general debate over the future of slavery in the upper South.

The legislation made manumissions more difficult and required anyone who freed slaves to pay for their transportation to Africa. The legislature also appropriated money to pay the passage for all free blacks who agreed to "go back" to Africa.

This type of legislation was never fully implemented, because many people opposed such a general program. Also, free blacks were too valuable as workers on the Eastern and upper Western shores for their employers to give them up willingly. But as the Civil War neared and tensions between the North and the South grew more strained, the debate on the status of free blacks in a slave society grew more intense.

Free blacks in Baltimore established a vital community during the early nineteenth century. Placing emphases on religion and education, free blacks tried to improve their lives.

Because of discrimination, the black members of several Methodist Episcopal congregations began meeting separately in 1787. They incorporated as a separate church, the Bethel African Methodist Episcopal Church, in 1816. The church's first ordained minister was Daniel Coker. He was born a slave in Frederick County, ran away to New York, was later ordained, and returned to Baltimore after his freedom was purchased. He chose to migrate to Liberia in 1820 and lived there until his death 25 years later.

In the late 1790s an African School was opened in conjunction with the Sharp Street Methodist Church, a black congregation within the regular Methodist Episcopal connection. Daniel Coker taught there before he joined Bethel. In this and a number of other day and Sunday schools, black and white teachers taught black pupils throughout the antebellum period, when other schools were closed to them.

Toward a More Democratic Culture

In the early nineteenth century Maryland was a national religious center. During the same period there were also important developments in education, literature, and the arts. The thousands of immigrants who brought with them their language and their cultural and religious traditions also influenced the state's culture.

Religious Diversity

The democratic sentiments that followed the Revolution combined with the end of an officially established Anglican church in Maryland to encourage religious diversity. Many denominations flourished. Several brought about nationwide change.

Maryland's Catholics, under the leadership of men like Charles Carroll of Carrollton, had won political equality in the constitution of 1776. In 1790 Baltimorean John Carroll, a cousin of Charles Carroll of Carrollton, was consecrated the country's first Roman Catholic bishop. He was determined to build a thoroughly American Catholic church. Bishop Carroll worked with other religious leaders on a variety of educational and civic endeavors. This set an important precedent in interdenominational cooperation, which is traditional in America but not in many other countries.

The state was a center of Methodism, as well. In fact, American Methodists officially separated from the Church of England at a conference held in Baltimore during Christmas 1784. They chose Francis Asbury, who had come from England as a missionary in 1770, as their first American bishop. At the same conference, they passed a resolution calling slavery "contrary to the golden Law of God. . . . as well as every principle of the Revolution" and declared that all Methodists should free their slaves.

Despite the abolitionist stand of the Methodist church, many congregations began to discriminate against black members. For example, black members were forced to sit in an upstairs balcony separated from the rest of the congregation. Such practices led black Methodist leaders from Maryland and Pennsylvania to form the new African Methodist Episcopal Church in 1816.

Like blacks, and like Catholics before the Revolution, Jews faced discrimination. Although they had served in the armed forces and had contributed generously to the war effort during the Revolution and in 1812, Jews still could not vote or hold public office in Maryland. The injustice of this was recognized by a legislator from Washington County, Thomas Kennedy. From 1818 to 1826 he pressed the General Assembly to get the law changed. Shortly after Jews were enfranchised in 1826, two popular Baltimore businessmen, Jacob Cohen and Solomon Etting, were elected to the Baltimore City Council.

Education

Before the Revolution some Marylanders had discussed the need for a system of public education, but the state did not act until 1826. In that year the General Assembly authorized a public school system. Even then it voted very little money to support the system. Furthermore, all counties were allowed to vote in a referendum to decide whether they wanted to participate. Most chose not to spend the money.

Baltimore City made the commitment first. In 1829 one school for girls, with 34 students, and two schools for boys, with 235 enrolled, began offering instruction. Some other towns supported public schools, but no statewide system existed until after the Civil War.

Education was available, however. Most counties had private academies for students who could pay the tuition. Furthermore, private donors and churches both supported schools that students could attend free of charge. As a result, more Marylanders were literate than people in states farther south, but not as many Marylanders could read and write as people could in northern states where free education was more readily available.

Maryland's record in higher education was a bit better. Washington College, founded in Chestertown in 1782, and St. John's College, which opened in Annapolis in 1784, offered a liberal arts curriculum. The Medical College of Maryland opened its doors in Baltimore in 1807.

By 1850 people desiring education at all levels were more able to obtain it than they had been in 1790, but many Marylanders still grew up without an education. Over half of Maryland's children went to work on farms or in industries at ages when they are now required to be in school.

The Literary Scene

Maryland made contributions to the nation's literature, but the state was not a literary center. Edgar Allan Poe, writer of fantastic tales and often called the father of the modern mystery, did some of his writing in Baltimore. He was the most famous Maryland writer of the period.

BENJAMIN BANNEKER: INVENTOR

Benjamin Banneker lived between 1731 and 1806. He was a distinguished mathematician, a maker of scientific instruments, and an author who published an annual *Farmer's Almanac* between 1792 and 1802. President Thomas Jefferson was one of many Americans who recognized and appreciated his genius.

Banneker's accomplishments were all the more remarkable because he was a free black in a slave society. He was born in Ellicott Mills and received the help of a local Quaker family in obtaining his early education. The quality and originality of his mind led him to continue to learn through independent study and scientific experimentation throughout his productive life.

All sizeable towns published their own newspaper. Annapolis, Cambridge, Cumberland, Easton, Elkton, Frederick, and Hagerstown, for example, all had newspapers in the 1830s. Newspapers, journals, and almanacs enjoyed a wider circulation than books generally did. *Niles' Weekly Register*, published in Baltimore by Hezekiah Niles, won nationwide respect. Thomas Jefferson was impressed with the quality of the *Almanac* that was published by Benjamin Banneker, a free black from Howard County.

Newcomers from Abroad

Economic opportunity lured some people to travel across the Atlantic Ocean to Maryland. Hardship drove others from their European homes to the haven of a growing country that needed their labor. By 1850 more than 50,000 Maryland residents had been born abroad. Almost all of these immigrants came from Great Britain, Ireland, or Germany. All brought with them a cultural heritage that added to Maryland's diversity.

Irish immigration grew gradually through the early nineteenth century, but then the potato famine in Ireland during the 1840s forced a massive emigration by people faced with starvation and disease. Most of those who came to Maryland were rural people who arrived with little or no money, and most of them settled in Baltimore, where they had to take the lowest-paying unskilled jobs. Many immigrant men signed on to work on big construction jobs, and they helped build roads, canals, and railroads across the state.

Although these Irish immigrants settled in a state with a long Catholic tradition, they met with discrimination in jobs and housing. Churches and the Hibernian Society, which was sponsored by earlier immigrants, including some Scotch-Irish Protestants, provided what help they could.

Some German immigrants were luckier. Some came with savings and could buy a farm. Those who knew a craft could earn a decent wage. While large numbers of Germans stayed in Baltimore, many journeyed farther west, toward Frederick. The Maryland German Society helped the newcomers find jobs.

Germans came in such large numbers that German-language newspapers were published. German communities supported schools in which all instruction was given in German. The German immigrants came from a variety of faiths: Catholic, Lutheran, German Reformed, and Jewish. All brought their traditions of worship with them and, for a while, conducted services in German.

In 1850, 70 percent of the state's foreign-born population lived in

Baltimore City. Many of the other immigrants settled in western Maryland, where they, like native-born migrants, found a growing economy. Very few immigrants went to the Eastern Shore or southern Maryland at this time.

Political Reform and Dissension

The growth of cities, with their commerce and manufacturing, the immigration of new workers, the decline of the tobacco economy and slavery, all had an impact on politics. Demands grew for more democratic institutions such as public education and wider suffrage, which would be achieved by ending property requirements to vote.

As the Republican party continued in power after the War of 1812, its leaders moved more and more toward cooperating with business leaders. Gradually some men, calling themselves Democratic-Republicans and later Democrats, split off from the old party. When they nominated Andrew Jackson for the presidency in 1824, they described themselves as the party of the common man.

Within 10 years the anti-Jacksonian forces formed a new party called the Whigs. Instead of Federalists and Republicans, the two major political parties of the early 1830s were Whigs and Democrats. This new political rivalry would continue into the 1850s.

Democrats and Whigs

Although the Democrats called themselves the party of the common man, wealthy men and ordinary men were active in both parties. The one real difference in party makeup was that most immigrants tended to support the Democrats.

After the property requirement for voting was removed in 1803, more and more people participated in politics. All white men could vote—but no women, few blacks, and no Jews.

The parties responded to the new voters by making politics both enjoyable and rewarding. They held barbecues and hired bands for political rallies. They repaid faithful supporters with government jobs, called patronage jobs. Responding to demands for greater popular participation in the nomination process, the parties began to hold conventions to choose both state and national candidates. Baltimore became a favorite site for national conventions because of its proximity to Washington, D.C.

Jacksonian Economics

President Jackson's economic policies made Whigs of many Marylanders. Two policies stand as examples. The first was Jackson's failure to support internal improvements. At a time when most Marylanders would benefit from new roads, canals, and railroads, Jackson maintained that the federal government had no power to spend money on those things.

Local opposition to the Jacksonian Democrats also grew because the Democrats opposed the Bank of the United States. Jackson believed that the bank exercised too much power over the nation's finances, so he closed it down. This triggered bank failures in Maryland and elsewhere in 1833 and 1834. Many lost lifetime savings. Business failures and wide unemployment followed. An angry group of citizens destroyed the homes of some bank directors.

Until 1835 political debates centered on economic issues. Maryland voted predominantly against Jacksonians and for the Whigs through this period and into the early 1850s.

The Reform Act of 1837

After 1835 questions of reform dominated Maryland politics. The pressure for greater democracy, which had begun during the revolutionary era, increased. Members of both parties worked to end the longtime control of politics by the state's rural landed gentry. Throughout this period, however, political participation remained limited to adult white males.

Sweeping change came in the Reform Act of 1837, which restructured Maryland's political system and made it more democratic. Beginning in 1838, the state senators, one from each county, were chosen by popular vote. The governor, William Grason, also for the first time, was elected by all eligible voters. To give equal representation to the state's three regions, the governorship would rotate among the Eastern Shore, southern Maryland, and western Maryland.

The Constitution of 1851

Demand for a new state constitution came in response to an economic crisis in Maryland. The government had borrowed a great deal of money to pay for internal improvements: the roads, canals, and railroads people had wanted. In the 1840s the state owed over $40 million that it could not pay.

A debate raged between Whigs, who wanted to levy a tax to raise the necessary money, and Democrats, who offered two different proposals. Some Democrats suggested that the state simply renounce the debt, but many believed that course too irresponsible. Some suggested that the government cut back on its programs to save money that could then be used to pay off the debt. The slogan of these Democrats came to be "retrenchment and reform."

The economic problems convinced many early opponents of the need for constitutional reforms, and men began to talk seriously about holding a convention to write a new state constitution. Only four counties opposed adopting a new constitution: Charles, Dorchester, Prince George's, and St. Mary's. A convention was held, and the Maryland Constitution of 1851 was adopted.

The constitution that went into effect in 1851 specifically prohibited the state from incurring any indebtedness greater than $100,000. It also shifted yet more political power to Baltimore City and western Maryland. It provided for one Senate seat for each county and for Baltimore City. It also specified that the seats in the House of Delegates be allocated according to each county's population. Baltimore City could have up to four delegates more than the largest county. The governorship, with a term of four years, would still rotate among the state's three regions.

This constitution further democratized the political process by allowing the popular election of local governments. It also provided that judges be elected instead of appointed.

Beyond 1850

The constitution of 1851 remained in effect until 1864. It established the form of the state government that would face the problems that led to the outbreak of Civil War in 1861.

During the 1850s Marylanders turned some attention to the national problems that would soon tear the country apart. In some ways Maryland represented the country as a whole during this time. Maryland's people included planters and small farmers, slave owners and strong opponents of slavery. Although most counties were still devoted to agriculture, the cities had grown in importance. The industrialists, merchants, and workers had concerns similar to those of urbanites farther north.

These different interest groups could not find a peaceful way to settle their disagreements. The decade that followed was one of steady progress toward war.

MARYLAND		THE NATION AND THE WORLD
	1850	Compromise of 1850
New Maryland Constitution adopted Gorsuch raid	1851	
	1852	Harriet Beecher Stowe's *Uncle Tom's Cabin* published
B & O Railroad reaches Wheeling	1853	
	1854	Kansas-Nebraska Act
Know-Nothing Millard Fillmore carries Maryland	1856	
	1857	Democrat James Buchanan becomes president
Know-Nothing Thomas Hicks becomes governor	1858	Dred Scott decision
John Brown's raid	1859	
Democrat John Breckinridge carries Maryland	1860	Republican Abraham Lincoln elected president South Carolina secedes from the Union
Baltimore mob attacks federal troops John Merryman case	1861	Lincoln becomes president Confederate government formed Fort Sumter, South Carolina, fired on Lincoln calls for 75,000 volunteers
Battle of Antietam	1862	
First Maryland draft First black regiments organized	1863	Emancipation Proclamation First draft instituted Battle of Gettysburg
New Maryland Constitution adopted Jubal Early's raid	1864	
	1865	Confederacy surrenders at Appomattox, Virginia Lincoln assassinated
Democrat Thomas Swann becomes governor	1866	Reconstruction begins
New Maryland Constitution adopted Wicomico County formed	1867	
Black men vote	1870	15th Amendment ratified: enfranchisement of black males

CHAPTER 4

Maryland in Peace and War, 1850–1870

The years from 1850 to 1870 were critical ones in Maryland. Divisions within the state were stronger than ever before or since. The state served as a battleground for the Union and Confederate armies during the Civil War. Because Maryland was a border state, some of its residents fought for the South, although a majority joined the Union army. In both cases, families were disrupted as relatives faced each other across battle lines. Of necessity, Maryland women replaced men on the farm, and, in some instances, in factories and shops.

Politics changed during these years. In 1864 and again in 1867 Marylanders rewrote their constitution. Parties changed, too. The Whig party, which had been powerful in the 1830s and 1840s, disappeared. For a brief period a new organization called the Know-Nothing party emerged, but by 1860 it, too, had ceased to exist. State politics were dominated in the 1870s by two durable organizations: the Democrats and the Republicans.

For 90,000 slaves the Civil War meant freedom. In 1864 white adult male Marylanders accepted, although by a tiny margin, a new constitution that ended slavery. In theory blacks were free, but in practice they were not. They joined the state's free black population of 84,000 in a social and economic system based on white domination.

Despite these changes, many aspects of life stayed the same. The daily lives of some Marylanders did not change much in this period. Most Marylanders still earned their living in agriculture, and farmers continued to raise wheat, corn, and tobacco in the same ways their fathers had. The state's industry and commerce were still concentrated in Baltimore. Even though they were "freedmen," blacks remained in subordinate roles. So did women, who could neither vote, nor, if married, control property or any wages they earned.

Politics during the 1850s

More so than today, political parties defined the public activities of Marylanders in the mid-nineteenth century. Parties held nominating conventions, controlled newspapers, and organized rallies and parades that thousands of Marylanders attended. Because elections were frequent and competition was intense, politics entered into everything.

Political Affairs

Typical of the political events during this period was a grand rally held in Baltimore's Monument Square in 1856. According to newspapers, 50,000 people (of the city's total population of 200,000) crowded into the square for a preelection rally. Many had marched there carrying banners and torchlights and singing war songs. Once in the square, these partisans, or party supporters, listened to their leaders' campaign speeches, in which they were encouraged to turn out at the polls.

Stimulated by such activities, Marylanders voted in great numbers. In the presidential elections of 1856 and 1860, 72 percent of the eligible voters cast ballots, and even in state and local contests, 60 percent did so. Of course, relatively few Marylanders could vote during this period because the constitution of 1851 had limited the franchise to free white male citizens of the United States over age 21 who had lived in the state one year and in their county six months.

In these elections voting was hardly secret. Voters handed a printed ballot that listed the party's candidates to an election judge. Observers could see which ballot the voter selected.

The American, or Know-Nothing, Party

After Andrew Jackson was elected president in 1828 and a competitive two-party system was established, for many Marylanders their attachment to a particular party became a lifelong commitment. But throughout the nation in the early 1850s the Whig party declined, and a new party called the Americans, or Know-Nothings, became the state's most important political organization. The name Know-Nothing, which is certainly not complimentary, resulted from the party's origins. Because it began as a secret society, its members responded to questions from outsiders with the phrase "I know nothing."

The Know-Nothing societies grew out of changing conditions in the cities. The arrival of large numbers of newcomers in urban areas meant stiff competition for jobs. Native-born whites, free blacks, and immigrants often found there were not enough good positions to go around. Newly arrived immigrants, desperately in need of cash, would often get jobs by accepting lower wages than native-born workers had been earning. This situation soon resulted in organized hostility against the immigrants by groups like the Know-Nothings. In addition, there was a misunderstanding that all Catholic immigrants (the Irish and some Germans) held a political allegiance to the Pope.

Much to the surprise of many political observers, in 1854 the Know-Nothings won the Baltimore mayoral race and control of the General Assembly. Then, in 1857, Thomas Hicks, a Know-Nothing farmer from Dorchester County, was elected governor. In 1856 Maryland was the only state in the Union to cast its electoral votes for the Know-Nothing presidential candidate, Millard Fillmore. Know-Nothing candidates ran better in the city of Baltimore and western Maryland than they did on the Eastern Shore and in southern Maryland, where Democrats were strong.

For a number of reasons Marylanders gave more support to the Know-Nothings than did citizens of other states. Certainly the party's anti-Catholic and anti-immigrant doctrines had a strong appeal to voters. The fear that America was being taken over by Catholic foreigners attracted Protestants and native-born workingmen, who competed with immigrants for jobs. It also appealed to those who insisted on conformity to what they believed were traditional standards of behavior and thinking. Some Marylanders were offended, for example, when Germans held festivals on Sundays and when Irish Catholics set up new churches. Seven Irish Catholic churches were established in Baltimore between 1851 and 1858.

In Baltimore by 1860 one of every three residents was either foreign-born or Catholic. In some areas of the city, the second ward, for example, there were more Irish-born and German-born people than native-born. By this time the Germans and the Irish had organized social clubs and newspapers, along with a commercial network of stores.

Throughout the 1850s Know-Nothing leaders like Governor

In this pro-Know-Nothing cartoon, Irish and German immigrants, labeled whiskey and beer, make off with the ballot box, while other foreigners (who voted Democratic) beat up Know-Nothing supporters.

Thomas Hicks and Congressman Henry Winter Davis urged a longer naturalization period for immigrants. They proposed to lengthen the number of years of residency required for a foreigner to become a citizen. They also emphasized the importance of "Americans ruling America." Such platforms attracted many who feared that the Union would become divided over the issue of slavery and who sought a political diversion from agonizing national concerns.

The Democrats

The Democrats, Maryland's other major party in the 1850s, believed that Know-Nothing promises appealed to prejudice and emotion and were therefore demagogic and anti-American. To Democrats their opponents' insistence on secrecy as well as their nativist, or anti-immigrant, doctrines violated the national ideal that the United States should be a haven for all.

Moreover, according to Democrats, the Know-Nothing political clubs depended on violence to win elections. Certainly force was used in some elections during the 1850s. During Baltimore's 1856 mayoral election, rifles, bats, and even cannons were employed by both sides to intimidate voters, and a pitched battle took place, complete with rifle charges, cannon fire, and organized companies. As a result of this political rioting, 17 died and 67 were wounded.

The 1850s was a period of political realignment. Voting allegiances were in flux. Local party platforms also were changeable, and they were often vague. Politics was perceived as a matter of personalities as much as a matter of issues. In the early 1850s some Democrats still looked back to Andrew Jackson as their hero and therefore remained loyal to his party. Immigrants generally voted for Democrats as the opponents of the Know-Nothings.

As the decade progressed, more and more Marylanders came to see the Democratic party as the party of slavery. Particularly in southern Maryland and on the Eastern Shore, Marylanders voted for Democrats to support the institution of slavery.

Election Fraud and Reform

One major issue of the time was election fraud and violence. Although the Know-Nothings were usually held responsible, violence on election day was a bipartisan affair during the 1850s. Both parties encouraged the formation of political clubs whose names conveyed their intentions: the Bloody Tubs, the Butt Enders, the Rip Raps, and the Gladiators. Especially in Baltimore, both Democrats

Rivalry between Know-Nothing and Democratic clubs often resulted in violence. This 1856 cartoon pictures a gang of armed men known as Plug Uglies aboard a coach named after the Know-Nothing mayor of Baltimore.

and Know-Nothings stuffed ballot boxes and bought votes, which usually sold for a dollar.

By the late 1850s some Marylanders were repelled by such tactics and worked to reform elections. By state law, election officials checked lists in each ward to make certain that those men who wanted to vote were in fact legal voters. Even so, illegal voting and intimidation persisted. In Baltimore merchants and businessmen formed a nonpartisan league to increase the number of polling places and to tighten registration procedures. For the most part, however, changes in election procedures were postponed until after the Civil War.

Other Issues

Know-Nothings and Democrats also clashed over the issue of religion in the public schools. During the 1850s Roman Catholic parents insisted that their children be permitted to use their own version of the Bible in the classroom instead of the Protestant one. When a Catholic archbishop asked for public funds for parochial schools, Know-Nothings were convinced that Catholics had overstepped the boundary between church and state.

Issues such as religion in schools, immigration, and election reform had little to do with the growing national conflict over slavery. Temperance, or prohibition of the use of alcoholic beverages—a cause that some Know-Nothings supported—was also peripheral to the slavery issue. As late as 1858 many Marylanders concentrated on local issues and tried to avoid national problems like the extension of slavery into the territories or the growing independence of the South. Community concerns had a more direct impact on their daily lives.

Given that Maryland was a slave state located geographically between the North and the South, Marylanders had nothing to gain from taking extreme positions. In general, they spent little time debating the questions that divided the country. While many Marylanders opposed slavery in theory by the 1850s, few spoke out against the institution or its spread into the territories. Thus, during the 1850s Marylanders supported the Union and avoided the sectional controversies that would soon split the nation in two.

Maryland's Economy: The Old and the New

Maryland's economy during the mid-nineteenth century consisted of two different kinds of systems, one traditional, the other modern. The two functioned side by side during this period.

The Traditional Economy

Maryland's small farms were the backbone of the traditional economy. Such farms ranged from an acre or so to 70 acres and were largely self-sufficient because the men and the few women who farmed them did not raise crops to sell. Instead, these small farmers traded or bartered any surplus they had. Although they existed throughout the state, such farms were usually far from the major arteries of transportation: roads, railroads, and canals.

The families who comprised the traditional economic system raised corn, potatoes, wheat, and vegetables, and they kept livestock, as well. They could afford neither iron plows nor the new steam harvesters that had appeared on large farms during the 1840s. Nor could they pay the dollar a day that it cost to rent a slave or hire a neighbor's son at harvest time. In fact, they sometimes served as day laborers themselves or hired out their sons to more prosperous farmers.

Often their problems were as fundamental as trying to drain the marshes of tidewater lands in order to put more land under cultivation. They struggled against natural disasters of drought, flood, and, in 1853, the invasion of an especially malevolent insect, the Hessian fly.

From a modern perspective their lives seem tedious and difficult. They lived in small single-story wooden or log houses, which were often no more than cabins. Glass was expensive, and there were no screens. In these homes a wooden table and bedstead were prized possessions. In fact, visitors to the state often commented on the poor living conditions of these farmers. One observer of southern Maryland wrote, "This area is dreary and made up of uncultivated wastes, a barren soil, . . . lean and hungry stock, a puny race of horses and houses falling to decay."

The Modern Economy

By comparison, a modern economic system depended on both farming and commerce. In this arrangement large farms produced surpluses of tobacco, corn, grains, and, especially on the Eastern Shore, fruits and vegetables. While a traditional farmer rarely used money, a large producer might be paid thousands of dollars for his surplus. In turn, this cash was used to buy provisions, seed, agricultural tools, and clothing.

The wealthy used their large profits to build brick and stone houses, and even to import furniture and expensive household goods from England. By the 1850s large country villas existed in western and northern Maryland as well as on the Eastern Shore. The richest Maryland families depended on slaves to do the endless and time-consuming household tasks.

Increasingly, the money that these families had left over provided the capital necessary for nineteenth-century commercial ventures. Men like Charles Reeder and John Pendleton Kennedy, whose fathers had been prosperous farmers, invested in railroads and canals as well as in manufacturing establishments.

The large land units owned by wealthy farmers could be efficiently run and produce a surplus mainly because the landowners could afford to introduce new technology to farming. For example, on the Eastern Shore, Edward Lloyd VI's Wye plantation contained 3,629 acres. Across the Chesapeake Bay in Prince George's County, Charles Calvert raised tobacco and grain on more than 2,000 acres. Both Lloyd and Calvert had sufficient funds to try new methods of agriculture and to use new fertilizers to preserve their

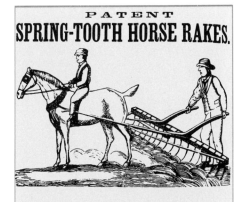

With a spring-tooth horse rake, a farmer was able to rake hay 10 times faster than he could rake it by hand. Springs moved the teeth up over rocks, so the teeth were less likely to break off.

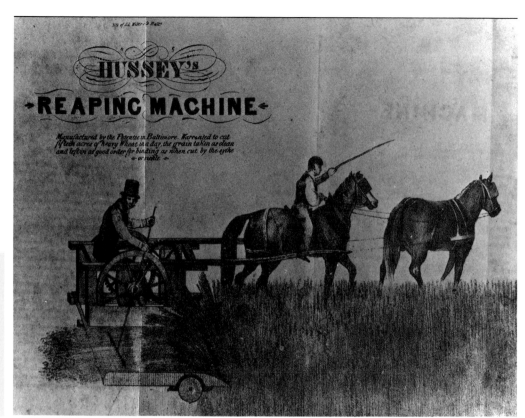

It took a farmer using a scythe two to three weeks to harvest a 40-acre field. With Hussey's reaping machine, pictured here, or McCormick's reaper, a farmer could harvest the same field in two and a half days.

land's fertility. Like most large-scale planters, Lloyd and Calvert depended on slaves for their labor. Lloyd owned 210 slaves, and Calvert more than 100. They, like other Maryland planters, especially in southern Maryland and on the Eastern Shore, ran farms that resembled southern plantations.

The raising of crops for cash, whether on the Eastern Shore or in western Maryland, depended on an efficient transportation system to get perishable goods to market. By the 1860s Maryland farmers moved their harvested crops into market by roads (some mud, some plank, a few macadam or concrete), canals, rivers, and, increasingly, railroads.

When the Baltimore and Ohio reached Wheeling, Virginia, in 1853, markets in previously isolated areas became available. The B & O tapped into the local midwestern transportation network of railroads, river boats, and wagon routes. Smaller lines went north and linked Maryland with Philadelphia and New York. Of course, the Chesapeake and Ohio Canal still operated.

Baltimore

Baltimore stood at the hub of this more modern economic system. By 1860 nearly one out of every three Marylanders lived in the city, and its population of 212,000 made Baltimore the third largest city in the United States.

In a slow but persisting process, thousands of Marylanders, people from other states, and German and Irish immigrants left the countryside to find employment in shipbuilding yards and in iron and textile mills.

While the white population in Baltimore more than doubled, the white population in southern Maryland and on the Eastern Shore stayed roughly the same from 1840 to 1860. Baltimore's combined free and slave black population increased more than 30 percent during these same twenty years.

Baltimore's port supported the city, where commerce was still more important than industry. Cumberland coal, flour from local mills, tobacco from southern Maryland, and grain from the Eastern Shore came to the busy docks of Baltimore's harbor and Fells Point. By railroad and ship, these goods were then transported throughout the world. The city had an especially brisk trade with South America, exchanging agricultural goods such as high-grade flour, as well as finished textiles, for coffee and guano, a natural fertilizer.

Baltimore was not only an international trading depot; it was also at the center of an important interior trade. Products from overseas such as coffee and copper ore arrived in Baltimore and then were sent throughout the United States by railroad, wagon, and canal barge. In the 1850s these goods more and more frequently were sent to the North and West, rather than to the South.

Encouraged by this trade, Baltimore businessmen built factories in order to change the natural products of the farm into finished goods. The city became well known for its sugar refineries, tanneries (where leather goods were produced), and clothing factories, as well as its iron mills. In 1860 Baltimore employed more than half of the state's industrial workers and produced more manufactured goods than any southern city, including St. Louis.

On a lesser scale, the state's towns and other cities, especially in the western and northern parts of the state, also participated in this new modern economy. By 1860 Frederick, the state's second largest city with 8,000 inhabitants, and Annapolis, with 4,500 people, also served as transportation and trading centers. Small workshops and homes that produced goods gradually were replaced by factories. Then, as now, however, the state's economy was dominated by Baltimore, where most of the state's industry and commerce was concentrated.

Table 4.1. Leading Free Black Occupations in Baltimore, 1850 and 1860

Occupation	1850	1860
Barbers	91	96
Blacksmiths	31	27
Bricklayers	63	93
Butchers	16	9
Carriage drivers	33	34
Carters, draymen, etc.	385	331
Carpenters	26	13
Caulkers	75	63
Cooks	22	26
Grain measurers	27	17
Hod carriers	14	10
Hucksters	19	28
Laborers	799	571
Ostlers	11	9
Oystermen	24	50
Porters, waiters, etc.	236	226
Rope makers	12	1
Sawyers	146	47
Seamen	94	107
Seamstresses	20	4
Shoe makers	24	11
Shopkeepers	21	13
Stevedores	35	34
Washers	260	142
White washers	70	62

SOURCE: Matchett's *Baltimore Directory*, 1849–50 (Baltimore: R.[ichard] J. Matchett, 1849), pp. 439–73; *Wood's Baltimore City Directory* (Baltimore: John W. Woods, [1860]), pp. 427–59. Courtesy of the Maryland Historical Society.

Industrial Workers

The diverse labor force on which this production depended was a mixed, and typically American, one. Many of the unskilled workers, who earned as little as 50¢ a day, were recent Irish and German immigrants. Others were free blacks. Still another labor source consisted of slaves who were hired out by their masters, who then collected their wages. In his autobiography, Frederick Douglass describes how each Saturday night he was compelled to deliver every cent he had earned that day to his "Master Hugh." In return, he received board and some clothing.

For all these workers, the hours were long, usually more than 10 hours a day. To protect themselves, some groups of skilled workers organized workingmen's associations. Especially important were the efforts of two groups, the Association of Black Caulkers and the Society of Employing Shipwrights, whose members were white. Before the Civil War, Baltimore was famous for its workers' strikes, for shorter hours, usually a 10-hour day, and higher wages.

Yet, wages remained low throughout this period. In 1860 William Finsley paid each of the 20 women in his textile mill near the Jones Falls $5.05 per month, while male workers in a cabinet shop earned $16.00 each month. Wages of $5.00 per month plus board were common for domestic servants, and storeowners calculated that this was the cost of keeping a slave. During this period, it cost about $4.50 a week for a family to survive, or at least this was the amount of money allocated by Baltimore's Association for the Improvement of the Condition of the Poor.

Daily Life at Midcentury

For the most part, the lives of Marylanders centered around their families. Much larger than families of today, a typical midcentury Maryland family consisted of parents and four children. The romantic image of the nineteenth-century family as one in which grandparents, parents, children, and other relatives all lived in one contented household is incorrect. In fact, nuclear families, families made up of just parents or stepparents and children, prevailed, although many Maryland families did have servants and slaves living under the same roof with them.

Fathers had extensive legal and economic powers in what are called patriarchal, or male-dominated, domestic arrangements.

Only by a special legislative bill could married couples end their marriage. Mothers had no custody rights, because fathers were the automatic legal guardians of their children. In practice, long-term separations often took the place of a legal divorce.

Health

Death was more likely to divide the family than voluntary separations, and in some cases families were reformulated by remarriage. One of every four children could be expected to die before age 16 from malaria, diphtheria, typhoid, whooping cough, and a host of bacterial infections now treated by modern antibiotics. Today's Marylanders live into their 70s, but the average life expectancy in midcentury Maryland was less than 35 years. For those who lived in the tidewater regions of southern Maryland and the Eastern Shore, as well as for slaves throughout the state, life expectancy dipped into the 20s.

Throughout the period, epidemics of cholera, yellow fever, and typhoid were a terrifying part of Maryland life. Because no one knew the cause of these epidemics, there was no way to combat them. The commonly held belief that germs were airborne led people to shut their windows and stay inside. In 1855, when Baltimoreans heard of the yellow fever epidemic in nearby Norfolk, Virginia, they did everything from sniffing rags dipped in vinegar to holding public prayer meetings to try to avoid getting the disease.

Because there were few hospitals, few trained doctors, and fewer treatments, one of the important tasks of Maryland women was to nurse the sick. Their remedies often involved what is called "invalid cookery," that is, homemade medications created from herbs and edibles.

The Role of Women

Women cleaned, laundered, raised the young, and, especially farmers' wives, clothed their families. If they lived in the country, they tended the animals, made butter, and generally provided their households with goods that today are bought in stores. One Maryland woman in the 1850s wrote, "I am so harried that I can say no more. I have to finish a pair of tweed pants commenced this morning."

Despite their contributions to the household, wives had no legal standing. According to the ancient doctrine of coverture, a woman was "covered" by her husband and had no right to sign contracts

MEDICAL THERAPIES

Medical care in the nineteenth century differed in many ways from the medical care of today. Some of the treatments employed by doctors threatened life more than the home remedies did. One example involved bleeding a patient by using small knives, or lancets, and even the bloodsucking worms called leeches. Bleeding supposedly restored the body to its proper balance.

Doctors also used massive doses of drugs. Thus, the prescription for cholera included laudanum (an opium derivative), camphor, and calomel. One Maryland doctor advised taking a dose every five minutes "until vomiting ceases," at which time the patient was to be bled.

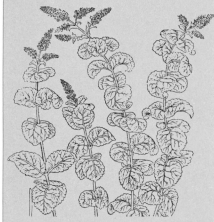

Home remedies were based on herbal preparations. Mint was used as a remedy for nausea and vomiting. Rhubarb stalks boiled with saffron were thought to cure dysentery. Cooked cabbage leaves were rubbed on boils. Ergot, a rye fungus, was used to bring on labor. Some of these home cures were effective, and some of them were not. Generally they were not as dangerous as techniques like bleeding.

or convey property. Unless she and her fiancé signed an agreement before their marriage, a woman had to turn over all she owned to her husband. Married women who worked outside the home did not control their wages. Nor could women control their inherited or earned assets until 1882, when the Maryland legislature finally passed a Married Woman's Property Act.

Single women who lived in the city often worked outside the home. For example, in the textile mills in Phoenix, in Baltimore County, and along the Jones Falls, young single women, some as young as 10, made up more than half of the work force. Female workers were sought after in the textile industry because of the supposed dexterity of female fingers. In Baltimore in 1860, young single women were most likely to be employed as live-in servants, cigar wrappers, laundresses, and textile spinners.

Schooling

Mid-nineteenth-century Maryland had several different kinds of schools. In private all-male academies, the sons of the wealthy were taught Greek and Latin. Women were responsible for teaching their children to read and write at home in areas of the state where there were no district schools.

Although there was no statewide school system, more and more communities used public taxes to support one-room schoolhouses for students of all ages from 5 to 21 and all levels of ability. Especially in Baltimore and the larger towns, these classrooms were presided over by strict disciplinarians, who did not hesitate to use whips and rods. Learning was based on the concept that the mind, like a muscle, strengthened with use. Therefore most material had to be memorized and recited in a question-by-teacher, answer-by-student procedure.

The idea of a public "high" school supported by taxes was new. By the 1850s there were several such institutions in Baltimore, with separate schools for boys and girls. Yet in the city only one out of every four school-age children was in school, and a college education was rare and generally limited to the wealthy. This did not mean that school children attended school every day for at least five hours. Boys in farm areas often stayed home during planting and harvest time, and frequently girls left school to help their mothers with a new baby or to help during family illness. Only after the Civil War did Maryland pass regulations about school attendance.

Before the war, blacks received less formal schooling than whites. Slaves were educated at the whim of their masters. Sophia Auld, for example, "very kindly" taught Frederick Douglass the alphabet before her husband forbade it. By the 1850s Baltimore's large free black community had established several schools for blacks, and in this endeavor they were aided by white congregations. The most successful of these schools in the mid-nineteenth century, the Wells Free School, survived until the city finally used local taxes to support segregated institutions late in the century.

Religion

Churches helped to define the lives of mid-century Marylanders. The state has always been associated with Roman Catholicism because of its original Catholic proprietor and settlers. During the 1850s, largely as a result of immigration, Catholics increased their numbers as well as the number of institutions they supported. So too did Protestants, and there is no doubt that in 1860 most Marylanders were Protestant, with the largest denominations being Methodists, Lutherans, and Presbyterians. By the mid-nineteenth century, churches played a prominent role in the essential ceremonies of most Marylanders' lives. For example, in colonial Maryland marriages took place at home, but by 1850 weddings and funerals, as well as celebrations of national holidays, were usually held in churches.

Slavery in the "Free State" in 1850

Just as their ancestors had, many white Marylanders continued to support slavery, and in 1860 the institution was more than 200 years old. Some slaves were emancipated by their owners, however, while others won their freedom through self-purchase or being purchased by relatives. Some Maryland slaves were sold to plantations in the South. As a result, there were fewer slaves and more free blacks in Maryland in 1860 than there had been in the early 1800s.

Emancipation Efforts

By the 1850s few of Maryland's whites agreed with the abolitionists, who believed that slavery should be abolished immediately. One who did was William Gunnison, a Baltimore merchant who suffered economically and politically for his principles. Among

Table 4.2. Maryland Population by Condition and Color, 1860

County	White	Free Black	Slave	Total County Population
Allegany	27,215	467	666	28,348
Anne Arundel	11,704	4,864	7,332	23,900
Baltimore[a]	231,242	29,911	5,400	266,553
Calvert	3,997	1,841	4,609	10,447
Caroline	7,604	2,786	739	11,129
Carroll	22,525	1,225	783	24,533
Cecil	19,994	2,918	950	23,862
Charles	5,796	1,068	9,653	16,517
Dorchester	11,654	4,684	4,123	20,461
Frederick	38,391	4,957	3,243	46,591
Harford	17,971	3,644	1,800	23,415
Howard	9,081	1,395	2,862	13,338
Kent	7,347	3,411	2,509	13,267
Montgomery	11,349	1,552	5,421	18,322
Prince George's	9,650	1,198	12,479	23,327
Queen Anne's	8,415	3,372	4,174	15,961
St. Mary's	6,798	1,866	6,549	15,213
Somerset	15,332	4,571	5,089	24,992
Talbot	8,106	2,964	3,725	14,795
Washington	28,305	1,677	1,435	31,417
Worcester	13,442	3,571	3,468	20,481
Total	515,918	83,942	87,009	686,869

SOURCE: Eighth U.S. Census, 1860.
  [a] Includes city.

slavery's supporters, the term "Old Gunny" became an epithet of ridicule. Gunnison could no longer afford to send his children to school, was taunted in the streets, and received many threatening letters telling him to leave the city. Nevertheless, Gunnison continued to speak out against slavery.

Earlier in the century, Marylanders had supported efforts to send blacks to Africa, but by the 1850s few Marylanders believed that colonization was the solution. Instead, most feared that ending slavery would disrupt the Union. Although only one of every six Maryland households owned slaves, whites worried about the high number of blacks—free and slave—in the population. While many whites were sympathetic to the position that slavery was wrong in theory, in practice, slavery was too imbedded in the culture for them to give it up.

Like other aspects of Maryland society, slavery was a regional institution. In southern Maryland's five counties, where 10 percent of the state's whites lived, 50 percent of the state's slave population was concentrated. The Eastern Shore accounted for another 30 percent of Maryland's slaves. In the northern and western parts of Maryland, there were few blacks, slave or free. In Baltimore slaves accounted for only 3 percent of the city's total population. Some former slaves found sanctuary amid Baltimore's free black population of 29,000, the largest free black community in the United States.

Slave Life

Slaves generally did not learn to write, so they left few records. Thus, the reconstruction of their daily lives is exceedingly difficult. Oral histories given by their descendants do indicate that their condition varied according to where they lived, what they did, and who their master was. But the terrible fact of their existence was that they were property. They could be, and often were, sold South. They had control over neither their lives nor their bodies. Even the simplest of activities, such as walking to town, required a pass.

Yet, in different ways, they struggled to be free. Some ran away, while others protested their condition by destroying tools and burning their master's barns. Some worked obediently in order to be able to buy themselves from their masters.

Because it bordered the free state of Pennsylvania, Maryland became an avenue to freedom. The famous Liberty Line, or Underground Railroad, used stations such as the Orchard Street Church in Baltimore. Free blacks in Maryland helped fugitive slaves reach the North, although this violated the provisions of a stringent federal fugitive slave law that was included in the Congressional Compromise of 1850.

$50 Reward.

Runaway on Saturday the 17th inst. a coloured woman by the name of

EASTER,

Who was formerly the property of Arthur Hill, near Reisterstown;—the said Easter is rather between a mulatto and black, short chunky, with thick lips and somewhat freckled in her face; she is about 22 years of age; she had on a light calico frock when she went away, and a cloth over coat, olive colour. She has some relations living in Baltimore at Fell's Point, where she is expected to be lurking at this time. If she is taken in Baltimore County and secured so that I get her again I will give 25 dollars, and if out of the State 50 dollars.

JACOB WOOLERY,

Within four miles of Winchester.

Dec. 14, 1855.

Many slaves ran away to escape their bondage. In this advertisement, Jacob Woolery offered a reward for the capture of a 22-year-old runaway named Easter.

THE UNDERGROUND RAILROAD

One way that many men and women rebelled against slavery was to escape. A network called the Underground Railroad aided runaways as they made their way northward to freedom. En route "conductors" helped the fugitives, who were sometimes hidden under hay in a farmer's wagon or in the hold of a boat. Often they traveled only under cover of darkness. Sometimes the fugitives even pretended to be a conductor's slave.

The conductor led one or a small party of slaves from one "station" or safe hiding place to another. Stations were sometimes the home of a free black or Quaker family, sometimes a free black church, sometimes even a boat that sailed the Chesapeake Bay. Many people hid fugitives in their homes, frequently at great risk to themselves. These people often built a special trap door to the basement, covering it with a rug and perhaps a table or chair. The runaways then could hide in a secret underground room until it was judged safe for them to move on to the next station.

Maryland's most famous conductor on the Underground Railroad was Harriet Tubman of Dorchester County. After her own escape to the North in 1849, she returned many times to lead between 200 and 300 others to safety. Her most frequent route took her from southern Maryland through the Delmarva Peninsula and on to Philadelphia. After 1850, when the federal Fugitive Slave Act required that northern states return escapees, the Underground Railroad network reached through the northern states to Canada.

Harriet Tubman, born a slave in Dorchester County, became Maryland's best-known conductor on the Underground Railroad. She lectured to abolitionist societies throughout the North between raids.

Even for those slaves who did not have any outside help, Maryland was a critical junction. For example, two Georgia slaves conceived an ingenious plan for escaping in the early 1850s. Dressed as a man, the light-skinned Ellen Crafts posed as an ailing planter on his way north to be treated. Attending her was a faithful black servant, who was in fact her husband, William Crafts. The plan worked, but not before some tense moments in a Baltimore train station, where the supposed planter was required to post a bond in case "his slave" escaped in Maryland.

Newspapers tell the story of the efforts of white owners to get back what they considered their property. Sometimes owners tracked their runaway slaves themselves. Sometimes they hired slave hunters, and in the 1850s there were many such men loitering on the streets of Baltimore. According to the Compromise of 1850, suspected runaways were to be brought before United States marshals who decided, without testimony from the blacks themselves, if the runaways should be returned to their masters. The marshals received more money if a slave was returned than they did if he or she was not returned.

Tension over Slavery

In 1851 Edward Gorsuch, a Baltimore County slave owner, pursued four former slaves into Pennsylvania, even though his uncle had freed them. In a battle between blacks living near Christiana in Lancaster County, Pennsylvania, and Maryland whites, Gorsuch was killed in an exchange of gunfire. In the increasingly tense atmosphere of the late 1850s, this incident provoked the supporters of slavery, who sought more protection for their human property.

Eight years later another incident involving slavery occurred, this time in Maryland. On an October night in 1859, John Brown and his small band of black and white abolitionists attacked a federal arms depot at Harpers Ferry. Their intention was to arm slaves, who could then fight for their own liberation. But Brown, who believed that he acted as God's lieutenant in a struggle against "the sin of slavery," was captured by the militia. He was convicted of murder and treason, and he was hanged. But before his death he made a grim prophecy: "I John Brown am now quite certain that this guilty land will never be purged away but with blood."

Brown's raid had failed, but it alerted Marylanders to the seriousness of the slavery issue and the disagreements between North and South. For weeks, grim headlines incorrectly linked Brown to the Republican party, and public opinion condemned Brown as a fanatic. Largely because of the exaggerations of the press (one news-

Escaping from slavery meant walking through woods and swamps in all kinds of weather, often under cover of darkness. This drawing of fugitives escaping from the Eastern Shore of Maryland indicates the discomfort but not the danger of an escape.

SLAVE SONGS

Slaves used music to express feelings they could not express openly and to convey messages. The following is a song Frederick Douglass wrote down. It shows the slave's sense of unfair treatment by the planter.

We raise de wheat,
Dey gib us de corn;
We bake de bread,
Dey gib us de cruss;
We sif de meal,
Dey gib us de huss;
We peal de meat,
Dey gib us de skin
And dat's de way
Dey takes us in.

Some spirituals told of an escape or were used to signal such an escape.

Steal away, steal away,
Steal away to Jesus;
Steal away steal away home,
I ain't got long to stay here.

My Lord calls me
He calls me by the thunder
The trumpet sounds within my soul
I ain't got long to stay here.

Green trees abendin'
Poor Sinner stands a tremblin'
The trumpet sounds within my soul
I ain't got long to stay here.

Steal away, steal away,
Steal away to Jesus;
Steal away, steal away home,
I ain't got long to stay here.

paper exaggerated Brown's band of 17 into "250 abolitionists"), whites saw a freedom fighter in every black.

These anxieties led slave owners on the Eastern Shore and in southern Maryland to try to end freedom for all blacks. Curtis Jacobs, a delegate from the Eastern Shore to the lower house of the assembly, introduced a bill on the subject two months after Brown's raid. This bill would have prevented all Marylanders from freeing their slaves and would have forced free blacks to hire themselves out to whites in permanent contracts.

Jacobs's bill passed the legislature but failed in the popular referendums that were required before it was put into practice. Many white Marylanders voted against it because they opposed having blacks, either free or slave, in their communities. They believed that the bill would make black labor a permanent feature of their counties. Jacobs insisted that his legislation was a test of whether Maryland was a southern or a northern state. The time was coming when Marylanders would have to decide.

Politics during the 1860s

Although Marylanders avoided the issues raised by slavery in the 1850s, they could not do so during the national election of 1860. Previously, citizens from other states had made national policies regarding fugitive slaves and the extension of slavery into the territories a central feature of their politics. The doctrine of popular sovereignty, which gave local residents the authority to decide whether slavery should be allowed in their community, had stirred great debate elsewhere. Marylanders demonstrated a firm desire to avoid such sectional controversies.

Partisan Differences

The differences between North and South emerged early in 1860, when the Democratic nominating convention in Charleston, South Carolina, could not agree on a platform or a candidate. As a result, it met again in Baltimore in the spring. At this convention a rehearsal of the Civil War took place when the party split into a northern wing, led by Stephen A. Douglas of Illinois, and a southern wing, led by John C. Breckinridge of Kentucky.

Baltimore was a favorite convention city throughout the nine-

PARTY PLATFORMS IN THE PRESIDENTIAL ELECTION OF 1860

Crowds throng the 1860 Republican Nominating Convention in Chicago.

Sections of the 1860 presidential party platforms addressed the problems of slavery and union in similar ways. Each party wanted the language to be as vague as possible so the platform would not offend any voters.

Constitutional Union Platform: Resolved, that it is both the part of patriotism and of duty to recognize no political principle other than the Constitution of the Country, the Union of the States and the Enforcement of the Laws.

Democratic Platform of 1860 (Douglas): Resolved: inasmuch as a difference of opinion exists in the Democratic party as to the nature and extent of the powers of a Territorial Legislature, and as to the powers and duties of Congress under the Constitution of the United States, over the institution of slavery within the Territories that the Democratic party will abide by the decision of the Supreme Court of the United States upon these questions of Constitutional Law.

Democratic Platform of 1860 (Breckinridge): That is the duty of the Federal Government, in all its Departments, to protect when necessary the rights of persons and property in the Territories.

Republican Platform of 1860: That the new dogma that the Constitution of its own force carries slavery into any or all of the Territories of the United States is a dangerous political heresy at variance with the explicit provisions of that instrument.

teenth century, and in Baltimore a new compromise party was organized. Some said this Constitutional Unionist party was a successor to the Know-Nothing party. Certainly many of its Maryland leaders, including Henry Winter Davis and John Pendleton Kennedy, had supported the Know-Nothings in the 1850s. But this new party said nothing about immigration or Roman Catholics. Instead, in a short and very vague announcement of its principles, it confined itself to supporting the Union and the U.S. Constitution and opposing sectionalism.

Throughout the summer and fall of 1860 Republicans, the two wings of the Democratic party, and the Constitutional Unionists discussed issues critical to all Americans, but especially to Marylanders, who lived in a border state located between the North and the South. Did Congress have the right to control slavery in the territories? Were blacks property, as the Supreme Court had ruled in the Dred Scott case? Did states have the right to leave the Union? Did the Republican candidate Abraham Lincoln intend to destroy slavery? What did loyalty to the Union mean? What was the proper relation of a border state to the South?

The Election of 1860

In November the results of the presidential election demonstrated how Marylanders would answer these questions. First of all, the state rejected the Republicans, whom they incorrectly associated with abolitionism. In fact, throughout the campaign Marylanders harassed Republicans and disrupted their meetings by throwing eggs and bricks. No one was surprised when Lincoln got only 2 percent of the state's vote. The Douglas Democrats did only slightly better in Maryland. They had no organization, because most state Democrats preferred Breckinridge, and efforts to merge the two factions failed.

The real contest for Maryland's eight electoral votes was between John Breckinridge and John Bell, the candidate of the Constitutional Unionist party. Both men proclaimed their support of Constitution, Union, and enforcement of the laws. Both opposed extremism, and both avoided making specific statements about their future intentions. A vote for Breckinridge, however, was generally considered a vote for the extension of slavery throughout the West. In the end, Breckinridge won narrowly over Bell by 522 votes out of some 93,000 votes cast.

One way to interpret the results of this election is to see both Bell and Breckinridge as conservatives who appealed to Marylanders because they pledged to support the Union. Both men were also attractive to Marylanders because they were from border states and might be expected to avoid war. People believed that these men understood the dilemma of a slave state located between the North and the South whose economic ties favored the North and the West.

In Baltimore, which Breckinridge carried, local issues explained some voting decisions. By 1860 many Baltimoreans identified the Democrats as a reform party and voted for that party's candidate because they wanted an end to corrupt elections, not because they were taking a stand on national policies.

In another interpretation the election outcome can be seen as a pro-southern statement. Some Marylanders believed that Breckinridge was the southern candidate, and it is certainly true that his supporters used the slogan "Maryland Must and Will Be True to the South." The anti-Breckinridge vote in Maryland, however, represented 56 percent of the total. A minority of Marylanders had actually voted for the southern rights position, if that is what Breckinridge represented.

Postelection Tensions

Usually after a presidential election the losers accept the winners, but there was great uncertainty in Maryland following Lincoln's election. This was a response to the activity of southern states. South Carolina and six other states seceded, that is, left the Union, before the new president was inaugurated in March 1861. These states, along with four others, made up the Confederacy. Recognizing the importance of the border states, southern states promptly sent agents to Maryland to lobby for their new "nation."

A crucial debate now took place as an aftermath of the 1860 election. Should Governor Thomas Hicks, who had been elected as a Know-Nothing, convene the state legislature in order to discuss Maryland's future? Should Maryland secede? What should Marylanders do if a war broke out between North and South?

Different groups discussed these questions at public meetings. For example, in the winter of 1861, skilled workers in Baltimore signed a petition opposing secession. In nearby Reisterstown, farmers adopted the southern symbol of a blue cockade and named their military company the Confederate Minute Men. For the most part, businessmen opposed secession at their meetings. A group of citizens in Towson and Annapolis shouted their approval to resolutions supporting Union and Constitution. In January 1861 the editor of the *Baltimore Sun* wrote, "We are for the Union—for the restoration of the Union." But on the Eastern Shore, resolutions included a pledge saying that Maryland was "essentially a Southern state."

Maryland and the Union

The immediate effect of the political disagreements in 1860 and 1861 was to depress economic activity. Businessmen did not want to commit resources to any financial ventures during such uncertain times, and although seven states proclaimed themselves the Confederate States of America in February 1861, Maryland's trade with the South virtually ceased. Banks suspended specie, that is, gold and silver, payments; stocks dropped in value; and employment suffered.

Political Tensions

The General Assembly met biennially and was not due to convene until the following year, but the political pressure to call the Maryland legislature into a special session was intense. Governor Hicks resisted, however, believing that the pro-southern atmosphere in Annapolis would affect the delegates. He refused to see the commissioners who had been sent from southern states to encourage Maryland's secession. Hicks declared that he "would aid Lincoln with faithful advice." His policy has been called one of "masterly inactivity."

No matter what they thought about slavery or which side they favored, all Marylanders sought a peaceful resolution of the issues between the North and the South. Leaders as diverse in their politics as Governor Hicks, Congressman Henry Winter Davis, S. Teackle Wallis, and John Pendleton Kennedy opposed coercion of the South because, in their view, allegiance to the Union must be voluntary, not forced. "Let them go in peace" became a popular slogan in the winter of 1861.

War Begins

The decision lay elsewhere. On April 12, 1861, the Confederacy began the war by firing on federal property at Fort Sumter, South Carolina. Two days later President Lincoln called for 75,000 volunteers to suppress this insurrection. Marylanders who had hoped to avoid war immediately volunteered "to save the Union," according to the *Baltimore Sun*.

Another group of men believed that southerners could not be brought back into the Union through the use of force. They opposed the passage of any northern troops through Maryland, claiming that such passage violated states rights.

When northern troops had to pass through the state to get to Washington, D.C., these men encouraged their fellow citizens to prevent what they called a "Yankee" invasion. At meetings throughout the state, but especially in Baltimore, in southern Maryland, and on the Eastern Shore, leaders asked whether "Lincoln's" troops should pass over the soil of the Free State of Maryland. Often the response came back, "No, never," and it was this kind of thinking that led to the Baltimore riot of 1861.

The Baltimore Riot

On April 19, 1861, a bloody conflict took place when Baltimoreans attacked soldiers of the 6th Massachusetts Regiment and the Penn-

Baltimoreans rioted against the 6th Massachusetts Regiment as it traveled through town on its way to Washington, D.C., at the beginning of the Civil War. Sixteen people were killed.

Less than a month after the Baltimore riot, Union General Benjamin Butler and the 8th Regiment occupied Federal Hill, overlooking the city's harbor, to make sure Union supplies passed safely through the city.

Warned of an assassination plot in proslavery Baltimore, president-elect Abraham Lincoln traveled through Maryland to his inauguration in Washington by night so as not to be seen. This satirical cartoon shows him making the trip in disguise.

sylvania Militia who were en route to Washington. Like everyone who traveled from the North to the nation's capital, these soldiers had to change railroads in the city. A hostile mob surrounded the soldiers as they made the transfer between stations. At first just rocks, curses, and firecrackers were hurled. But soon there was gunfire, with soldiers returning the attack. When the riot was over, 4 soldiers and 12 Baltimoreans were dead, and many others were wounded. No one could predict the future course of Maryland.

After the riot, civil authorities moved to restore order. A meeting took place in Monument Square, where Baltimore's Democratic Mayor George Brown and Maryland's Know-Nothing Governor Thomas Hicks made a bipartisan appeal for an end to the violence. Standing next to the state flag, Hicks proclaimed his support of the Union: "I am a Marylander, I love my State and I love the Union." He also announced his opposition to "striking a sister state," and he meant by this any effort on the part of northerners to force the South back into the Union.

Shifting Opinions

Gradually the tide of pro-southern sentiment and neutrality shifted. Many of the most violent southern sympathizers went South to form a Maryland regiment. In Maryland, shouts for Jefferson Davis, the Confederate president, gave way to those for the Union, and Confederate flags and blue cockades disappeared. When the legislature finally convened in Frederick, away from southern sympathizers in Annapolis, the delegates overwhelmingly denied that they had the constitutional power to secede from the Union. Thus, Maryland had chosen the Union.

Maryland and the Confederacy

The election of a pro-Union governor, Augustus Bradford, in November 1861 did not end the struggle over Maryland's allegiance. Throughout the war, from 1861 to 1865, a small group of Confederate sympathizers continued to harass military and civilian officials.

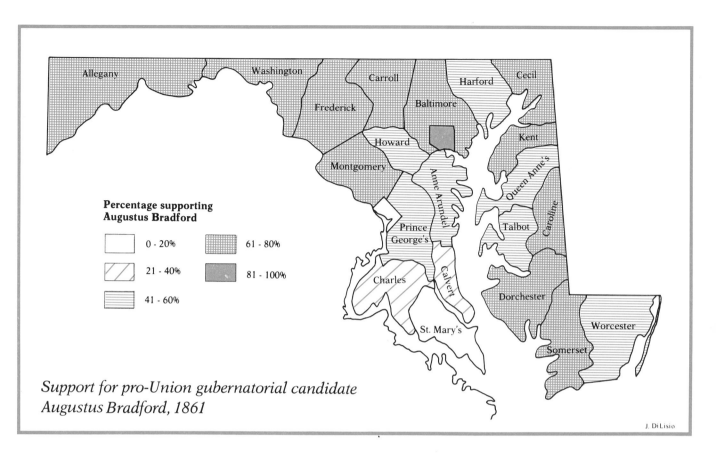

Percentage supporting
Augustus Bradford

- 0 - 20%
- 21 - 40%
- 41 - 60%
- 61 - 80%
- 81 - 100%

Support for pro-Union gubernatorial candidate Augustus Bradford, 1861

J. DiLisio

Early Conspiracies

Even before the war started, some Marylanders may have threatened Lincoln's life. Threats forced the president-elect to go through Baltimore at night and in disguise on his way to his inauguration in Washington. Some Marylanders engaged in sabotage. One Confederate partisan was Lincoln's assassin, John Wilkes Booth, who in October 1861 was listed as a suspected traitor and was freed only because he took the loyalty oath.

Another southern sympathizer was John Merryman, a well-known Baltimore County farmer, who destroyed railroad bridges in order to prevent Union troops from coming through "neutral" Maryland. Merryman was promptly arrested, but his case aroused a controversy between military authorities and civil officials that had a lasting effect on constitutional law.

First, Merryman was held in Baltimore's Fort McHenry without being charged. Military officials argued that their authority to keep him came from the wartime necessity of suspending the writ of habeas corpus. In peacetime this writ requires that no prisoner be held without being charged with a specific crime. Many Marylanders agreed with Lincoln that during war certain civil protections must be suspended.

Eventually, still without a trial, Merryman was released. But not before the chief justice of the Supreme Court, Marylander Roger B. Taney, wrote a stinging brief disagreeing with the government. According to Taney, habeas corpus was an essential protection for all free men. Without it, he said, governments degenerated into tyrannies, even during a civil war.

Differences of Opinion

The struggle between military and civilian authority reappeared in different forms throughout the Civil War. In some parts of the Eastern Shore and southern Maryland, Union troops patrolled near polling places. In September of 1861 military authorities arrested 27 members of the legislature who were considered disloyal and pro-southern. Imprisoned for a while in federal forts, the former legislators were released when they took the oath of allegiance. Throughout the war, some Marylanders believed that the federal government made a mockery of freedoms guaranteed to all Americans, but most considered these wartime violations of civil liberties a necessary price to pay for the Union.

A few southern sympathizers organized newspapers to express their opposition to the Union and Lincoln's policies. The most radical pro-southern newspaper was the *Baltimore South*, which was published only briefly. Not only did this paper oppose any limitations on the civil right to speech and assembly in the state, but it also openly sided with the South. Twice military commanders closed it down, for they believed that it had gone well beyond the limits of free speech.

One Marylander expressed pro-Confederate sentiments in a different way. James Ryder Randall, a Marylander from what is today Randallstown, was teaching in Louisiana when the war broke out in 1861. To a well-known German tune, he set the words that are still the state's anthem.

> The despot's heel is on thy shore, Maryland.
> His torch is at thy temple door, Maryland
> Avenge the Patriotic Gore,
> That flecked the streets of Baltimore.
> And be the battle queen of yore,
> Maryland, my Maryland.

Many people have found the choice of the pro-Confederate anthem odd in a state that remained loyal to the Union.

Marylanders in the Confederate Army

A small group of Marylanders went south in 1861, in some cases taking their families with them. Most of those who left were young and single, and they intended to fight for the Confederacy. By November 1863, 18,000 Maryland men were serving in the Confederate army, while approximately 53,000 Marylanders were serving in the Union army. The state's Confederates had hoped that their units would be organized into an all-Maryland brigade. Despite the formation of two infantry regiments, three cavalry units, and four artillery batteries, Marylanders did not usually fight together as a state unit, but instead were scattered throughout other units. For the most part, these troops were stationed in northern Virginia.

For all Civil War soldiers, months of tedium were interspersed with periods of excitement and terror. During the winter months, when fighting was suspended, camp life combined boredom with occasional danger. In vital matters such as food and clothing, Confederate soldiers were not as well supplied as soldiers in the Union army. Both armies suffered from diseases, especially dysentery.

The Civil War held special agonies for all Marylanders who fought in the army, whether they were Confederates or Yankees. They might, as did the dashing Confederate cavalry commander Harry Gilmor, fight near their homes and use their knowledge of the countryside as protection. Or, like William Goldsborough at the battle of Front Royal, Virginia, in 1862, they might find that the soldier across the lines was a relative. Confederate Major Goldsborough captured his own brother. Or they might end up as prisoners of war, with only the hope of being exchanged for a northern prisoner easing the bitter conditions of internment.

Maryland during Wartime

Marylanders had always known that any war between North and South would be fought on their soil, and this was one reason they were conservative politically. Not only did their state border the Confederacy, but it surrounded Washington on three sides. To most nineteenth-century military strategists, there was no more important target than the enemy's capital, which meant that Maryland would be a critical military theater.

As expected, for four years—from April 1861 to April 1865—the state served as just such a center of military activity. Vast armies

---

A SOLDIER'S DIARY

The following is an excerpt from the diary of a Maryland Confederate soldier. It reveals the tedium of life at the front as well as the problem of disease, which both armies encountered.

7th to 21st Sick in camp with the measles.

" 27th Having nearly recovered I received my discharge from the Hospital and proceed to join my Regt.

July 8th Second alarm in camp from pickets firing in the night all turned out in quick time ready for marching but quietness taking the place of noise and confusion, we return to our quarters and were soon again in the land of dreams.

" 12th Visited again by Brig. Gen¹. Bonham.

18th 19th 20th My regt laid these 3 days in the swamps of Bull Run, awaiting the enemy, half the time with half rations of hard bread and, muddy water, yet not a murmur is heard from one.

21st At night: A strange yet pleasing sight on a battlefield on returning from the pursuit of the routed enemy, we met a beautiful young lady in a buggy, and just a little farther on we are greeted by a sight of the cleanly shaven face of His Excellency President Davis, and give three cheers for both.

23rd to 31st My Brigade again take the advanced post.

1st to 15th August. My Company greatly reduced by sickness.

24th to 31st Make 3 forced marches from Centreville to near Fairfax Court House, in expectation of a battle each time but it was all a sham. During one of these marches I had the honour of seeing for the first time the renowned Stonewall Jackson, then in command of his Old Brigade.

Courtesy of the Maryland Historical Society.

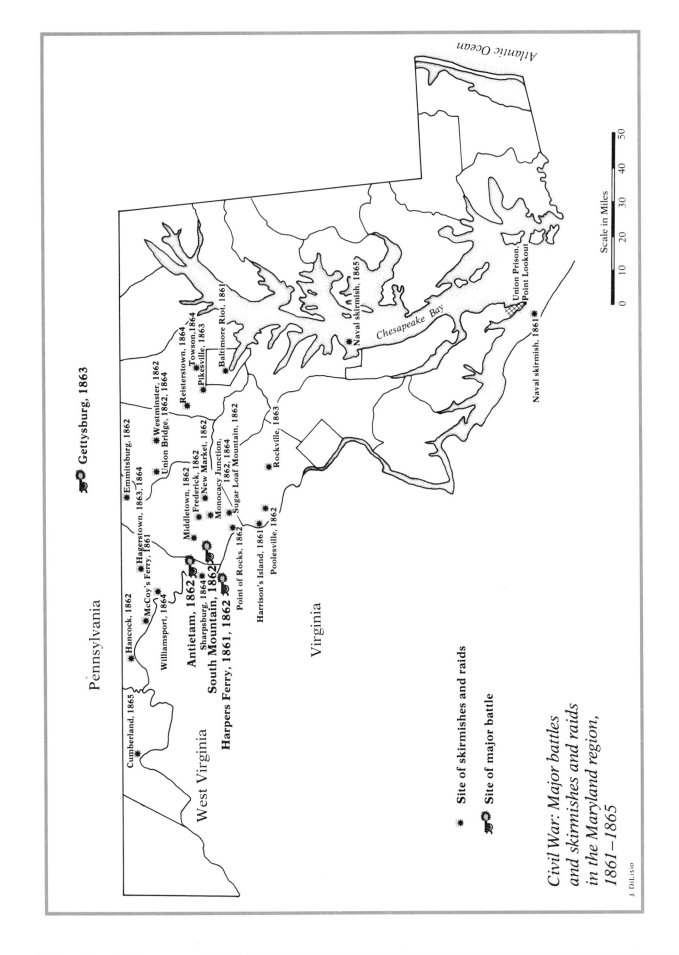

Pennsylvania

Gettysburg, 1863

West Virginia

Cumberland, 1865

Hancock, 1862

McCoy's Ferry, 1861

Williamsport, 1864

Hagerstown, 1863, 1864

Emmitsburg, 1862

Westminster, 1862

Union Bridge, 1862, 1864

Reisterstown, 1864

Towson, 1864

Pikesville, 1863

Baltimore Riot, 1861

Antietam, 1862

Sharpsburg, 1864

South Mountain, 1862

Middletown, 1862

Frederick, 1862

New Market, 1862

Monocacy Junction, 1862, 1864

Sugar Loaf Mountain, 1862

Harpers Ferry, 1861, 1862

Point of Rocks, 1862

Harrison's Island, 1861

Poolesville, 1862

Rockville, 1863

Naval skirmish, 1865

Chesapeake Bay

Virginia

Union Prison, Point Lookout

Naval skirmish, 1861

Atlantic Ocean

Scale in Miles

0 10 20 30 40 50

* Site of skirmishes and raids

Site of major battle

Civil War: Major battles and skirmishes and raids in the Maryland region, 1861–1865

J. DiLisio

Soldiers spent much of their time performing drills and enduring routine camp life. In this drawing, soldiers camped at Druid Hill Park in Baltimore are patronizing Sutler's Hut. They are probably buying goods not issued by the army.

marched across its territory. In addition to the 31 military engagements fought in Maryland, hundreds of minor raids and skirmishes made the fighting more than a matter of reading newspaper accounts of distant battles. It was not by chance that the war's first casualties were Baltimore civilians. Later, spies, blockade runners, and dealers in contraband, or smuggled, goods found the state a convenient base for their operations.

Although they knew that they would suffer during the war, Marylanders were swept up in the calls to glory and patriotism. Most believed the war would be short, more a summer adventure than the grim reality it became. Everywhere in the United States, young men enrolled in hastily organized units and went off to fight for the Union, not to end slavery.

Antietam and Gettysburg

It was fall 1862 before the state's civilians had a firsthand view of the horrors of battle, although they had read of field operations in northern Virginia and in the West during 1861 and early 1862. After defeating the Union General John Pope at Manassas in Virginia, Confederate Generals Robert E. Lee and Thomas "Stonewall" Jackson crossed the Potomac into Maryland. Not only did they hope to find provisions for their ill-fed army, but, according to Lee, they also expected to relieve Maryland "from her foreign yoke." This was a miscalculation, for the Confederate army found a hostile civilian population in western Maryland.

On September 17, 1862, near Antietam, the Confederate Army of Northern Virginia encountered Union General George B. McClellan's Army of the Potomac. Lee had divided his army, sending one part to Hagerstown and the other to capture Harpers Ferry. Somehow Lee's orders, wrapped around three cigars, were dropped, and a Union soldier found them. He passed them on to his superiors, who then planned their strategy with full knowledge of Confederate plans.

On a gentle rolling field crossed by a peaceful stream the war's bloodiest single day's battle took place. At dark, after a series of disjointed, uncoordinated attacks, 12,000 Union soldiers had been either killed or wounded, along with 11,000 Confederates. McClellan claimed victory, but, in fact, this was a defeat for both armies. The things that had separated these two warring sides disappeared, as the cries of dying men became a common denominator. Overnight the churches, barns, and meeting halls around Sharpsburg and Antietam were transformed into hospitals and shelters. In one day Marylanders had discovered the costs of war.

One reason for the high number of casualties was the state of warfare. While nineteenth-century technology had produced rifles that were effective at over one mile and artillery guns of longer range and accuracy, men still fought wars the same way they had during the American Revolution. They lined up and advanced in formations, only to be mowed down by new, improved breech-loading rifles. As a result, more Marylanders, and Americans, were killed during the Civil War than in all the other wars they fought in combined, until the Vietnam conflict of the 1970s.

As happened so often during the Civil War, neither side could claim a clear victory. Lee was forced to withdraw across the Potomac, but, much to President Lincoln's irritation, McClellan missed an opportunity to destroy the southern army.

Less than a year later, after a series of victories at Fredericksburg and Chancellorsville in Virginia, Lee invaded western Maryland. He was gambling again that this region would welcome his troops and that he could isolate Washington from the North. His offensive ended catastrophically at Gettysburg, Pennsylvania, in July 1863. This three-day engagement was the turning point of the war, although neither army had chosen the battle site. Indeed, it might be said that the South lost the Civil War in Maryland and in Pennsylvania, because every time Confederate troops took the offensive there, they endured heavy casualties that had disastrous effects on their army.

Burnside's Bridge across Antietam Creek was a focus of the September 17, 1862, battle that resulted in more than 23,000 casualties.

President Lincoln visited Sharpsburg, near Antietam, on October 3, 1862.

Clara Barton, who later founded the American Red Cross, worked as a nurse during the Civil War. She traveled through Maryland and Virginia with her mule wagons, carrying medicine, bandages, and food.

Jubal Early's Raid

A year after Gettysburg, Confederate General Jubal Early launched an invasion of Washington and Maryland. In July 1864 Confederate troops burned bridges, cut telegraph wires, plundered stores and farms, and stole horses. They even burned Governor Bradford's house in Baltimore County and demanded that Hagerstown and Frederick pay ransoms or risk having their towns burned. Jacob Engelbreck, a farmer who lived in Frederick, described the feelings of many Marylanders during the Civil War. "These are awful times. One day we are as usual and the next day in the hands of the enemy. But whatever is the final issue, I say come weal or woe, come life or death, we go for the Union forever."

Early's 1864 raid on Maryland was the last time that a Confederate force invaded the state. By the fall of 1864 General Ulysses S. Grant's army had placed relentless pressure on Lee in Virginia, and General William Sherman had slashed through Georgia.

Finally, in April 1865 at Appomattox in northern Virginia, Lee surrendered. The war was over for Maryland and the nation. The Union had been saved; now it had to be restored.

Life on the Home Front

For four years the war enormously affected every area of Maryland life. Families, of course, were split up when someone enlisted for military service. At first this was a voluntary decision, but in

ANNA ELLA CARROLL: MILITARY STRATEGIST

Anna Ella Carroll was a political pamphleteer and military strategist during the Civil War. A member of the distinguished Carroll family of Maryland, she became a champion of the Know-Nothing party. Her book *The Great American Battle* praised America and condemned Roman Catholicism as a foreign system.

Anna's preoccupation with public affairs was unusual for a woman of the time. Always interested in politics, she wrote editorials supporting the Know-Nothings. During the Civil War she recommended that Union forces travel down the Tennessee River to launch an invasion that would split the Confederacy. In fact, she drew up a precise military plan and sent it to Lincoln.

After the war she supported black suffrage. She acted as a private lobbyist in expressing her strong views to senators and congressmen, many of whom she knew well, to influence them to support political rights for former slaves.

1863 both Congress and the Confederacy passed a conscription, or draft, law. All able-bodied white male citizens between 20 and 45 were thereafter liable for military service. Only a few Marylanders were actually drafted, although the draft stimulated some to join rather than be conscripted. Also, the 1863 congressional act permitted those who were drafted to hire a substitute or to buy for $300 what was called a "commutation," or exemption, from the service, and many did so.

Women and the War Effort

At home, older men, young boys, and women took the places of men who went into the army. Some women who had worked inside the home took paying jobs. Rural women planted crops and tilled fields, and school-age children were often employed on farms and in factories.

Middle-class women who had servants had more free time to support the war effort. Especially in the state's towns and cities, they organized ladies' associations, which provided clothing for the soldiers. They served as nurses in Maryland's army hospitals, and they ran fairs that raised money for the troops. A wounded soldier outside Baltimore wrote admiringly of what he called the "Crinoline Brigade." One Maryland woman, Anna Ella Carroll, even became an expert on military strategy and sent Lincoln her plans for a military campaign in the West which would split the Confederacy in two.

Conditions at Home

The war led to shortages in goods and in food. Taxes increased, and in 1864 Congress instituted the first federal income tax in American history. This, along with the traditional local property taxes, strained the resources of many families at a time when there was no public welfare. Although wages increased (a Baltimore carpenter earning $1.75 a day in 1856 made $2.25 in 1864; a drug clerk's salary rose from $30 a month to $50), prices increased more rapidly. What had cost $1.00 in 1860, cost $1.82 by 1864.

One area of Maryland life—politics—remained much the same. The competitive two-party system of Democrats and Republicans endured throughout the war. Democrats insisted that federal troops interfered in favor of the Republicans, but, in fact, there were surprisingly few intrusions. In 1864 the Republicans, who in Maryland called themselves Unionists during the war, renominated Lincoln, and he defeated the Democratic presidential candidate General

SERGEANT MAJOR CHRISTIAN A. FLEETWOOD

During the Civil War, approximately 180,000 black troops fought in the Union armies. Before the struggle was over, 17 black soldiers and 4 black sailors had won the Congressional Medal of Honor. One of these was Sergeant Major Christian A. Fleetwood, 4th United States Colored Troops.

Fleetwood received his Medal of Honor for heroism in the Battle of Chapins Farm, Virginia, which was fought on September 29, 1864. His citation stated that he "seized the colors after two color bearers had been shot down and bore them nobly through the fight."

The son of free black parents, Fleetwood was born in Baltimore in 1840. He was educated in the home of a wealthy sugar merchant and at the Ashmun Institute (later renamed Lincoln University) in Pennsylvania. He served as secretary of the Maryland Colonization Society and visited briefly in Liberia and Sierra Leone. Fleetwood and some of his friends published a newspaper, the *Lyceum Observer*, in Baltimore. When the Civil War broke out, he enlisted in the Union Army.

George McClellan in a close election. Lincoln, who had gotten almost no support in the state in 1860, received 54 percent of the Maryland vote four years later.

Freeing the Slaves

Without doubt the most important result of the Civil War for Maryland was the emancipation of the state's 90,000 slaves. The 46,000 Marylanders who fought in the Union army fought to keep the Union, however. Emancipation was an unintentional result.

Throughout the war, many slaves freed themselves. When they learned of the existence of a federal army, they ran away from their masters. They tried to join the army, but they could not do so until 1863. Still, these former slaves lived in camps near armies or military installations. Sometimes they worked on fortifications as day laborers, digging the ditches and trenches that became more and more a part of the defensive tactics of both armies. Living conditions were often difficult, but these newly freed people correctly believed that the army would not return them as runaways.

National Policy

As early as 1861 some generals in Washington urged Lincoln to support the enlistment of blacks in the army. But public opinion in Maryland did not support recruiting slaves, and in state law slaves were still considered private property. Finally, in 1863, Congress passed a bill permitting blacks to join the Union Army, and by 1864 six Maryland regiments made up of former slaves and free blacks were defending the Union.

Blacks fought for their own freedom in a number of campaigns in northern Virginia and off the coast of South Carolina. But blacks were not accorded equal treatment in the army. In the first place, they were always commanded by white officers. And, while black units fought as bravely as any white units, black privates were paid $9 a month, compared to $13 a month for white privates. This kind of discrimination was a forerunner of the inferior treatment blacks received even after the Civil War.

Yet, attaining freedom for slaves was as much a political as a military battle. In 1862 Lincoln proposed that the federal government compensate each Maryland slave owner for his slaves, who would then become free, but he withdrew the plan. On January 1, 1863, Lincoln freed slaves in the Confederacy through his Emancipation Proclamation. But Maryland's slaves were not included because under the terms of the Emancipation Proclamation only those held in bondage in states "where the people were in rebellion against the United States" were to be "forever free." Maryland was not in rebellion, so its slaves remained in bondage.

Emancipation in Maryland

Increasingly, Marylanders saw that slavery must end. By 1863 a group of so-called Unconditional Unionists supported abolition of slavery without any conditions. They made this the central issue in Maryland politics in 1864. Abolition required a new state constitution, as the old one explicitly forbade ending slavery.

In 1863 Unconditional Unionists led by Henry Winter Davis and John Creswell began to campaign for a new constitutional convention. First, the Maryland legislature had to agree. Next, the people of Maryland had to vote for such a convention and elect delegates to it. Finally, the convention had to rewrite the slavery article of the state constitution.

The constitutional convention met throughout the summer, and then, in September 1864, white Maryland men went to the polls. They voted either to accept or to reject the new constitution, which included in its Declaration of Rights the article:

Hereafter, in this State, there shall be neither slavery nor involuntary servitude, except in punishment of crime whereof the party shall have been duly convicted, and all persons held to service or labor, as slaves, are hereby declared free.

Throughout the campaign for the new constitution Democrats opposed emancipation, arguing that such a provision was not necessary. In the end the vote was very close, but on November 1, 1864, Maryland's slaves were no longer property. At sunrise that day the guns at Fort McHenry signaled a day of emancipation as the state put its motto—the Free State—into effect. All over Maryland former slaves and free blacks, approximately 25 percent of Maryland's population, celebrated in churches, village groves, and city streets.

The Aftermath

Slaves did not automatically become the social, political, or economic equals of whites. A great deal of antiblack feeling remained in the state, and freedom was no assurance of equality. Nor did white violence against blacks disappear.

In the late 1860s blacks were frequently forced out of public facilities, especially trains, streetcars, and waiting rooms, into segregated and inferior facilities. Earlier this had not been an issue, in part because there were fewer facilities and in part because, as slaves, blacks often traveled with their masters as personal servants. Freedmen encountered discrimination in many areas. In 1867 a New York black sued the Baltimore Passenger Railway Company for damages, and won. The *Baltimore American* headline ran "THE CARS FREE TO ALL."

To some extent the Freedman's Bureau, a national agency organized during Lincoln's administration to help blacks, aided Maryland's former slaves. Freedmen turned to this organization for food, shelter, and medical care, and for protection from whites. The Freedman's Bureau also started schools and colleges. Howard University in Washington, D.C., was founded in 1867 as a teacher's college for blacks. Privately supported schools continued to teach black students in the early post–Civil War years.

Some white Marylanders found it difficult to accept the new status of their former slaves. They tried to continue slavery by insisting that their former slaves sign lifetime contracts that amounted to peonage. In some instances black Marylanders convicted of petty crimes were sold by the courts to local farmers for periods ranging from 6 to 18 months. Moreover, whites forced blacks who were younger than 21 to sign apprenticeship contracts that bound them to their former masters permanently. This, of course, violated the law, but by 1867 more than 3,000 black minors had been bound over to their former masters. Finally, after hundreds of complaints were made, Hugh Bond, a Baltimore judge, issued writs of habeas corpus freeing the blacks.

Postwar Politics and Society

After the Civil War, during the period called Reconstruction, the national government tried to bring the South back into the Union and to make sure that southern blacks were given some rights. As a Union state, Maryland avoided some of the problems that plagued southern states from 1865 to 1876. In a sense the state reconstructed itself in a process that began with the emancipation of slaves in 1864.

Postwar politics contained elements of both change and continuity. Only white males older than 21 could vote until 1870, when the Fifteenth Amendment, which enfranchised black men, was accepted by two-thirds of Congress and three-quarters of the states. Maryland was not one of these states; its legislature voted unanimously against giving blacks the franchise.

A two-party system was still in effect after the war. These parties were the Republicans (no longer called Unionists) and the Democrats. Methods of voting also remained the same, and so did the disproportionate power of rural counties. Thus, a delegate to the General Assembly from Charles County represented 6,000 white Marylanders. A delegate from Baltimore represented three times that number. Even after the Civil War, one of the state's U.S. senators (who were still elected by the state legislature) had to be from the Eastern Shore. Such representation gave that section more power than its population warranted.

One change in Maryland politics after the war was the growing power of the Democratic party. By 1868 the Democrats controlled the state legislature, the congressional delegation, and the governor's house. The Democrats' power was illustrated by the party-switching of Thomas Swann, who had been elected governor on the Unionist ticket in 1864 and 1866. Swann, a successful businessman before he went into politics, had been the Know-Nothing mayor of Baltimore in the 1850s, but in 1866 Governor Swann denounced the Republican party and became a Democrat.

Post–Civil War Issues

Swann explained that he was changing parties because he opposed the iron-clad oath, which had become one of the central issues of Maryland's politics in the 1860s. This oath required prospective voters to swear that in the past they had never sided with the Confederacy or aided it in any way. This was a wartime measure and was based on the belief that Confederate supporters should be excluded from voting.

After the war the oath aided the Unionist-Republican party. Many families in the border state of Maryland had relatives fighting for the Confederacy, so it had been difficult for them to avoid helping the rebels. Swann, along with other Democrats, believed that the requirement of past loyalty should be repealed. Furthermore, Democrats connected the oath to the other important issue of postwar politics, black enfranchisement. They believed Republicans were trying to replace Maryland's white voters with blacks, who of course had supported the Union and could take the oath.

THOMAS SWANN: WARTIME GOVERNOR

Born in Virginia in 1806, a member of an old elite family of that state, Thomas Swann moved to Baltimore in his early twenties. He bought stock in the Baltimore and Ohio Railroad, and subsequently became a director and then the president of that company during the period of its westward expansion.

He was equally successful in politics. As the Know-Nothing mayor of Baltimore in the late 1850s, he was responsible for many city improvements. During his administration, the inadequate volunteer fire department was replaced by a professional municipal fire department. Also, he established streetcar service in Baltimore. He is perhaps best remembered for acquiring Druid Hill Park, then on the outskirts of the city, to preserve some green space for the pleasure of the public.

Swann was elected governor of Maryland on the Unionist ticket and took office in January 1866. While governor he switched his allegiance to the Democratic party, and he ended his political career as a four-term Democratic congressman.

Like many Democrats, Swann now urged a new constitutional convention. In 1867 the Maryland legislature presented a new constitution to Maryland voters, who accepted it that fall. This constitution still stands as the state's basic charter. It repealed the iron-clad oath and, while rejecting blacks as voters, gave blacks the right to testify in court proceedings.

In many ways the document reflected the conservative views of new leaders like Oden Bowie, who was elected governor in November 1868 and took office in January 1869. He argued for the removal from the state's declaration of rights the clause stating that "men were created equally free." Because the apportionment of state delegates was based on nonvoting blacks, the new state constitution favored the heavily Democratic Eastern Shore and southern Maryland. For the rest of the decade, white male Democrats continued to control Maryland politics.

Postwar Society

Maryland life settled into familiar social and economic patterns. The war had done nothing to change landholding patterns, ways of making a living, family structure, and church associations.

Maryland's population had increased 13 percent in the decade from 1860 to 1870. As in the 1850s, Baltimore and the northwestern counties accounted for most of the gain. The populations of the tidewater counties of the Eastern Shore and southern Maryland remained stationary, while the city of Baltimore had 20 percent more people in 1870 than it had in 1860. Some of this urban growth was the result of freedmen leaving farms for the city. Yet, despite the turmoil of war, emancipation, and reconstruction, 6 of every 10 blacks still lived in southern Maryland and on the Eastern shore, while 2 of every 10 blacks lived in Baltimore.

Manufacturing, industry, and commerce continued to be centered in Baltimore and northwestern Maryland. In 1870, over 90 percent of the state's industrial production came from the region located north of the Patuxent River, nearly 75 percent of it from Baltimore City. This was the same proportion as before the war. Moreover, the same type of goods were produced, as iron foundries, flour and sugar mills, and clothing, cotton, and shoe factories accounted for most of the state's annual production. Certainly the war had stimulated mechanization in some areas, although probably mechanization in other industries was retarded because of the war.

Change and Continuity

Most Marylanders were still farmers, and they produced wheat, corn, tobacco, and dairy products in the same ways that they had before the war. They worried about the weather and the soil, although by 1870 the Hessian fly had given way to a different pest, the potato bug. While they no longer could depend on slaves, farmers still used black labor.

If work was much the same, so too was play. Costumed knights armed with lances competed in jousting tournaments, which had survived the war and flourished in rural areas. Farmers from all over the state flocked to the livestock and agricultural displays at the Maryland State Fair. In the city, communities of Germans and Irish enjoyed the activities of their ethnic associations.

There was, however, one compelling sign of change. On April 8, 1870, Elijah Quigley, a black man from Towson, placed his ballot in a Baltimore County voting box. The Fifteenth Amendment had passed Congress, and three-quarters of the state legislatures had ratified it. By the fall of 1870, 35,000 Maryland black men had registered to vote in the congressional elections. This signaled a new era of Maryland history.

Another sign of change came gradually. It was a shift in emphasis. Conflicts between regions and groups continued, but as the twentieth century approached, attention became focused on new developments: industrialization, urbanization, immigration, and reform. As the nation moved closer to the modern period, some of the old problems faded and new ones challenged new leaders.

MARYLAND		THE NATION AND THE WORLD
Garrett County formed	1872	
The Johns Hopkins University opens	1876	
	1877	Radical Reconstruction ends in the South
Arthur Pue Gorman elected to the U.S. Senate	1880	
Charity Organization Society founded in Baltimore	1881	
Married Woman's Property Act	1882	
Reform League organized	1885	Democrat Grover Cleveland becomes president
Steel plant opens at Sparrows Point	1889	
Harry Cummings, Maryland's first black elected official, elected to the Baltimore City Council	1890	
	1893	Financial panic and depression
Maryland Woman Suffrage Association founded	1894	
Reform Republican Lloyd Lowndes becomes governor	1896	
	1898	Hawaii annexed
	1901	Progressive Theodore Roosevelt becomes president
Poe Amendment defeated	1905	
Reform Democrat Austin Crothers becomes governor	1908	
Maryland urban population exceeds 50 percent of the total state population. Maryland passes the first injury compensation law in the nation	1910	
Reform Republican Phillips Lee Goldsborough becomes governor	1912	
	1913	Progressive Democrat Woodrow Wilson becomes president 16th Amendment ratified: the income tax 17th Amendment ratified: direct election of U.S. senators
	1914	World War I begins in Europe
	1917	United States declares war against Germany

CHAPTER 5

A New Century, 1870–1917

Reo Touring Car $1000

The outcome of the Civil War meant an end to a society based on bondage. Slavery had been eliminated and black men had been given the vote. People's lives were also changed by industrial development, which proceeded rapidly after 1870 and greatly altered the state's economy. Industrialization became the dominant force for change at the turn of the century.

As industries grew, cities also changed. People poured into Baltimore and other Maryland cities from the countryside, neighboring states, and overseas. Those who lived in the crowded cities faced problems of sanitation and safety; some of them experienced terrible poverty and discrimination. Politicians disagreed on how to meet the new needs and challenges of industrialization. Early in the twentieth century, reformers called Progressives sponsored programs that increased the government's responsibility for the public's well-being. With industrialization, urbanization, black voting rights, immigration, and political reform, Maryland and the nation had changed forever.

The New Industrial Society

Once the turmoil of the Civil War subsided, the nation turned its attention to building industry. Industries existing before the war were expanded, and new industries were begun. As the years passed, more people worked in industrial jobs and more people moved into the cities and towns where the factories were located. In their daily lives, people used increasing numbers of factory-made products.

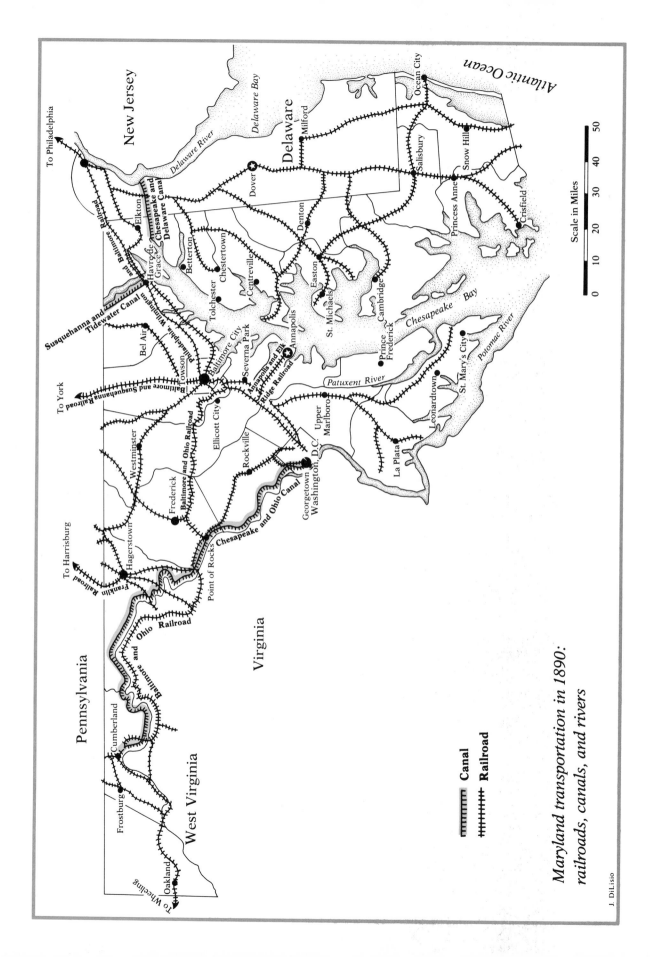

Maryland transportation in 1890: railroads, canals, and rivers

J. DiLisio

Canal
Railroad

Scale in Miles

0   10   20   30   40   50

Maryland's Industries

Maryland's industries developed at a moderate rate compared with the industrialization of the nation as a whole. The wide variety of industries that were established in the state made its economy more stable than an economy that depended on only one or two major products. Men's clothing was the industry that generally produced the greatest income and employed the most workers in Maryland from 1880 to 1916.

Iron, steel, copper, and tin were also important. The steel plant at Sparrows Point in Baltimore County was Maryland's largest single manufacturing establishment. Its first giant blast furnace began to operate in 1889. By 1892 the plant could produce 400,000 tons of steel annually and had begun to build ships. It made rails for the nation's rapidly expanding train system and for sale to foreign countries. One industry tends to lead to another. In this case, makers of foundry and machine-shop products took advantage of the available metals.

Processed agricultural products ranked high in Maryland's economy. Flour and grist mill products predominated until 1900, when canned seafood, vegetables, and fruit replaced them in importance. Chesapeake Bay oysters were canned during the winter months and sold throughout the country beginning in the 1840s. The rotation of oysters in the winter and fruits and vegetables in summer and fall gave steady work to the canneries. As canning techniques improved, fruits and vegetables surpassed seafood in total value. In the early twentieth century, slaughtering and meat packing also became major industries.

Baltimore's Leading Role

Baltimore's harbor played an important role in the national as well as the local economy. Domestic and foreign shipping produced vast revenues and many jobs. In 1870 Baltimore had $33 million worth of imports and exports; by 1900 the value of its foreign trade rose to $130 million, making Baltimore the third largest of all U.S. ports. Coal and grain were among the products that shippers sent through the Baltimore harbor.

SPARROWS POINT: A COMPANY TOWN

When the Pennsylvania Steel Company developed the Sparrows Point site, it also built a residential town for its workers. The 1,100 acres, located 14 miles out of Baltimore, were laid out according to the company's ideas about the lives and relationships of its workers.

The town had sidewalks, electric lights, water pumped from deep wells, and underground sewers. Trees and hedges were planted. A free kindergarten, a club house, and a manual training school all were progressive features. The company collected garbage and provided fire and police protection. The only store was company owned, however, and it accepted payment only in cash.

Three types of housing were available. Supervisors, technical and office staff, and teachers lived in detached houses with seven rooms, a bath, a furnace, and a cellar. Skilled workers qualified for houses with six rooms, stove heat, and cold water. Black skilled workers lived in a similar but segregated village across Humphrey's Creek. Unskilled, unmarried immigrant and black workers lived in barracks made of rough pine boards. Each 10-by-14 foot room contained two double bunk beds. Unskilled workers living here had to haul water from outside hydrants.

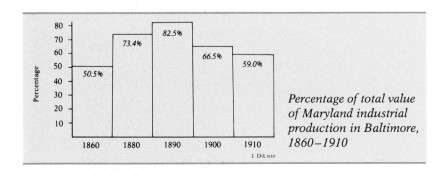

Percentage of total value of Maryland industrial production in Baltimore, 1860–1910

J. DiLisio

177

The Baltimore area dominated the state's industrial development until 1890. Then, for several reasons, towns in the rest of the state added new industries more rapidly than Baltimore did. A depression in 1893 and 1894 hurt many of Baltimore's industries. As transportation and electrical power improved, a number of manufacturing establishments moved nearer to their sources of supply. By moving, the companies also benefited from lower taxes, lower rents, and the space available outside the city.

Industrialization in Maryland's Smaller Cities

Until 1914 Cumberland was the second largest manufacturing center in Maryland. Its iron and steel industry benefited from nearby sources of iron and coal. A local supply of timber made Cumberland's lumber industry important.

In 1914 Hagerstown surpassed Cumberland in the total value of its manufacturing. It depended on a variety of industries, including machine shops, railroad repair shops, flour and grist mills, and manufacturers of furniture, organs, and knitted clothing. Frederick, which ranked fourth in manufacturing behind Baltimore, Cumberland, and Hagerstown, also had industries based on nearby resources. Because Frederick was located in the center of one of the state's major agricultural districts, flour mills and canning both flourished there.

Numerous industries sprang up in Maryland's smaller cities. There were a lumber industry and flour and textile mills in Salisbury; pulp mills, fertilizer plants, and canneries in Elkton; oyster packaging plants in Cambridge and Crisfield; and canneries and flour mills in Ellicott City.

Changes in Daily Life

In the long run industrialization strengthened the state's economy and led to higher living standards for most people. Food canning techniques freed the family shopper from the chore of visiting the market daily. Mass production made fashionable clothing available at affordable prices. A growing variety of consumer goods reached more and more buyers. Increasingly complex machines, like automatic washing machines and typewriters, eased life in both the home and the workplace.

The rapid industrial growth came at an enormous cost, however. Workers in industrial plants faced dangerous machines and an unhealthy environment. The population of cities grew so quickly that many of the cities' new problems could not be handled within the

Old-fashioned washtubs and hand wringers, like these used by women in Allegany County around 1900, were gradually replaced by indoor washtubs supplied with running water. Later, electric washing machines made washing clothes by hand a thing of the past.

The Valley Store Museum in Washington County is a re-creation of the old rural general store that sold everything. Customers would gather to talk or play checkers by the potbellied stove.

existing governmental structure. Industries filled the air with coal dust and the water with refuse. Cities grew ugly, but people still had to live in them. Natural resources were depleted and not replenished. In the short run, it sometimes seemed that the disadvantages of industrialization outweighed the benefits.

Cities and Immigrants

Industrial development drew people into cities and towns across America. The U.S. census of 1920 revealed that, for the first time, more people lived in cities of 2,500 or more than lived in rural areas.

Urban v. Rural

In Maryland, city dwellers first outnumbered the rural population in 1910. The state's total population grew, but cities grew faster than the rest of the state.

Not only did more people live in cities, but there were also more cities to live in. In table 5.1 Maryland's total population growth is broken down into growth in urban and rural areas.

Table 5.1. Population Growth, 1870–1920

Year	Total State Population	Percentage Urban	Percentage Rural
1870	780,894	37.8	62.2
1880	934,943	40.2	59.8
1890	1,042,390	47.6	52.4
1900	1,188,044	49.8	50.2
1910	1,295,346	50.8	49.2
1920	1,449,661	60.0	40.0

SOURCE: U.S. Census, 1870–1920.

The towns in table 5.2 and other towns increased in size during the years between the Civil War and World War I. By 1910, 15 incorporated towns boasted a population of 2,500 or more. Over half of all the people in Maryland lived in these towns. Baltimore clearly stood out as the major city in Maryland. It dominated both industrial development and population growth in the state. Because of the city's large population, urban changes were more accentuated in Baltimore than they were in other towns.

Table 5.2. Population of Selected Maryland Towns, 1870, 1890, 1910

City	1870	1890	1910
Baltimore City	267,354	434,439	558,485
Cumberland	8,056	12,729	21,839
Hagerstown	5,779	10,118	16,507
Frederick	8,526	8,193	10,411
Annapolis	5,744	7,604	8,609
Salisbury	2,064	2,905	6,690
Cambridge	1,642	4,192	6,407
Havre de Grace	2,281	3,244	4,212

People of Many Backgrounds

People from many different places who had many different backgrounds contributed to all phases of urban growth. Demography is the study of people, their numbers and their characteristics. A demographic study of Maryland and its cities is like a summary of many lives.

The following demographic information from the census taken in 1870 fills in a picture of the people of Maryland in that year. The total population of the state was 780,894. Slightly more than one-third of Marylanders lived in urban areas, while the majority lived on farms or in small towns. Of the state's total population, 22.5 percent were black. Over 10 percent of all Marylanders had been born in another country.

The black population was concentrated most heavily in agricultural southern Maryland and on the Eastern Shore. Baltimore's blacks belonged to a substantial community with very old roots. Few blacks lived in western Maryland.

The majority of foreign-born immigrants lived in urban areas, especially Baltimore. Of the major subdivisions, Baltimore City had the most foreign-born people, while Baltimore and Allegany counties had the second and third largest number of them. More than half of the immigrant population in 1870 had come from Germany. The next largest group was from Ireland. Germans, Irish, and others from northwestern Europe made up what is called the "old immigration."

Using 1870 as a base year, changes can be traced easily. After 1870 more and more people came to work in urban industries and related services. Rural Marylanders, both black and white, migrated to the cities seeking employment. People came from neighboring states, especially Pennsylvania and Virginia. Immigrants from abroad swelled the urban population even further.

When they arrived from Europe, newcomers had to wait to be processed by immigration and health officials. This photograph is of an immigrant pen at a Locust Point pier in the Baltimore harbor.

Immigrants

Immigration was responsible for much of the nation's growth during the late nineteenth and early twentieth centuries. In some large cities in other states, immigrants and their children outnumbered the native-born population and rapidly gained influence. Maryland's foreign-born population lagged somewhat behind the national average during this period. Immigrants made up about 10 percent of the state's total population between 1870 and 1900. In Maryland, as throughout the nation, immigrants tended to settle in the cities. Most, but by no means all, of these immigrants to Maryland lived in Baltimore City.

By the 1870s and 1880s a "new immigration" had begun. People from eastern, central, and southern Europe began to cross the Atlantic in greater numbers. Like the earlier immigrants, this group left their homes for a variety of reasons. Because of droughts, farm families in Italy faced starvation. Anti-Jewish pogroms, or riots, in Russia threatened both lives and property. Discrimination in the Austrian Empire drove people like Czechs to leave their homes in desperation. Others made the choice more freely and came to seek the opportunities they had heard existed in America. Maryland's major groups of new immigrants came from Russia, Poland, Italy, and the Austrian Empire.

Many urban newcomers arrived with only meager provisions. Political refugees, victims of religious persecution, disaster-stricken farmers, and former slaves whose ancestors had lived in America for generations, all lacked the resources to make a new start easily. Many immigrants neither spoke nor read English when they arrived. Many former slaves had been denied the chance to become literate in their native language. Some immigrants were ridiculed because they dressed or worshipped differently. Often they were able to attain only the lowest level of jobs. Foreigners and blacks alike faced discrimination in housing, education, and other areas, as well.

Although not all urban immigrants faced overwhelming problems, many joined the lower economic groups in the growing and increasingly diversified urban society. Their jobs were essential to the rapid industrial growth that was the basis for national prosperity. But they often did not share in that prosperity.

Problems of City Life

Living and working in American cities at the end of the nineteenth century could be quite an ordeal. Working-class people of all ethnic backgrounds earned low wages, resided in overcrowded dwellings, and endured generally unhealthy conditions.

Working-Class Life

Poor wages and long working hours severely limited the lives of many urban residents. From 1885 to 1900 an unskilled worker earned about $1.25 each day, and a skilled worker could bring home between $1.75 and $3.00 a day. Those who found seasonal employment in industries like construction often spent several winter months with no income. From their earnings, the average family in 1885 paid $78.00 rent per year. By 1900 this figure was closer to $100.00. Only 1 family in 10 could save any money, and 4 in 10 ended every year in debt.

Many women and children took jobs to help make ends meet. In Baltimore they worked most often in the clothing and canning in-

THE COMFORTABLE AND THE NOT SO COMFORTABLE

Contrasting descriptions indicate that pleasantness of life in Baltimore in the 1880s and 1890s was relative to financial standing. People who were financially comfortable described a different Baltimore than the city described by people who did not have even the barest necessities.

The Comfortable

Memories of a Baltimore Businessman of His Childhood (from *The Early Eighties*, 1924)

Baltimore of the eighties was a pleasant place. A charm of the old world pervaded the residential district; houses along St. Paul and Hamilton Streets, and elsewhere, had rose gardens. Piano music and snatches of song greeted passersby, for the study of music had a definite place in the upbringing of the young ladies of that day.

It cost less to live in those days! Posner's was one of the largest stores. M. Goldenberg was at 132 Lexington Street. I. Hamburger & Son, 104 W. Baltimore Street, offered "handsome Spring Overcoats $10.00," and Julius Gutman & Co., 120 W. Lexington Street, advertised "new summer silks, changeable effects, some very elegant designs in this lot, 50 cents." At 303 W. Fayette Street, table board [meals] was obtainable for $3.50 per week; a Help Wanted advertisement offered $10.00 a month for a "Girl, German Preferred, to do cooking, assist with washing and ironing," and Richard Walzl's Studio made "Elegant portraits $2.50 per dozen."

Memories of Journalist H. L. Mencken, Who Grew up in a Row House in a Middle-Class Neighborhood on Hollins Square (from *Happy Days*, 1940)

The city into which I was born in 1880 had a reputation all over for what the English, in their real-estate advertising, are fond of calling the amenities. So far as I have been able to discover by a labored search of contemporary travel-books, no literary tourist . . . ever gave Baltimore a bad notice. They all agreed . . . that its home-life was spacious, charming, full of creature comforts, and highly conducive to the facile and orderly propagation of the species. . . . There was some truth in all these articles, but not, I regret to have to add, too much. Perhaps the one that came closest to meeting scientific tests was [this]. Baltimore lay very near the immense protein factory of the Chesapeake Bay, and out of the bay it ate divinely.

The Not So Comfortable

Description of Early Immigrant Arrivals by Rabbi Isaac Fein (from *The Making of an American Jewish Community*, 1971)

There is a degree of suffering such as no pen can describe. Emigrants arrive every day almost from Europe in such numbers . . . and expect gold to be found in the streets. But when they have come, instead of gold, the picture is changed, and they find distress of every kind meeting them at every step. . . . [They] arrive without means, without a language, with new customs, often without a relative or even an acquaintance.

Description of the Immigrant Section of East Baltimore by a Local Reporter

A crowded place of tenement houses, saloons, filthy shops, foul odors, hideous noises. . . . Trees, flowers, lawns . . . gardens were sorely lacking . . . a saloon on this corner, a saloon on the opposite corner, a third saloon a few feet away . . . broken shutters and unsightly curtains.

They crowd into tenement houses, eat unwholesome food, breathe impure air, shun water and despise soap. Their children are covered with several layers of dirt. The women go unkempt, the men unwashed.

Memories of Hyman Blumberg, a Labor Union Organizer, of Life in the Sweatshops of His Youth

My father was a presser of pants making $8 a week when he worked. There were plenty of slack weeks. Unfortunately father's job was full of stoppages. I went to work at eleven to help support the family. My father was very religious . . . he believed that everything comes from God. . . . When I asked father whether he was satisfied with his boss's treatment, his answer was: "It is the will of God."

Children often had to work to help support their families. These boys worked in an oyster cannery, a hazardous place to work because the machinery did not have safety guards. Because they worked all day, they could not go to school.

Women worked in crowded garment factories such as this one, often earning less than a dollar a day.

dustries. In 1880 more than 6,500 Maryland children worked in manufacturing and mechanical industries. Many black women and some Irish women worked in domestic service. Women and children received as little as 40¢ a day for 10 to 15 hours of labor.

Poor working conditions resulted in health and safety hazards for all workers. In Baltimore's 400 sweatshops, where ready-to-wear clothes were assembled, workers were crowded into second-story and attic rooms that lacked proper light and ventilation. Canneries and other industries used machines without safety guards. A worker who was seriously injured at work generally was fired. There was no workmen's compensation or unemployment insurance to help workers get through hard times.

The Unhealthy Environment

Overcrowded housing and lack of urban services further threatened people's health and safety. Baltimore had no underground sewer system or sewage treatment facility until 1909. Human waste was channeled into cesspools that often leaked into the ground water that flowed into the city's drinking wells. Other waste flowed through the streets in open sewers, making its way slowly to local streams and rivers. Baltimore newspaperman H. L. Mencken wrote that in his childhood years, the Back Basin sewage stench "radiated all over downtown Baltimore."

Disease could spread rapidly because of the unsanitary water supply and the overcrowded housing conditions. Baltimore's smallpox epidemic of 1882–83 killed 1,184 people, most of whom lived in low-lying, densely populated areas like Fells Point, Canton, and South Baltimore. Other cities suffered similar outbreaks of disease.

Until 1910 Cumberland both drew its drinking water from and drained its sewage into the Potomac River. Thousands of cases of typhoid fever resulted every summer. Frederick in the 1880s lost over 50 children each summer to diphtheria that was spread by impure drinking water. Towson, the county seat of Baltimore County and a summer resort for some city residents, experienced several typhoid outbreaks in the 1890s when sewage overflow contaminated the drinking water there.

Fires presented another major hazard in this period. The largest fire in the state, Baltimore's great fire of 1904, demolished 140 acres in the downtown business district. An 1871 fire in Hagerstown leveled a prominent church and the county courthouse. The largest of several fires in Pocomoke was in 1888. Fires wiped out large areas of Cumberland and Frostburg during the late 1800s. Municipal fire

Little remained at Hopkins Place and Lombard Street after the great Baltimore fire of 1904.

THE BALTIMORE FIRE OF 1904

On Sunday, February 7, a fire broke out in the Hurst Drygoods Company on Liberty Street. Inside the warehouse, smoldering cotton exploded, spewing burning debris over the neighborhood. High winds and freezing temperatures determined the magnitude of the catastrophe. Before the fire stopped, 140 acres in the heart of Baltimore were destroyed. Miraculously, no one died. But the 1,545 destroyed buildings took records, wealth, and jobs with them. Estimated damage stood at $125 million.

The city's fire chief had complained of the dangerous conditions for several decades. He noted that the city's closely built warehouses stored kerosene, cotton, fertilizer chemicals, and grain side by side. In the downtown horse stables, hay was stored in the lofts. No regulations controlled storage or electric wiring.

After the fire, Mayor Robert McLane appointed an emergency relief committee, then the Burnt District Commission, to plan long-term rehabilitation. Baltimore took advantage of the destruction to modernize the downtown. Streets were widened and smoothly paved. Sewer connections were installed under the new streets. The fire department was enlarged and modernized. The fire helped win support for a new building code.

companies often lacked the equipment to put out fires, and as a result, large areas were destroyed. Cities often took advantage of the destruction to modernize the burned-out areas.

Discrimination

Discrimination based on race and religion increased the difficulties of certain groups within the population. Blacks faced the most severe problems. Many employers refused to hire blacks for skilled or professional jobs. Health care suffered because the few black doctors there were could not admit patients to most Maryland hospitals. As a result of the lack of medical care and poverty blacks lived in, the black mortality rate was twice that of whites in Baltimore City. Tuberculosis posed an especially strong threat in black neighborhoods because of overcrowding and poor sanitary conditions.

Segregation, although not as all encompassing as it was in the South, still limited access of blacks to stores, theaters, restaurants, and transportation. The state established segregated schools throughout Maryland. Several times the Baltimore City Council voted to require that housing be segregated by block, but all such laws nationwide were disallowed by the U.S. Supreme Court in 1917. It was still legal for neighborhood associations to keep out unwanted racial or religious groups, however, and many did.

Other groups faced similar discrimination. "Help wanted. No Irish need apply." was an advertisement that frequently appeared. Many employers refused to hire immigrants from southern and eastern Europe. Some neighborhood associations forbade the sale of houses to Jews, and some colleges set quotas that limited the number of Jewish students who could enroll. Many people used ethnic stereotyping to justify the rampant discrimination.

In this period many educated men and women espoused the philosophy of Social Darwinism. They believed that the best or "fittest" people rose to the top, and the inferior people remained at the bottom. The poverty seemed to support the idea that these people were inferior. Social Darwinists did not take into account how much such factors as the heritage of slavery or the lack of knowledge of the English language affected a person's position on the economic scale.

Life could be very cruel in urban Maryland and urban America at the turn of the century. The people who kept the nation's industries going suffered physically and emotionally. Some in America believed that these people should be helped, and they set out to do so.

Fighting Back

The initial response to poverty and prejudice arose very quickly. Help came from private organizations or individuals rather than from public institutions. The government had not yet assumed responsibility for the economic and social conditions of its citizens. Later in this period it would begin to do so. Until then, religious, ethnic, social, charitable, and labor groups filled the gap.

Immigrant communities often formed around a church or a synagogue that served some of the needs of newcomers. These institutions within the community tried to meet social and cultural needs as well as religious and economic ones. They provided something small and familiar in a large city in a strange land. The most complex immigrant communities in Maryland grew up in Baltimore, where most of the newcomers settled. Other Maryland cities followed the same pattern, but on a smaller scale.

Ethnic Communities: Immigrants and Blacks

Germans, who made up Maryland's largest immigrant group, had the advantage of established and prosperous predecessors. The German Society, founded in the eighteenth century, continued to give assistance to immigrants from Germany, Austria, and Switzerland. The society helped people find jobs and provided financial aid in times of crisis. The strong German community convinced the Maryland legislature in 1868 to have every general law published in German as well as in English, and to have German translators available at all trials. In both Baltimore and Cumberland, German-language churches, schools, and newspapers served the community. German savings and loan associations helped immigrants become homeowners instead of renters.

Irish newcomers enjoyed the double advantage of a prior community and fluency in English. The Hibernian Society provided some financial and medical aid to the needy. The Hibernian Free School, which was founded by John Oliver in Baltimore, educated approximately 12,000 boys and girls. Respected religious leaders like Baltimore Archbishop James Cardinal Gibbons, whose parents were Irish immigrants, gave a strong voice to the community. Still, many Irish immigrants faced poverty and discrimination all their lives.

Russians, Italians, Poles, Czechs, Greeks, and other "new" immigrants to America were not met by a group of their countrymen.

ALLEYS AND ROW HOUSES

Many newcomers to Baltimore lived in alley housing, where rents were lowest. Although schools and many transportation and shopping facilities were segregated, housing was not. European immigrants and native-born blacks frequently lived in the same alley block.

Some working-class families, including many immigrant families, realized the dream of owning their own home. Baltimore's reasonably priced row houses made home ownership more attainable there than in most other cities. Leasing the land through low-cost ground rents lowered the total price. Families who bought these homes often were helped by loans from neighborhood building and loan associations. Home loans usually were paid off in five years.

Henrietta Szold began an evening school in Baltimore where immigrants could study English after work. Her school became a model that was copied all over the United States.

The first to come tended to cluster together. They built a church or synagogue as soon as possible. The largest numbers of all these groups settled in Baltimore, the port of entry for most of them.

The early Italian arrivals of the 1870s rented housing near the waterfront and then moved into the neighborhood still known as Little Italy. Archbishop Gibbons dedicated St. Leo's Roman Catholic Church there in 1880. The church and the parochial school became the community's focal point. Lodges and self-help and social clubs grew as the population increased. Poles, Greeks, and others followed a similar pattern, creating churches and societies to support their communities.

Jewish newcomers, mostly from Russia and Poland, moved into the old German-Jewish neighborhood along Lombard Street. Many of them worked 12 to 14 hours daily making clothing in the East Baltimore sweatshops. Several charitable groups raised substantial funds to meet the needs of these people. Henrietta Szold, daughter of a Hungarian immigrant rabbi, was a pioneer in establishing a self-help program that was later adopted by cities throughout the nation. She initiated the first adult evening classes in Baltimore, where English and various skills were taught to immigrants to allow them to get better jobs and thus move up the economic ladder.

Although Maryland blacks were descended from many generations who had been born in the United States, segregation and discriminatory practices led to the establishment of institutions for them which were similar to those of the immigrants. Black churches played a particularly strong role. In Baltimore, several local black doctors raised the funds to build Provident Hospital, which opened in 1894. They believed that a black hospital was necessary because of the discrimination against both doctors and patients in white hospitals. Three black newspapers merged to form the *Afro-American*, still one of the nation's leading black newspapers.

Charities and Social Workers

In addition to the ethnically based groups, many private charities tried to ease the burdens of urban, industrial life. They offered help to all ethnic and religious groups. These private efforts led to the formation of a group of experienced and professional social workers. Before 1880 most charitable work throughout Maryland had consisted of giving alms and other physical necessities to the poor. Allegany County charities, for example, opened soup kitchens during the depression of 1877–78.

This situation began to change when the Charity Organization Society was founded in Baltimore in 1881. Mary Richmond, a pioneer in the field of social work and general secretary of the society, developed the techniques used in case work today. Social workers visited people in their homes and taught job skills, homemaking, and budgeting. Richmond kept records of clients which indicated their needs and their progress.

Settlement houses, which had already succeeded in cities like New York and Chicago, opened in Baltimore after 1895. Volunteers and professionals opened houses in poor neighborhoods where they conducted cooking and sewing classes, kindergartens, and clubs for all age groups. They offered English classes for foreigners. They emphasized skills for self-betterment.

Women led the way in many of the activities for improving the lot of working people. Local leaders like Elizabeth King Ellicott, Etta Hayne Maddox, and Anna Lloyd Corkran worked through groups such as the Maryland Federation of Women's Clubs and the Consumers' League. They fought to abolish child labor and to require inspection of health and safety conditions in factories. They campaigned to make water pure and milk safe to drink. They lobbied for underground sewers to get the filth off the streets. The Women's Cooperative Civic League, a black organization in Baltimore, worked for similar aims. It sponsored a day nursery for working mothers which was run by Sarah Collins Fernandis, an early black social worker. Today's standards came only after long battles in which these women took the lead.

Labor Unions

Workers joined together in labor unions to fight back in a different way. They sought higher pay, shorter hours, and better working conditions. They lobbied for legislation abolishing child labor and requiring compulsory education. They campaigned for laws to create workmen's compensation for injuries received on the job.

Many companies blacklisted employees who joined a union. They fired them and put their names on a list that was circulated among all area employers so the activists would never be able to get work.

Unions grew nationally and in Maryland during the 1870s. Industrial workers in Baltimore and coal miners in western Maryland formed the backbone of the state's union strength. The Knights of Labor organized its first local district assembly in Baltimore in 1878. This national union was unusual in that it welcomed all workers, skilled and unskilled, men and women, white and black.

Violence characterized nineteenth-century labor protests such as the B & O strike of 1877.

THE B & O STRIKE OF 1877

In July 1877 railroad workers took home only one-half the wages they had earned monthly before 1873. Four pay cuts had reduced daily wages from $3.00 to $2.25 to $1.75 to $1.58. On the road, men had to pay 30¢ for a meal. Hard times in 1877 left the men working only 14 to 18 days a month, but the B & O appeared to be making a profit.

Accidents, against which there was no insurance, took a terrible toll. Railroad shop machinery mangled hands and cut off fingers. Landslides buried men who were digging tunnels. Railroad cars crushed men who were trying to couple them together.

The fourth pay cut was the last straw, and on July 16, B & O workers in Cumberland began the protest. Pennsylvania Railroad workers followed. The strike spread nationwide, including to Baltimore. Strikers succeeded in stopping all freight traffic in Maryland.

B & O owner John Garrett asked the governor to send the state militia to Cumberland, where a train has been stoned. Then he persuaded the governor to issue a general alarm. As soldiers started to leave the Sixth Regiment Armory in East Baltimore, a crowd turned them back. The soldiers lost control and fired into the crowd. Nine people died.

Another crowd disabled an engine and tore up track in South Baltimore. They cut fire hoses so the hoses could not be used to control the protesters. The next day was quiet as more than 2,000 federal troops arrived. That night a crowd tried to burn the B & O foundry at Mount Clare and did set fire to a coal oil train.

The company refused to make wage concessions. Rail traffic finally resumed, although trains required military escorts for safety. The workers had lost.

The Knights of Labor declined in the 1890s, however, partly because of labor violence elsewhere and partly because a nationwide depression in 1894 made workers less willing to risk their jobs through union activity.

In 1883 some 32 craft unions joined Baltimore's Federation of Labor. By 1900, 65 trade unions in the city were affiliated with the American Federation of Labor (AFL). Members generally were skilled workers, male, and white. They relied on the strike as their chief weapon.

The AFL staged almost 200 strikes, with 30,000 participants, between 1881 and 1900. These strikes were frequently met with violence. Factory owners often hired private guards, who rode on horseback into crowds of strikers, beating and sometimes killing the defenseless workers, who were on foot.

For the unions, gains came slowly and only after great struggle. In 1886 the building trade union won a 9-hour workday. In 1892 clothing workers failed to abolish sweatshops, but they did gain a 10-hour workday. By 1914, however, one-third of all Baltimore workers still labored 60 hours a week, Monday through Saturday.

Modern Amenities:
The Brighter Side of City Life

Utility services that we take for granted were virtually nonexistent in 1870. After that time, gas and electric service, telephones, and water systems modernized the major towns of Maryland. New educational and cultural institutions opened up to everyone opportunities that previously had been enjoyed only by the wealthy few. Popular amusements proliferated in parks and vacation areas. Commuter transportation allowed some people to enjoy the urban amenities while living in suburban spaciousness. Urban life improved slowly, first for those with money and then for everyone.

Utilities and Sanitation

Utilities brought a whole new lifestyle to city dwellers. Instead of filling the stove with wood or coal, people could turn a burner on with the twist of a knob. Instead of filling lamps with kerosene and trimming wicks daily, people could flick switches that brought light to every room. Privately owned utilities opened for business in the late 1870s, and services spread quickly. Gas and electric power came to Baltimore, Cumberland, Frederick, Salisbury, and Westminster by 1890.

Baltimore's first telephone exchange began operating in 1879. Westminster had one in 1884, Chestertown in 1885, Salisbury and Rockville in 1895. Installations came slowly at first. Baltimore in 1890 had about 2,000 telephone subscribers, in 1900 over 4,000, and then, in 1910, almost 40,000.

Utility companies began small. They served wealthier citizens

Magneto Bell Telephone. Loudest talking, clearest tone and best constructed magneto phone on the market. As no batteries are required with this phone, the current being generated by means of a powerful generator in the telephone box, a large part of the expense of maintenance is eliminated. Suitable for use for exchange or private lines of any length. This instrument cannot be excelled in general excellence, nor in appearance. The boxes being of highly polished hardwood, and metal parts of nickel, plated or oxidized. Full directions for putting up the phone and constructing lines accompany each instrument. Prices quoted below are for phone complete and do not include any materials for line construction. Weight, each phone, 15 lbs. Price, per phone......$18.00
Price, per pair, complete for two stations 35.00
For quotations of wire, insulators, etc., see No. 24218.

Telephone advertised in the 1895 Montgomery Ward catalog.

In public baths such as this one, urban working-class people whose homes did not have running water bathed themselves and washed their clothes.

Indoor plumbing, as in this 1910 bathroom, was commonly found in middle-class homes in the early twentieth century. Gradually the luxury became standard.

first, the masses later. Small companies gradually consolidated into larger ones, which dominated increasingly wide areas. Then the government began to take an interest in their rates and the quality of their service.

Two urban services essential to community health are water and sewer systems. Improvements in these services began in the late nineteenth century, as cities looked for new sources of drinking water and opened water works to treat and pump the water. Wealthy homes in Baltimore had enjoyed running water for a number of years, but after the Gunpowder River was dammed in 1881, relatively pure drinking water was widely available in the city for the first time. Baltimore's first sewage treatment plant opened at Back River in 1909. In towns throughout Maryland, running water became available in the late nineteenth century. The quality of the water depended on its source.

Education

Cultural institutions also improved the quality of urban life. Both private philanthropy and government legislation created institutions that benefited cities and rural areas nearby.

Public education was the institution that touched the greatest number of individuals. Baltimore City had created a school system in 1829, and the Maryland Constitution of 1864 had mandated a statewide system of public schools. Nevertheless, Maryland lagged behind most states in public education, since many counties and towns chose not to collect taxes to fund education. Even Baltimore's system excluded black students until 1867. Throughout the state, education remained racially segregated until the Supreme Court made that practice illegal in 1955.

Public schools at the turn of the century differed greatly from today's public schools. The General Assembly decided not to require attendance. Some children worked all day because their families needed the extra money. Others stayed home to help with household chores or to care for younger brothers and sisters. Some could not afford the book fees charged. In Baltimore City in 1870, only 28 percent of those aged 5 to 19 were enrolled in public schools. By 1900 the figure rose to 43 percent, still less than half. In 1902 the state legislature responded to political pressure from Baltimore City and Allegany County and required all children aged 8 to 12 in those jurisdictions to attend school. In 1912 the assembly extended compulsory attendance to all but six counties.

JOHNS HOPKINS: PHILANTHROPIST

Johns Hopkins, a nineteenth-century philanthropist, founded Baltimore's internationally known hospital and university. Born in 1795, he grew up on a large farm in Anne Arundel County. The family performed all their own labor after Hopkins's Quaker father freed his slaves. It is said that Hopkins always placed an especially high value on education because he had so little time for it.

At age 18, Hopkins came to Baltimore to work with his Uncle Gerard, a commission merchant and grocer. Later he opened his own wholesale provision company. Hopkins invested in the development of the city's port and in the B & O Railroad. At the time of his death, he was the railroad's largest stockholder. He supported B & O President John Garrett's pro-Union stand during the Civil War and contributed $50,000 to furnish transportation facilities to the Union.

Hopkins never married. When he made his will, he left 1 million dollars to friends and various local charities. He divided the rest of his 8-million-dollar estate between the hospital and the university that bear his name.

Philanthropy

Throughout the country during this period, men and women who had grown rich in business and industry sponsored the building of institutions for the public benefit.

Johns Hopkins was one of many such philanthropists in Maryland. He donated funds to build a university and a hospital. The university opened to students in 1876 and quickly gained a worldwide reputation. The medical school opened later, in 1893, because of lack of funds. In an unusual step, it agreed to admit female students. The women's committee raised the money needed to open the school, which gave them the necessary leverage to demand that women medical students be admitted.

The doctors who served both the hospital and the medical school contributed to the public well-being. Dr. William Osler and Dr. William Henry Welch brought their influence to bear on issues of pure water, sewage disposal, and treatment of infectious diseases. They were early activists in cleaning up the city.

Another philanthropist, George Peabody, a banker who had accumulated much of his fortune in Baltimore, donated funds for a cultural center. The Peabody Institute opened with a library, an art gallery, and an academy of music.

Enoch Pratt, a Baltimore merchant, gave the city money to open a free library. Pratt stated that the library's books were "for all, rich or poor, without distinction of race or color."

During the same period, black Methodists and others gave to Morgan College. These funds allowed the institution to grow from a seminary into a liberal arts college.

Although the largest philanthropic gifts were made in Baltimore, where the greatest wealth was concentrated, a similar pattern prevailed throughout the state. Both private gifts and tax dollars supported an increasing variety of public institutions.

For example, citizens of Frederick in 1888 collected money to build a public park around the county courthouse. In Cumberland in the 1890s, local women helped establish the Western Maryland Hospital to take care of victims of railroad accidents.

In 1901, Salisbury business leader William H. Jackson gave the land and money for the construction of the second and modernized Peninsula General Hospital. Also in 1901, the Washington County Free Library, endowed by Benjamen F. Newcomer, opened in Hagerstown. Librarian Mary Lemist Titcomb made history when she established the nation's first bookmobile. The horse-drawn wagon, loaded with books, traveled throughout the rural areas of Wash-

The Washington County Free Library's bookmobile, first horse drawn, then motorized, brought books to people in rural areas. It is shown here stopping at the Old Road House in Indian Springs around 1915.

ington County. Philanthropy, large and small, added much to the quality of life at the turn of the century.

Transportation for Vacations and Suburbs

Post–Civil War advances in transportation caused people's lives to change in several major ways. One such change was the opening of vacation areas to city dwellers. Trains and steamships carried people to resorts throughout the state. The Deer Park Hotel, built in 1873 in the mountains of Garrett County by John Work Garrett, president of the B & O Railroad, provided an elegant escape from hot city summers.

In Kent County, across the Chesapeake Bay from Baltimore, enterprising businessmen built beach resorts at Tolchester and Betterton. Hotel guests and day-trippers alike crossed the Bay in excursion boats throughout the summer months. Maryland's largest resort town, Ocean City, was one of a number of oceanfront subdivisions advertised in 1875. Several small hotels and a few cottages housed vacationers who traveled across the Bay by steamship and the Eastern Shore by train. By 1900 Ocean City supported two country stores, two churches, and one amusement center, where the Trimper family had installed a large merry-go-round.

Advances in transportation also made suburbs possible. First horse-drawn trolleys, then railroads and electric street railways, allowed people to live outside the crowded center cities and still

In Ocean City around 1910, boardwalk strollers wore suits or dresses and hats. Bathers covered up also, as dictated by rules of modesty at that time.

The main street was busy with horse-drawn traffic in Taneytown, Carroll County, around 1896.

commute to work and to enjoy urban culture. The first commuter facility in the Baltimore area, the City Passenger Railway, was chartered in 1858. Other lines, serving Catonsville, Hampden, Highlandtown, and Pikesville, followed.

More and more people moved into the "Belt," the area of Baltimore County which surrounded the city. Many of them used city services and sent their children to city schools but continued to pay the lower county taxes. After much conflict, Baltimore City annexed 17 square miles of the Belt and its 35,000 people in 1888. After further controversy, the city expanded to its current bound-

New methods of transportation, both public and private, are evident in this photograph of the Hagerstown Public Square in 1912.

aries in 1918. Both annexations required a majority vote in the areas affected.

Baltimore City and County were not the only areas affected by the national movement to build suburban communities. Workers from Washington, D.C., began building houses in neighboring Montgomery and Prince George's counties. In Anne Arundel County, towns like Severna Park grew after the railroad established connections with Baltimore and Annapolis. In western Maryland, Cumberland had both electric streetcars and suburbs in the 1890s.

At the turn of the century, Marylanders living in cities had begun to experience many elements of today's urban lifestyle. Utility service, public transportation, public education, a wide range of cultural institutions, vacations, and suburbanization all were familiar parts of life. Maryland's rural population was also touched by these changes, but far less than city people were.

Turn-of-the-Century Life outside the Cities

During the urban boom, many rural Marylanders continued to live close to the land in the manner of their parents and grand-

Entire families worked in the fields. Laura Petty, six years old, earned two cents a box for berries she picked in Montgomery County in 1909.

parents. Their lives centered on their farms and local communities. In western Maryland, coal miners formed a distinct society that in some ways resembled an industrial community. Around the Chesapeake Bay, whole communities drew their livelihood from the bounty of the waters.

Maryland's Farms

Following the Civil War, the majority of Marylanders still lived in rural areas. Counties like Montgomery, Prince George's, Anne Arundel, and Baltimore, which today house dense suburban populations, were still mostly farmland in 1900.

Farm products varied across the state. On the Eastern Shore, Worcester County produced corn, wheat, and potatoes; Wicomico County grew corn, potatoes, melons, and berries. Kent County's big crop in the 1880s was peaches, followed by tomatoes, pears, wheat, corn, and potatoes. First steamboats and then, beginning in the 1870s, railroads carried the produce to market in Baltimore, Philadelphia, and New York. As the Eastern Shore prospered, a new county, Wicomico, was carved out of two older ones in 1867.

The wages of Eastern Shore agricultural workers, whose employment was seasonal, were comparable to those of urban industrial workers. In Worcester County from 1890 to 1918, the average farm worker earned $1 daily. In peak seasons, good workers could do better. When canneries opened to process Eastern Shore produce, the demand for labor drew immigrants from Baltimore to work in temporary summer jobs. Four weeks in a tomato cannery could yield $175 in wages.

Montgomery and Prince George's counties supplied much of the food for Washington, D.C. Wheat, corn, potatoes, fruits and vegetables were raised on these Maryland farms. Tobacco fields still covered significant areas of Prince George's and St. Mary's counties. Many former slaves left the area and moved to Washington and Baltimore, and a paid labor force took over the work. The transition from the pre–Civil War tobacco economy to a more diversified agricultural economy took place gradually.

On farms from Frederick to Hagerstown, wheat was the dominant crop at the turn of the century. Dairy farming and animal husbandry were growing in importance. Late in the nineteenth century, Baltimore County farmers still drove their sheep and cattle down the York Turnpike through Towson to market in Baltimore City. From Harford County, trains carried dairy and meat products to Baltimore and returned with fertilizers and machinery. Canning

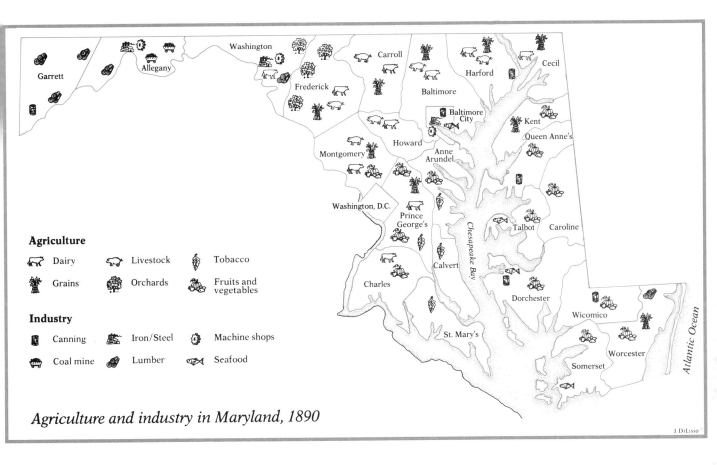

Agriculture and industry in Maryland, 1890

houses in Havre de Grace and Aberdeen employed hundreds to process corn and tomatoes.

In rural Maryland, small general stores dotted the countryside. One-room schoolhouses served the larger towns. High schools opened slowly. The county seats and larger towns began constructing utility networks soon after Baltimore did, but most rural areas did not enjoy gas, electric, telephone, public water, or sewer service at all before World War I. Many counties did not have hospitals until well into the twentieth century.

Mining in Western Maryland

In 1900, Allegany County ranked third in the state in county population. The rapid growth spurred by the coal mines and railroads lasted from 1865 to 1920. The population expanded so fast that a new county, Garrett County, was carved out of the western part of Allegany County in 1872. It was named for the B & O's John Work Garrett.

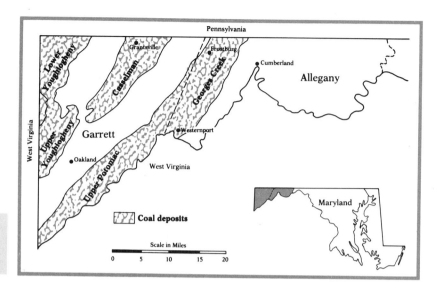

Major coal deposits in Maryland. Inset: *The shaded area shows Garrett and Allegany counties.*

In 1880 Maryland was the fifth largest coal producer in the United States. Maryland coal, shipped out first by barge along the C & O Canal and later by railroad, fueled East Coast industries, naval stations in the British West Indies, and was even shipped to Alaska during the gold rush there. Towns in the coal region, like Frostburg and Lonaconing, prospered. Agriculture, local timber, and the iron industry were also important to the area's economy.

Maryland's miners enjoyed a better life than many coal workers elsewhere. Their wages were higher than the wages in neighboring Pennsylvania and West Virginia. One-third of Maryland mining families owned their homes. Most miners raised a garden and kept some animals. Generally, they were free to live and shop where they wanted. Elsewhere, miners often had to shop at a company-owned store and rent company housing, both at inflated prices.

Despite the relatively higher standard of living, Maryland miners shared numerous hardships with their colleagues in other states. At work for 10 to 12 hours each day, they breathed in the foul air of the dark, wet mines, as well as the toxic fumes from their oil lamps. Boys worked the same long hours at half the adult wage. Mining towns shared the sanitation problems prevalent in other towns at the time. For example, Lonaconing's streams were polluted with waste from houses and stables.

One major problem miners faced was fluctuation in wages. Their pay rose and fell with the price of coal. Often they protested lowered wages with a strike. Strikes organized by the Knights of Labor and later by the United Mine Workers only occasionally resulted in higher pay.

Early-twentieth-century coal miners prepare to enter the mines of the Consolidated Coal Company, George's Creek, Allegany County. Many miners were young boys, who were paid only half of what men earned for their labor.

The Potomac River at Williamsport, Maryland, in 1903. Towns developed along the banks of the C&O Canal, because it provided transportation of goods to the coast and water power for mills and factories. Here coal is being loaded into canal boats from cars belonging to the Western Maryland Railroad.

The miners' other source of influence was the political system. Beginning in the 1870s, miners elected sympathetic representatives to the state legislature, which passed laws that covered a variety of abuses. An 1876 law regulated ventilation in the mines and provided for an inspector. This law was strengthened in 1902 with the Mine Inspection Act. In 1910 Maryland passed the first law in the nation requiring compensation for injuries as well as for death on the job. In 1912 the state limited the age and regulated the working conditions of children in the mines.

Life on the Water

Around the Chesapeake Bay and its tributary rivers, the watermen harvested the oysters, clams, and other seafood for which Maryland became famous. Railroads and refrigerated rail cars made nationwide shipment of the seafood possible. A steam canning process in use after the Civil War allowed oysters to be a staple in the gold fields of California and Colorado.

Business took a major leap when John Woodland Crisfield, U.S. congressman and president of the Eastern Shore Railroad, connected Somers Cove, later renamed Crisfield, with Philadelphia. By 1872 the town of Crisfield had become the largest oyster center in the state. Twenty to 30 railroad cars full of oysters left the town every day but Sunday. In 1870 around 16,000 people statewide worked in oyster-related jobs. By 1891 the number had doubled.

Watermen, both black and white, were leaders in their communities. The men who braved the cold and dangerous Chesapeake Bay all winter long had to be strong and independent. In good times, oystering yielded a substantial income. In the 1870s watermen earned 25¢ a bushel, shuckers 20¢ a bushel. Packers sold shucked oysters for $1 a bushel and invested their profits in other businesses like real estate and stores.

Because their income depended on how much they harvested, watermen competed vigorously for the available supply. Boats with dredges that scraped oysters off the bottom tried to sneak into rivers where only hand tonging was legal. Marylanders and Virginians crossed state lines, often in the dark of night, to raid their neighbors' oyster beds.

Illegal dredging and raiding resulted in widespread violence, often called the Oyster Wars of the Chesapeake Bay. Marylanders and Virginians shot each other. So did dredgers and tongers. In 1868 the Maryland General Assembly created the Oyster Navy to bring order on the Bay and its tributaries. Then all types of watermen shot at the oyster police.

TONGERS AND DREDGERS

Tonging and dredging are the two major methods used to harvest Chesapeake Bay oysters. Tongers extend a 30-foot-long scissor-like rake into the water and pull out up to a third of a bushel of oysters. The work is done by hand.

Dredgers drag a sharp metal rake along the Bay's bottom to pull the oysters from their bars. The dredge is so efficient that its use nearly wiped out the oyster population. Since 1865, Maryland has allowed dredging only from boats powered by sail.

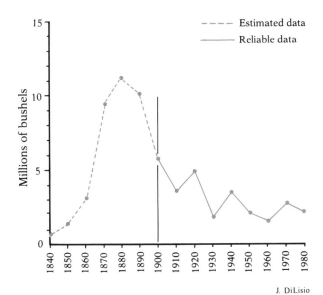

J. DiLisio

Maryland oyster harvest, 1840–1980

One major cause of the rivalries and bloodshed was the depletion of the oyster supply. Competing watermen plundered the oyster beds, and the beds were not reseeded with oysters. Beginning in 1885, the harvest decreased. This depletion of resources led to hard times for oystermen and their families and resulted in the illegal and violent behavior. The oyster industry has never fully recovered from the overharvesting of the nineteenth century.

Political Competition

Throughout the nation in the late nineteenth century, politics was complicated and often confusing. The many new problems facing America left people perplexed about the government's role. The government gradually became more involved in social and economic problems as the years passed. Sectional politics, which preceded the Civil War, had confused old alliances. Blacks enfranchised by the Fifteenth Amendment in 1870 added a new force in elections. Large numbers of European immigrants sometimes changed the political balance.

Men making political decisions faced the difficult problems of the period. In many places, political organizations known as machines used a tight, structured hierarchy to bring order to the political process. The machines enjoyed considerable power and provided specific benefits to their supporters.

Political Machines

The organization of a political machine resembled that of the army. A boss, who might or might not hold public office, possessed the highest power. Under him was a hierarchy of ward leaders, precinct leaders, block leaders and, at the bottom, ordinary voters.

Politicians most of all wanted votes. In exchange for votes, they met various needs of the people who supported them. To people at the lower end of the economic scale, the political machines offered emergency aid like food and coal in times of trouble. To many supporters, the machines offered jobs: cleaning the streets, teaching in the public schools, working in government offices. The machines also helped shopkeepers and peddlers obtain licenses. They got streets repaired and the garbage collected. Political organizations sponsored boat rides and picnics, sent wedding presents and funeral flowers. For many people, machines represented the only source of help in times of need and the only contact they had with the government.

Machines raised the money they needed for election campaigns and their other activities in a variety of ways. Officeholders generally contributed a set portion of their salary. Companies seeking contracts with city or state governments usually contributed heavily.

Democrats and Republicans: A Two-Party State

In Maryland a Democratic party group known as the Old Guard came closest to the machine political organization. Many urban workers, including immigrants, supported the organization. Owners of utilities and other businesses that relied heavily on government contracts also gave their support. Most Marylanders who had favored the South during the Civil War voted Democratic. This rather odd coalition of urban workers, businessmen, and old Maryland conservatives provided the major support for the Democratic Old Guard.

Maryland's Republicans, the main opposition to the Old Guard, also united a coalition of several interest groups. These included many western Marylanders and others who had favored the Union during the Civil War. Most blacks voted for the party of Lincoln and Reconstruction. Businessmen who favored the Republicans' national economic policies often supported local candidates, as well.

This second party challenged the domination of the Old Guard. Never a majority party, the Republicans nevertheless were able to prevail when enough Democrats defected and joined their ranks. Issues of political corruption and social reform often moved many Democrats to do just that. Maryland therefore never became a true one-party state in the manner of the states farther south. Nor could organization bosses ignore the protests of outsiders.

Voters

By 1870 all male citizens, black and white, over 21 years of age were able to vote in Maryland. Maryland's women, however, could not vote in the nineteenth century. The Maryland Assembly repeatedly spurned women's efforts, and, in fact, even declined to ratify the Nineteenth Amendment to the U.S. Constitution, which finally gave women the vote nationwide in 1920.

The Old Guard at Work

From the 1870s until 1906, Arthur Pue Gorman headed Maryland's Democratic organization. Gorman, who was elected to the House of Delegates from Howard County in 1869, consolidated his power during the following decade. He chaired the Democratic State Central Committee, which controlled party nominations. In 1880 he was elected to the U.S. Senate by the General Assembly. Gorman gained national fame in 1884 from the major role he played in Grover Cleveland's successful bid for the presidency. Cleveland was the first Democrat elected president after the Civil War, and his victory gave Gorman more political patronage jobs to hand out in Maryland.

Senator Gorman worked with a coalition of county Democratic leaders like Elihu Jackson of Wicomico County and John Walter Smith of Worcester County, both of whom later became governor. Fred Talbott of Baltimore County, another organization leader, enjoyed strong support from conservative countians. He had served with Harry Gilmor in the Confederate army.

Baltimore City's boss, Isaac Freeman Rasin, headed the largest and most powerful urban organization. His machine, which controlled the city, worked closely with Gorman's statewide organization. Rasin worked his way up through ward leadership in the city. In 1867 he was elected clerk of the Court of Common Pleas, the only elective post he ever held. In the 1871 election Rasin was lucky enough to support two winners, William Pinkney White for governor and Joshua Vansant for mayor. Rasin thus came to control pat-

Senator Arthur Pue Gorman headed Maryland's Democratic organization from the 1870s until his death in 1906.

Isaac Freeman Rasin, an ally of Arthur Pue Gorman's, controlled the Baltimore City Democratic organization until he died in 1907.

ronage jobs in Baltimore City. He served his working-class constituents by giving strong support to labor legislation. He was responsive to the city's varied ethnic groups and worked closely with many businessmen.

Although the machines provided order during the post–Civil War period, they often used illegal means to assure their power. Elections held many temptations. In parts of Maryland, faithful supporters of the machine spent the whole day voting all over the state at different polling places. "Vote early and often" was more than just a slogan! Sometimes dead people's names were left on the registration lists so party regulars could vote in their place.

In some states, machine leaders acquired personal fortunes through bribes, kickbacks from contracts, and other fraudulent means. Many went to jail. Maryland's organization leaders generally avoided the worst abuses. Some of their appointees were competent men who served Maryland's interests well. But sometimes the public suffered because political allies got jobs that they were not qualified to perform.

Machine politics never totally controlled Maryland. The power of Gorman, Rasin, and their allies faced repeated challenges. After the death of Gorman in 1906 and Rasin in 1907, John J. "Sonny" Mahon assumed the position of boss. His influence, however, was never as great as that of the earlier leaders.

Reformers Challenge the Old Guard

Throughout the nation, reform groups quickly challenged the control of the political machines. They decried the machines' corrupt practices, the political payoffs, called graft, that were made, and the favor swapping that went on. They criticized the politicians for tolerating dirty streets and hazardous working conditions. Most of all, the reformers wanted to throw out the "bad guys" and put the reins of power into the hands of the "good guys," their own. Often the reformers won elections on a popular issue and then were turned out of office two or four years later as the machine pulled together its supporters.

As their power grew, the reformers came to be called Progressives. Early in the twentieth century, reformers dominated a number of state governments. Progressives like Theodore Roosevelt and Woodrow Wilson were elected president.

Although the antimachine effort in Maryland began in the 1870s, it gained much of its momentum in the 1880s and 1890s. In Baltimore County a coalition of reform Democrats and Republicans known as the Potato Bugs beat the machine in 1875, but the machine Democrats regained control in 1877.

The Reform League in Baltimore

In Baltimore City in 1885, leading opponents of Gorman and Rasin joined together in an organization called the Reform League. This group gained enough strength to provide an effective challenge over the years. Many of its leaders came from educated upper-class and professional families. Often the same people worked in other areas of reform, like health and education. Some had been hurt directly by the machine's power.

Charles J. Bonaparte led the Reform League in many of its early endeavors. He was the grandson of Napoleon's youngest brother, Jerome, and Betsy Patterson Bonaparte, daughter of the prominent Baltimore merchant of the revolutionary period. He had supported early efforts to enact civil service reform by putting government jobs under the control of a nonpolitical, nonpartisan commission instead of the bosses. Bonaparte later served as secretary of the Navy and attorney general in the cabinet of President Theodore Roosevelt.

Charles J. Bonaparte was a leader of progressive reform in Maryland.

Crusading Journalism

The Maryland reform movement gained momentum when Charles H. Grasty bought the *Baltimore Evening News* in 1891. Like many crusading journalists of the time, Grasty used his newspaper to attack abuses and reveal scandals about well-known public figures. The *News* attacked the high prices and poor service of the Consolidated Gas Company. It criticized the telephone and streetcar companies for their high rates and poor service and suggested that a public utilities commission be created to regulate the operations of all such companies.

Grasty published an exposé on the city's street-paving contracts: who got them, why, and how much money changed hands as part of the deal. He ran a series of articles on slums, pointing up the city's failure to regulate housing standards and to collect garbage in poor neighborhoods. He revealed the inner workings of the Policy, a lottery run by the Democratic party to raise cash for campaigns.

The Reformers' First Victory

Through the combined efforts of Republicans and reform Democrats, support for the Progressive movement grew. Finally, in 1895, the reformers' first big victory came as reform candidates swept elections across the state. Republican Lloyd Lowndes of Cumberland won the gubernatorial election, and Republican Alcaeus Hooper became mayor of Baltimore. Other Republicans won election to the state legislature and to many city and county council seats. In 1896 Maryland sent Republican congressmen to Washington. Democrat Gorman lost his Senate seat to Republican George L. Wellington from Allegany County.

Once they had gained power, the Republicans enacted several major laws that they hoped would change the state's political balance. In 1898 the General Assembly required the use of the Australian ballot in elections. This kind of ballot lists the names of all the candidates on one long ballot and is still in use today. The Australian ballot replaced the older, single-party, ballots. It allowed truly secret voting and made it easier for a vote to be split between candidates of the two parties.

The 1898 legislature also repealed the old requirement that one of Maryland's two U.S. senators come from the Eastern Shore. The new law opened selection of both senators to men from the entire state. Republicans especially welcomed the change because the Eastern Shore was heavily Democratic.

The Old Guard Retaliates

When machine boss Gorman and the Democrats regained control of the General Assembly in 1901, they began to make plans to prevent another Republican victory. They figured, correctly, that Maryland's black voters contributed substantially to the strength of the Republican party. Their plans to prevent future reformer victories, therefore, centered on disenfranchising blacks. They came up with a series of schemes that they hoped would keep blacks from voting.

In 1901 legislators voted to remove party emblems from the ballot. Without the party emblems, Democrats hoped, illiterate blacks might not know which party to vote for. But Republicans opened schools to teach recognition of the word *Republican*, and blacks continued to vote. In 1904 Democrats voted to remove all party identification from the ballot, but that effort also failed to confuse black voters.

Finally, John Prentiss Poe introduced a constitutional amendment that would require all voters except those whose grandfathers had voted to pass a test on the U.S. Constitution. He stated outright that the grandfather clause would exempt most white voters from the test. Maryland law required that this amendment be submitted to the voters in a referendum. The Poe amendment, and two similar ones that followed, were all rejected by Maryland's voting public.

All Republicans (black and white), reform Democrats, and many recent immigrant groups joined to defeat the Poe amendment. This is noteworthy because states farther south did, at this time, disenfranchise most black men and thereby assure Democratic control. Of the states that had enslaved blacks, Maryland was one of the few to allow black men to vote and run for public office continuously after 1870.

Decline of the Machine

Even before the Poe amendment was defeated, the solidarity of the Gorman-Rasin machine was cracking. Both in 1903 and in 1904, Gorman and Rasin supported opposing candidates and split the machine vote. By 1905, when the Poe amendment came up, the Old Guard no longer worked as a tight unit. In 1906 Arthur Pue Gorman died, and Isaac Freeman Rasin died the next year. Machine politics continued, but Old Guard strength was never the same. Political organizations across the state had to nominate some reform-minded men for the top jobs and support some reform legislation or risk losing all their power.

The Progressive Program

In Maryland and across the nation, as reformers gained power they began to enact their programs. After 1895 a number of Progressive measures became law in Maryland. These changes came during both Republican and Democratic gubernatorial administrations. Many reforms took place during the administrations of three Progressive governors, Republican Lloyd Lowndes, Democrat Austin Crothers, and Republican Phillips Lee Goldsborough.

The variety of these programs reflects the wide interests of the reformers. Measures were enacted to conserve natural resources and to provide people with a healthier environment. New laws regulated working conditions and protected laborers from some of the worst abuses. Other laws changed the political process to move

HARRY SYTHE CUMMINGS: CITY COUNCILMAN

In 1890, Harry Sythe Cummings, a black lawyer, won election to the Baltimore City Council. The grandson of Baltimore County slaves, Cummings became Maryland's first black man elected to public office.

Cummings and five other black Republicans served on the city council during the next four decades. They provided the only elected representation for Baltimore's black community in the political system. Education, health, and housing issues were of special concern to these councilmen. In both Annapolis and Cambridge black men were also elected to city councils between 1906 and 1912.

power out of the hands of machine leaders and thus preserve the opportunity for further reforms. All these changes took place gradually.

The Environment and Health

Conservation of the environment was a priority for some Progressives. Maryland's General Assembly in 1896 established a Geological and Economic Survey to investigate the potential for the development of the state's resources. Ten years later, in 1906, the legislature passed the first of a series of oyster conservation measures designed to prevent the destruction of this product of the Chesapeake Bay.

Baltimore City in 1904 authorized a major park-building program that put green spaces in Baltimore's most heavily populated neighborhoods and added many acres to large parks like Druid Hill, Clifton, and Patterson. Maryland's State Forest and Park Service began to operate during the same period.

In 1906 John and Robert Garrett, sons of B & O tycoon John Work Garrett, donated 2,000 acres in Garrett County to Maryland, and the state created a Board of Forestry, the first step toward scientific management of the state's forest lands. In 1910 the state Conservation Bureau came into existence.

Many environmental concerns centered on areas affecting the public health. Members of the state's medical community joined political reformers to effect change. Shortly after the state Board of Health was created in 1888, local boards of health were developed to cooperate with the state board in planning local measures. Maryland gained national fame for its program to treat tuberculosis, a disease that was still a major killer well into the twentieth century.

Construction of sewers and sewage treatment plants did much to improve public health. Baltimore was the last major city in the nation to build underground sewers. The new reservoir at Loch Raven and the new filtration plant at Back River finally assured the city of good quality drinking water.

Better Working Conditions

Progressives believed they had a responsibility to protect workers, children, and women, all of whom they saw as the weaker elements in society. Since working conditions posed grave dangers to the population's health and safety, Progressives sponsored a number of reforms in this area. Maryland pioneered the development of

DAVID J. LEWIS: REFORMER

David J. Lewis, state legislator and U.S. congressman, led the way in winning some early legislation to help working men and women. The son of a Welsh miner, he himself began to work in the Allegany County coal mines at age 9. At 19, he began studying law. He continued to work in the mines to support himself until he became a practicing attorney.

As a lawyer, he fought for the miners. When leaders of a 1900 miners' strike were tried for conspiracy, Lewis served as their defense attorney. Although the court decided against the strikers, Lewis became well known and popular. In 1901 he was elected to the state Senate as a Democrat from the predominantly Republican county.

Lewis pressed for and won the passage of a mine inspection bill. He saw to it that Maryland enacted reform laws requiring compulsory education for children, primary elections, and a minimum age of 14 to work in mines and factories. Elected to the U.S. Congress in 1908, Lewis returned to Annapolis two years later and lobbied successfully for an injury compensation bill.

a workman's compensation program. David J. Lewis, a state legislator and later a U.S. congressman from Allegany County, led the fight to provide financial compensation to people who were disabled on the job and to families of people who were killed at work. The Maryland law benefited coal miners first, in 1910, and extended to workers statewide in a few years.

Progressives were eager to get children out of the factories and mines and into the schools. Specific laws came gradually, but by 1912 most of the state's school-age children were required to be in school. In 1906 the General Assembly prohibited all children under age 12 from working in factories and required children aged 12 to 16 to obtain work permits certifying their health and literacy.

During Goldsborough's administration, a new law was passed that prohibited women from working more than 10 hours a day. Progressives argued that longer hours harmed the health of the women workers and also harmed their families, who depended on them. A long series of complicated laws were necessary to release people from the oppressive conditions of nineteenth-century labor.

Reforming the Political System

Much Progressive effort went into reforming the political process itself. Reformers wanted to make politics more open and to assure the selection of qualified people for government jobs. The year 1898 saw the introduction of the Australian ballot and the estab-

Matthew A. Henson, who was born on a farm in Charles County, worked his way to greatness despite the limitations imposed by segregation. He went to sea at age 12 as a cabin boy, worked his way up to able-bodied seaman, and then joined the team of Admiral Robert Peary, the Arctic explorer. Henson learned Eskimo dialects, and he was the only non-Eskimo chosen by Peary to accompany him to the North Pole in 1909.

lishment of a Board of Estimates and a Board of Awards to oversee Baltimore's budget and the awarding of the city's contracts. Baltimore's charter of 1898 also established a nonpartisan school board that was to be responsible for modernizing curriculum and facilities. Teachers and administrators were to receive appointments on the basis of merit. Before that time, teachers got their jobs because they knew a politician, not because they could teach.

During Governor Crothers's administration, Maryland passed a Corrupt Practices Act, authored by Attorney General Isaac Lobe Strauss, which set punishments for politicians on the take. The assembly also established a Public Service Commission to regulate and fix rates on railroads, ships, gas and electric service, telephones, and telegraph service. A primary election law, establishing elections as the procedure for nominating candidates in all jurisdictions except Baltimore City, was also passed by a majority of those in the legislature.

When Goldsborough was governor, the state initiated presidential primaries. It also extended the right of citizens to petition for a referendum on state legislation allowing them to vote directly on certain measures.

The Omissions of the Progressive Era

Despite all the victories for reform, Maryland fell short in several areas. Blacks and women still suffered severe discrimination at the end of the Progressive era. Both groups failed to attain some of their primary goals.

By the outbreak of World War I, Marylanders still lived in a largely segregated society. Schools and most public facilities were both racially separated and unequal. Health care facilities for blacks were often inferior. Although black men continued to win election to a few public offices, these few representatives often could not win majority support for the needs of their community. Blacks faced discrimination in jobs and housing. Despite the leadership of a growing black professional class, blacks did not enjoy equality in any sense of the word.

Women as a group did make some gains. In 1882, when the Maryland legislature passed the Married Woman's Property Act, married women finally won the right to control their earned and inherited assets. But women failed to gain their major objective, the vote.

During the late nineteenth century, when women won the franchise in some states, Maryland's women organized to push for enfranchisement. One group formed the Maryland Woman Suffrage

Association in 1894. Groups in Baltimore and other cities actively supported women's suffrage. Leaders like Emma Maddox Funck, who was president of the Maryland Woman Suffrage Association for 16 years, and Elizabeth King Ellicott, first president of the Maryland Federation of Women's Clubs, devoted many years to the cause of suffrage.

In 1910 leaders presented a women's suffrage bill to the General Assembly. Etta Hayne Maddox, sister of Emma Maddox Funck and the first woman to pass the Maryland bar exam and become a lawyer, drafted the bill. The measure never even came to a vote because it was tabled in committee in the House of Delegates and was never presented in the Senate. Maryland women were finally able to vote in 1920, when the Nineteenth Amendment was ratified.

Suffrage leaders believed that women needed the vote to press effectively for reforms in many areas. Women all along had been strong proponents of change. Women's organizations had worked hard for the abolition of child labor, for compulsory education, for safer and healthier living and working conditions. Even without the power of the vote, women were influential in many of the reforms of this period.

The reforms accomplished by Progressives often did not go far enough. At the outbreak of World War I blacks and women were unequal citizens. Many people still worked long hours under hazardous conditions, and many improvements were still to be made in areas such as public health, management of natural resources, and political reform. Clearly progressivism did not bring a perfect society. However, Progressives did, for the first time, put the responsibility for the general welfare into the hands of the public authorities. In the future, the government would be part of every social change.

Toward a More Complex World

During the decades since the Civil War, American life had grown more complex. New people, new industries, bigger cities with all their problems, had changed forever the old, agrarian way of life. As the nation moved into the second decade of the twentieth century, yet another force would make its impact felt. From 1870 to 1917 Maryland and the nation were occupied largely with their own problems and their own adjustments. Suddenly, in 1917, the outside world appeared in everyone's home in the form of World War I.

MARYLAND		THE NATION AND THE WORLD
Maryland National Guard begins training	1916	
	1917	United States declares war against Germany Bolshevik Revolution in Russia
Coldest winter on record	1917– 1918	Armistice in Europe
	1919	18th Amendment ratified: prohibition
Democrat Albert C. Ritchie becomes governor	1920	19th Amendment ratified: women's suffrage
	1921	Republican Warren G. Harding becomes president
United Mine Workers strike in western Maryland	1922	
	1923	Harding dies; Calvin Coolidge becomes president
Potomac River flood destroys C & O Canal	1924	
	1925	Scopes trial
	1927	Lindbergh flies solo across Atlantic Ocean
Drought cripples Maryland farmers	1929	Republican Herbert Hoover becomes president Stock market crash
Baltimore Trust Company fails	1931	
	1932	Reconstruction Finance Corporation Act
23,000 Baltimore families on relief	1933	Democrat Franklin D. Roosevelt becomes president "100" Days programs of first New Deal 21st Amendment ratified: prohibition repealed
Republican Harry Nice becomes governor Murray case overturns segregation at University of Maryland Law School	1935	Federal Relief Act creates Works Progress Administration
Congress of Industrial Organization organizes in Maryland Glenn L. Martin Company and Bethlehem Steel get orders for war materials from Europe	1937	
	1939	World War II begins in Europe
	1940	Peacetime Selective Service Act
	1941	Japanese bomb Pearl Harbor; United States declares war
	1945	FDR dies; Harry S. Truman becomes president Germany surrenders (V-E Day) Atom bomb dropped on Hiroshima and Nagasaki; Japan surrenders (V-J Day)

CHAPTER 6

Prosperity, Depression, and War, 1917–1945

On Good Friday, April 6, 1917, the headlines of the Baltimore *Evening Sun* read "PRESIDENT PROCLAIMS WAR!" The changes that took place during World War I, and in the three decades that followed it, touched every aspect of Marylanders' lives. These crisis-filled decades were marked by the death and destruction of two world wars and by the economic hardships of the nation's worst depression.

Lasting changes occurred during these years. Wartime industries brought economic expansion. Peacetime production introduced new consumer goods that made daily life easier. Americans continued their movement away from the countryside and into the cities. As the cities became more crowded, people who could afford to began moving to the suburbs, where urban amenities were combined with fresh air and green space.

War and depression both led to increasing government involvement. State and local government undertook responsibilities they had never considered before. The federal government played a more active role in state and local affairs. Despite all the changes, Maryland still retained many of its local characteristics. Eastern Shore and southern Maryland watermen and tobacco growers kept their old ways, in sharp contrast to the modern industrialization of Baltimore City and the Baltimore and Washington, D.C., suburbs.

Maryland during World War I

When President Woodrow Wilson proclaimed war, no one was surprised. War preparations had been underway in Maryland for many months. Citizens had been sharpening their marksmanship

Every Man!

Between the ages of 18 to 45 [both inclusive], except those previously registered,

Must Register

FOR THE

Selective Service Draft

SEPTEMBER 12

~ 1918 ~

→ *Penalty for Failure to Register* ←

is one year imprisonment, and NO man can exonerate himself by the payment of a fine.

Patriots Will Register ~ Others Must

REGISTER PROMPTLY!

skills under the direction of the National Guard for almost a year. Two weeks before President Wilson signed the war resolution, the National Guard had been mobilized. Men with rifles guarded train tracks entering Baltimore. Companies of the 5th Regiment were on duty at the Loch Raven, Clifton Park, and Montebello reservoirs to make sure that German spies did not drop poison into the city's drinking water.

The war changed forever the lives of soldiers and civilians both. Soldiers traveled abroad to fight, while the population at home became more concentrated around urban centers. Maryland activities became increasingly integrated into regional and national ones. At the same time, the federal government intervened in state and private activities to ensure efficient planning during wartime. The war brought prosperity to industry and agriculture, as they met wartime production needs.

War Begins: America Chooses Sides

Few Marylanders foresaw the extent of these changes when war broke out in Europe in August 1914. Long before the United States declared war in April 1917, however, Maryland citizens were drawn into the European struggle.

The first tie to Europe was economic. The status of Baltimore as a major port closely linked Maryland's well-being to European events. The city's shipping and manufacturing benefited from neutral trade with western Europe. After war broke out in Europe, Baltimore's labor force and exports tripled, while capital investment in manufacturing doubled. The Bethlehem Steel Company bought Sparrows Point and began to expand its production capacity. The Baltimore Drydock and Shipbuilding Company purchased half of Locust Point. Many other industries bought land around Baltimore's outer harbor and expanded production. Increased wartime trade brought prosperity to an economy that had been in the doldrums.

Maryland's mixed population of recent immigrants and older ethnic communities was the second factor that pulled the European war closer to Maryland. Each side in the European struggle had Maryland supporters.

Many Americans had good reason to sympathize with the Allied nations of France, England, and Italy. American Jews feared German anti-Semitism and hoped the Jewish homeland in the Palestine would be established, as the British had promised. Polish-Americans, whose homeland had been occupied by Germany, waited hopefully for an American response.

Irish-Americans, however, who resented England's control of Ireland, feared an American alliance with England. And German-Americans did not want to take up arms against friends and relatives from their homeland. Many Americans hoped the United States would remain neutral.

Nevertheless, American sympathy increasingly sided with the Allies. German use of submarine warfare against civilian ships was shocking. Propaganda appealed to emotions by portraying the Allies as fighting for democracy and making the German Kaiser and German soldiers seem like inhuman beasts. All things German became suspect. The German language disappeared in Baltimore schools. When the United States declared war, German Street in Baltimore was renamed Redwood Street, in honor of the first Maryland officer to fall in battle in World War I.

Maryland Military Participation

Once this country entered the war, Marylanders united to help the Allies achieve victory. The state provided 62,424 men and women to serve in the United States Army, Navy, and Marine Corps during World War I. A small number of white women, fewer than 1,000, served as army nurses or as naval clerical workers.

Blacks made up 11,500 of the military volunteers, or 18.4 percent of the total. For Maryland's black community, military service was initially a matter of pride. At first most blacks served in noncombat jobs, and very few blacks were able to become officers. Nationwide pressure from black leaders led to the formation of black combat units and officers' training units in the army. The navy had no black officers, because only the positions of messman and cook were open to blacks.

When war was declared in April 1917, the Maryland National Guard was already on duty in the state. The first Maryland unit of the guard arrived in France in February 1918 and joined the regular army which was already there. At first the Americans fought in trenches, alongside French soldiers. Trench warfare was particularly brutal. Men waited in deep ditches, which were sometimes muddy and cold, for a chance to fight. When the fighting came, it was often man to man. Bayonets and guns brought blood and death.

As the tide of battle turned, the troops moved toward Germany. The 115th Regiment, made up mostly of Marylanders and under the command of Maryland Colonel Milton A. Reckord, joined with other units of the 29th Division of the U.S. Army in breaking through the German lines north of Verdun, France. Another Maryland unit,

As World War I began, men enlisted in the army and learned a new way of life. For this photograph, taken at the Camp George G. Meade training center in Anne Arundel County, a quartet of cavalrymen posed in their new uniforms before shipping out to France.

known as "Baltimore's Own" because of its large component of Baltimore men, helped capture Montfaucon, one of the most strategically important French towns along the German front.

The army and the navy built many forts, camps, and bases within Maryland to train officers from all over the United States. Perhaps the most important of these was Camp Meade. This training center was located in the rural area between Baltimore and Washington because of the number of railroads that passed nearby. More than 100,000 men received training there before the war was over. At Camp Holabird, located near the new town of Dundalk, the army built a center to train soldiers to use its new motorized vehicles.

The War at Home

The "War to Make the World Safe for Democracy" was fought on the home front, too. Despite the long period between the start of the European fighting and American entry into the war, mobilization, getting personnel and military equipment ready to enter the war, did not begin until late. As the nation rushed to provide the food, clothing, and heavy artillery needed for war, shortages affected civilians in every part of their lives. Prices rose, and people began to hoard food, clothing, gasoline, and other necessities. Strikes in the coal fields and the heavy demand for coal for industry led to a fuel shortage in the winter of 1917–18. An unusually cold winter made the fuel shortage particularly painful.

Most Marylanders plunged in to help the war effort. Women's clubs organized sewing parties and made miles of bandages to send "over there." Children grew victory gardens that supplied produce. Banks and schools throughout the state promoted war bond drives to help finance the war. Maryland farmers plowed and planted new fields. They recruited schoolchildren and women as laborers to harvest the bumper crops needed to feed the American armies and the European civilian population.

Labor shortages brought a patriotic response from women, who moved into new types of work to free men for military service. Women became telephone operators, typists, and stenographers. A few even moved into the factories. In Cumberland, women "hustled" freight cars, switching them from one train to another, and replaced war-bound men in local industries. The United Railways in Baltimore hired 150 women to drive streetcars.

War bond sales raised billions of dollars for the war effort.

FOOD AND FUEL FOR VICTORY, 1917

Nothing brought wartime closer to home than the effort to reduce domestic consumption of scarce items. Fuel shortages caused the most hardship. Gasoline shortages did not affect the majority of citizens, for automobile ownership was not yet widespread. Scarcity of coal was a serious problem, however. Train transportation was needed for war materials, and coal cars were put on sidings when troop transports needed to use the rails. Stores were closed on Mondays to conserve electricity and fuel, and lights were blacked out on Mondays in parks, on streets, and in businesses. On special "lightless" Mondays and Thursdays, all but one light in each home had to be put out by 9 P.M.

Allied troops and the European civilian population badly needed agricultural goods. House-to-house canvasses were conducted to explain to American house-wives how they could voluntarily conserve wheat, sugar, and milk products. Whole wheat bread was banned in homes and hotels. Instead, hungry citizens were limited to two ounces daily of "victory bread," made of 75 percent wheat and 25 percent substitutes.

During the war, all three meals on Tuesdays were meatless. On Thursdays and Saturdays, families agreed to eat one meatless and one wheatless meal. Fridays were porkless. Christmas 1917 was a meatless day, although the Food Administration announced that it did not classify turkey and other fowl as meats. "Your conscience will be perfectly patriotic if you eat them," the agency stated. But since many workers—carpenters, teamsters, longshoremen, clothing workers, laborers—earned between $10 and $15 a week, and turkey cost 60¢ a pound, only the well-to-do could afford a patriotic Christmas turkey.

The End of War

A transatlantic cable from Europe on November 7, 1918, announced that an armistice had been signed. But Baltimore's celebration ended quickly when a later cable revealed that the first one had been false! When the real armistice was signed on November 11, the celebration began again, with singing and dancing in the city streets. The news did not arrive in Cumberland until early the next morning, but citizens partied in the streets until the following midnight. The war was finally over. In all, 1,752 Marylanders lost their lives, half of them from disease unrelated to battle. By early in the summer of 1919, the troops who had survived were home, ready to return to "normalcy."

Return to Peacetime Pursuits

Normalcy, for most people, meant attempting to return to the way things had been before the war. For Progressives, this meant enforcing the reforms already achieved. For businessmen, the postwar period was one of expansion and prosperity. Business was stimulated in part by growth of transportation networks in the state. In every industry, new technology and new plants brought new jobs to the Maryland economy.

Prohibition

The world war itself had helped to bring about some of the Progressive reforms. Many reformers advocated prohibition, the passage of a constitutional amendment forbidding people to sell or consume alcoholic beverages. Maryland Governor Albert C. Ritchie and Baltimore journalist H. L. Mencken were national leaders of the "wet" faction, which opposed prohibition. Baltimore Roman Catholic Bishop James Cannon was a leader of the national "dry" crusade. Most of the rural counties in Maryland voted themselves dry. On the other hand, Baltimore citizens, many of them immigrants whose cultural heritage included beer and wine, opposed prohibition. The Maryland General Assembly was dominated by rural county legislators, however, and the state voted overwhelmingly to ratify the Eighteenth Amendment in 1918.

The amendment was ratified nationally in 1919; however, Maryland did not pass a law of its own to provide for its enforcement. Governor Ritchie believed that prohibition was an attack on the liberties of the individual. Maryland's attorney general ruled that local police could not arrest people who violated the Volstead Act, the federal law enforcing the prohibition amendment. As a result, although Progressives succeeded in making prohibition a national policy, they could not force Marylanders to observe it.

Baltimore, the headquarters of opposition to the law, disregarded it openly. Baltimore natives knew that a restaurant displaying a red hard crab sign served beer with its seafood. The city's 42 miles of shoreline provided plenty of opportunities for smuggling liquor from Canada or Cuba, and Maryland became an eastern center for the distribution of liquor. Federal agents arrested 1,000 violators of the law each year without help from local law enforcement officers.

Women's Suffrage

Many of the same organizations of Progressive women that supported a prohibition amendment also worked hard for women's suffrage. They wanted a national constitutional amendment allowing women to vote. Maryland women had campaigned for a national amendment every year since the twentieth century began. Male state officials, led by Governor Ritchie, opposed a federal amendment for women's suffrage. They believed the issue involved "state's rights."

In 1917 many American women used the patriotic rhetoric of wartime to argue for their right to participate in a democracy through voting. When the Maryland General Assembly met in special session to pass emergency wartime legislation, women again tried to get the legislators to pass a bill allowing women to vote in presidential and primary elections. On the first day of the session, Dorothy Ford reenacted Paul Revere's ride by galloping into Annapolis on horseback with the message "Keep not liberty from your own household."

All of this activity gained moderate support for women's suffrage among Maryland women but failed to convince the men who controlled the election processes. Maryland refused, on the basis of state's rights, to ratify the Nineteenth Amendment. When 36 other states ratified it in August 1920, it became the law of the land and Maryland women finally were able to vote. The first woman elected to the Maryland House of Delegates, Mary E. W. Risteau, won election as a Democrat in 1921. Governor Ritchie later appointed her to the state Board of Education, and in 1934 she became the first woman to be elected to the Maryland Senate. Maryland finally ratified the Nineteenth Amendment in 1941.

Transportation Changes in Maryland

Wartime demands had accelerated an expansion of Maryland highway and rail networks connecting the state to its neighbors. In the 1920s Baltimore increased its importance as a world port, by shipping products from the entire nation to world markets. At the end of the war, the city had ranked seventh in the nation in foreign trade, but by 1926 it was third, behind only New York and New Orleans. Baltimore became both more dominant in the state's economy and more important in the nation.

One of Maryland's two canals fell into disuse during this period. A flood in 1924 made transportation of freight on the Chesapeake and Ohio Canal impossible. Baltimore's growth brought new interest in modernizing the Chesapeake and Delaware Canal, which connected the upper Chesapeake Bay to the Delaware River basin. Deepening its channel and eliminating its locks would enable heavier freight vessels to travel from Baltimore to Philadelphia in an inland waterway. During World War I the federal government purchased the C & D canal and began extensive improvements on it.

Consolidation, or merging many companies into a few, marked the development of rail transportation in Maryland in the first half

THE FLOOD OF 1924 AND THE C & O CANAL

On March 29, 1924, the waters of the Potomac began to rise. Deep snowfalls in the mountains from the winter were melting and running off toward the sea. Heavy rainstorms also swelled the river. The water level in the river rose 30 inches every hour. In Williamsport, the western end of the Chesapeake and Ohio Canal, the river was 28 feet above flood level. As the crest of the river reached Cumberland, the entire valley became a wall of water. The banks of earth which separated the river from the canal disappeared beneath the surface.

Freezing temperatures the night of March 30 stopped the rising waters, and flood damage to the cities of the Potomac River valley was minimal. But the canal was badly damaged. Locks were destroyed by the force of water and flood debris. In many places the canal banks were destroyed, the towpath washed away.

The B & O Railroad, which owned the canal, used this flood as an opportunity to end the expenses of running it. Since 1890, barge traffic and canal profits had declined as western Maryland coal deposits were used up. An era of inland water transportation had come to an end.

A few repairs were made to the canal's locks and banks in the Georgetown area, but the rest of the canal was left as a "magnificent wreck" until it was taken over by the National Park Service in 1938. In 1971 it became a national historic park and its towpath has become a recreation path for thousands of Maryland citizens.

of the century. Two major lines, the Baltimore and Ohio Railroad and the Pennsylvania Railroad, absorbed smaller lines and dominated the state's rail transportation. A third, the Western Maryland Railroad, became a subsidiary of the B & O in 1927. All three had grain elevators and port facilities in the Baltimore harbor, at Locust Point, Canton, and Port Covington. The capacity of these facilities doubled between the first and second world wars. In addition to hauling freight, railroads provided passenger service. A regular commuter traffic developed between Washington and Baltimore.

Prosperity brought with it increased leisure time for Maryland citizens, and railroads provided the link to the Atlantic Ocean beaches. Here, too, rail lines were consolidated in the early part of the century. The Baltimore, Chesapeake, and Atlantic Railroad, and the Maryland, Delaware, and Virginia Railroad controlled between them the operations of 33 Bay steamers. These boats carried passengers and freight from Baltimore to the Eastern Shore terminals at Love Point and Claiborne. During the 1920s, as many as 1,000 passengers rode the train to Ocean City on a hot summer weekend.

Existing railroad and water systems in Maryland competed in this period with new modes of transportation, especially the automobile. In 1910 there were only 4,000 cars in Maryland, but by 1917 there were 55,000 cars and 4,000 motor trucks. The prosperity of the 1920s made it easier for more people to own automobiles, and by 1945, 375,000 automobiles were registered in the state. Maryland spent a great deal of money, some of it from a four-cent-per-gallon gasoline tax, building a new system of highways. The 3,000-mile state road system was thought to be one of the best in the nation in the mid-1930s.

The Growth of Business

Better land and water transportation spurred the growth of Maryland manufacturing, trade, and food production. Baltimore led the way, although Kelly Springfield Tires introduced a new industry to the city of Cumberland. Other plants brought new industrial jobs to Frederick and Hagerstown.

Baltimore's first growth in this period was a physical one: in 1918 the city annexed, or legally added to its territory, 46.5 square miles of Baltimore County and 5.4 square miles of Anne Arundel County. Baltimore's residential areas stretched out into former farmlands. Large areas for industrial development were opened up, as well. The industrial sites built in the 1920s were large and roomy, with giant machinery taking the place of closely packed workers.

At the new Bethlehem Steel plant at Sparrows Point, the number of workers declined after the end of the war, but the plant's steel production rose. The old industrial district of Canton became a major center for growth because real estate was less expensive there. A new Standard Sanitary plant was built in Canton, and Western Electric built a factory to make telephone parts on the site of the old Riverview Amusement Park. Across the outer harbor, the American Sugar Company built a modern new refining plant. In the inner harbor, Coca-Cola built a bottling plant, and McCormick Spice opened a factory. In suburban Towson, the Black and Decker Company opened a huge concrete and steel factory filled with the latest labor-saving mass production machinery.

Aircraft manufacturing was another thriving industry in Maryland during the 1920s and 1930s. Air travel had its start in Maryland in 1908, when the Wright brothers persuaded the U.S. Army Signal Corps to experiment with flying machines at College Park, in Prince George's County. College Park Airport was a stop for airmail service between Washington and New York and a testing ground for development of the helicopter. Baltimore's Logan field, built in 1919, was supplemented with a municipal airport in 1929. Fairchild Industries built a large aircraft plant in Hagerstown. The Glenn L. Martin Company of Cleveland built a major aircraft factory on land along the Middle River.

Postwar Problems: The Roaring Twenties

Marylanders experienced postwar problems along with prosperity. People who did and people who did not want change opposed each other bitterly. Many Maryland businesses found that their workers were determined to share in the new prosperity. Labor unrest raised fears of radicalism among some Americans. The Ku Klux Klan attracted some Americans, who joined partly to preserve their definition of "Americanism," which meant exclusion of some racial, ethnic, and religious groups. Black Americans also became targets of postwar fears. The rise of a youth culture of new dances, clothes, and hairstyles caused many parents concern.

Labor Unrest and Postwar Hysteria

During the war, labor had agreed not to strike. After the war, as business improved, wartime controls on prices were lifted, but controls on wages were not. The postwar years became an era of labor unrest and strikes as unions sought to preserve the gains won during wartime. These included union recognition, increased wages, and improved working conditions. These strikes often resulted in violent clashes between the strikers and the guards hired by the owners.

In 1922, the United Mine Workers in western Maryland went out on an unsuccessful strike for union contracts and better wages. The strike lasted for eight months and shut down 65 mining companies. President Warren G. Harding urged Governor Ritchie to call out the National Guard to protect the mines when they reopened. Ritchie protested that the state could solve its own problems "without the aid of bayonets."

Other strikes, against the B & O Railroad, the Western Maryland Railroad, the Maryland Drydock Company, and Kelly Springfield Tire, also ended in failure. Workers who participated sought to protect the union shop, a workplace in which all of the workers were enrolled in unions, which bargained with the factory owners for the workers' interests.

During the early twenties, the labor movement weakened. The membership of the American Federation of Labor dropped. The steel, shipbuilding, and construction industries used new machinery to lower costs and weed "troublemakers" out of their work force. Although labor lost many key strikes, Maryland citizens were frightened by the violence that accompanied the workers' demands to share in the postwar prosperity.

The Rise of the KKK

Marylanders as a whole seemed more concerned about the rise of a group at the other end of the political spectrum. The Ku Klux Klan, or KKK, was a secret organization formed after the Civil War to terrorize former slaves. The Klan experienced a major national revival during the 1920s. It blamed Communists, blacks, immigrants, Catholics, Jews, and others outside the organization for America's troubles.

In Maryland, the Klan attracted membership in both the cities and the countryside. A *Baltimore Sun* reporter concluded that many who joined were "mainly perfectly good, kindly people, gen-

COMING!

Western Maryland Field Day
Saturday, May 23, 1925

Women of the Ku Klux Klan
Cumberland, Md.

The Biggest Event in the History of Klancraft.
Patriotic Americans Everywhere are Planning to Come.
We Have Perfected an Amazing Programme, Which
Will Last Throughout the Day.

Aerial, Stunt Flying, Day and Night, Aerial Fire
Works, Night and Day, Ground Fire Works

Speakers of National Renown in Ku Klux Circles Will Lecture at
Intervals throughout the Afternoon. Also Many Added Attractions you Can't Afford to Miss.

Music Will be Furnished by an Orchestra

Spend an American Patriotic Day in the Heart of the Allegany
Mountains, Surrounded by Historic Interest, and Scenic Beauty.

THE MEXICO FARM

SIX MILES SOUTH EAST OF CUMBERLAND, MD.

Come——Men   Boys   Women   Girls

FREE EATS

Patriots, Don't Miss the Biggest Day of the Year in the Klan
Jubilees. The Largest Naturalization Ever Staged in Western
Maryland. Women and Girls.

Special Trains to Grounds Throughout Day, by B. & O. Railroad

THE KU KLUX KLAN

Klan membership in Maryland grew rapidly in the 1920s, from a "few picked men" chosen by the first local King Kleagle, H. P. Moorhead, to the 33,000 boasted of by Frank Beale in 1925. The Klan grew in part because its organization provided an opportunity for social activities. Klansmen sponsored days filled with picnics and parades and speeches, like this patriot's day rally in Cumberland in 1925.

But innocent public ceremonies and social events coincided with more dangerous attempts to enforce the Klan version of public morality. The Klan did not believe that Catholics, Jews, or blacks could be truly American. The viciousness of Klan activities and scandals within the organization led to the Klan's decline in the late 1920s.

erally without anything to occupy their minds when they quit work . . . attracted by the idea of something mysterious, perhaps a little thrilled at the suggestion that they are members of a band pledged to support 'Americanism.'" In 1922 robed Klansmen paraded in Frederick and Baltimore and held a huge rally in Annapolis. In 1925 the Maryland organizer, Frank Beale, known as the King Kleagle, boasted that state membership had reached 33,000.

Klansmen burned crosses in front of black churches on the Eastern Shore. Blacks, Catholics, and Jews were targets of Klan violence, which ranged from destruction of property to lynchings. Opposition to Klan activities came from Maryland's active Catholic organizations and Archbishop James Curley, Maryland's 75,000-member Jewish community, and the growing and increasingly disadvantaged black population.

Black Marylanders Face a Dilemma

During the twenties, blacks found their position in society increasingly eroded. For one thing, Maryland agriculture brought low prices because of overproduction, and black tenant farmers in southern Maryland and on the Eastern Shore found it difficult to pay farm costs as well as feed and clothe their families. In addition to economic difficulties, rural blacks faced increasing hostility from their white neighbors. Black citizens accused of crimes were occasionally lynched by crowds who were encouraged by Klan charges against the blacks.

Many Maryland blacks moved from the counties into Baltimore City to try to find employment in expanding industries. Jewish, German, Italian, and other ethnic groups had begun to move out of the densely packed inner city. But blacks remained squeezed into crowded housing because of strictly enforced racial housing codes. Population density in black neighborhoods was estimated at 1,000 residents for every 113 homes. Blacks were refused service at many stores and were prevented from attending theaters with white patrons. Many were kept in menial jobs. Their children often were crowded into dilapidated schools that had been condemned for use by white children.

Baltimore's black community developed its own identity and services. Pennsylvania Avenue became the focus of black economic and cultural activity in the city. Black retail stores, laundries, theaters, a YMCA, and other businesses there served the needs that the larger business community would not meet. Near Pennsylvania Avenue stood Frederick Douglass High School, noted for its high academic standards. Along Pennsylvania Avenue an entertainment district grew up which hosted a Baltimore "Harlem Renaissance," the term used to describe the remarkable flowering of the arts in the black community in the 1920s.

The Roaring Twenties

Most Marylanders were not very interested in the problems of labor unions and blacks or concerned about the excesses of the Ku Klux Klan. They concentrated on their own lives. Transportation and communication networks brought new ideas and styles from the cities to the remotest corners of the state. Telephone, radio, indoor plumbing, automobiles, and electricity steadily became necessities of daily life. After the intense idealism of the "War to Make the World Safe for Democracy," the state joined the rest of the nation in a period of disillusionment and self-indulgence.

The state's failure to enforce prohibition was both a cause and a symbol of a growing cynicism among many citizens. Young people began to question older values. The new values became embodied in new fashions that seemed to be most attractive to the young. Women cut their hair and shortened their skirts. Young men rebelled against parental restraint by drinking homemade liquor at illegal bars. Jazz music, with the sexy sound of the saxophone, be-

The famous novelist F. Scott Fitzgerald lived in Baltimore during the 1920s with his wife, Zelda, and their daughter. His best-known works are The Great Gatsby *and* This Side of Paradise.

came the rage of the young. They danced to its strains with an abandon that was reflected both in the wild energy of the Charleston and in the shocking close embrace of couples dancing to the slower music.

Music, literature, and theater all chose themes of realism, rebellion, and explicit sex. Maryland audiences supported the new art forms. F. Scott Fitzgerald, a novelist who celebrated this new morality, lived in Baltimore during the period. Baltimore built extravagant theaters that attracted 30,000 patrons a week to see the new moving pictures.

H. L. Mencken came to represent the cynicism of the nation more than any other person. Born and raised in Baltimore's German community, Mencken fought against prohibition and censorship. He was outraged by many of the moral inconsistencies of the twenties, and used his sharp wit to expose the ridiculousness of much of the older American "genteel tradition."

The prosperity of the 1920s gave many people the financial resources to spend on amusements. Improved transportation and an increase in private car ownership made it easier for people to take advantage of entertainment. Moving pictures drew large crowds, spectator sports, especially baseball, grew in popularity, and film and sports celebrities became popular heroes.

H. L. MENCKEN: NEWSPAPERMAN

As he wrote newspaper and magazine columns in Baltimore and New York, H. L. Mencken's cynical wit gained him a large following among the rebels of the 1920s. This excerpt from a piece he called "The Good Man" shows how he loved to tear down anything that people held sacred.

Man, at his best, remains a sort of one-lunged animal, never completely rounded and perfect, as a cockroach, say, is perfect. If he shows one valuable quality, it is almost unheard of for him to show any other. Give him a head, and he lacks a heart. Give him a heart of a gallon capacity, and his head holds scarcely a pint. The artist, nine times out of ten, is a dead-beat. . . . The patriot is a bigot, and, more often than not, a bounder and a poltroon. . . . The intellectual giant has bad kidneys and cannot thread a needle. In all my years of search in this world, from the Golden Gate in the West to the Vistula in the East, and from the Orkney Islands in the North to the Spanish Main in the South, I have never met a thoroughly moral man who was honorable.

George Herman "Babe" Ruth (lower right), pictured here when he was a member of the 1914 Baltimore Orioles, International League. Born in Baltimore on February 6, 1895, the Babe went on to have a legendary career in major league baseball, setting records that lasted for over a generation.

James Emory "Jimmie" Foxx was born in Sudlersville, in Queen Anne's County, on October 22, 1907. In this photograph, he is wearing the uniform of the Easton minor league baseball team, which was in the old Eastern Shore League. Jimmie played for Easton in the summer of 1924, after his junior year of high school, before beginning his major league career.

Maryland and the Great Depression

Economic expansion ended in the 1930s when a worldwide depression brought severe public and personal hardships that neither individual communities nor the state could remedy. The economic crisis of the Great Depression had been foreshadowed in the slowed agricultural economy of the late 1920s. Businesses lost confidence and began to lay off workers in 1929, after the New York Stock Exchange crashed. By the end of 1932, one-fourth of Maryland farmers were near bankruptcy, and 100,000 people in Baltimore had no income.

Problems of Farmers and Watermen in the 1920s

For farmers, the depression began shortly after the end of World War I. Despite the nation's industrial growth during the war, one-

Workers harvest string beans in 1937 on a farm near Cambridge. After World War I farmers grew more and more fruits and vegetables for the expanding urban markets.

Fruit production was introduced into western Maryland as the area's lumber industry declined. In this 1920 photograph, men are spraying an apple orchard at Maples Fruit Farm in Chewsville, Washington County.

fourth of Maryland's families still relied on agricultural income. After the war, overseas demand for crops dropped, and so did prices. Some farmers in central Maryland shifted from grain to dairy farming. Farmers in the western counties and on the Eastern Shore began producing more fruits and vegetables for urban markets. But the majority of farmers still depended on grain and tobacco crops, which were affected by the shrinking export market.

Farmers already deeply in debt were in no shape economically to withstand the drought of the summer of 1929, the worst drought in the state's history. The blistering heat finally helped reduce the grain surplus that had kept prices down, but slightly higher prices did nothing for individual farmers whose grain crops shriveled and cattle died. Maryland farm losses that year reached $38 million.

For watermen, the 1920s brought a declining supply and demand for seafood. Over-harvested oyster beds yielded fewer oysters, and American consumers began eating fewer shellfish. Increasing pollution of Bay waters had an impact on the shellfish trade, also. A 1924 outbreak of typhoid in Chicago, Washington, and New York was traced to contaminated raw oysters and brought the Chesapeake Bay oyster industry to a standstill. Between 1924 and 1929, the annual value of the Maryland oyster trade dropped by one-third. Some watermen switched from oystering to crabbing, but even the quadrupling of crab production could not make up for lost oyster revenues.

The Great Crash and Its Impact on Maryland

Newspaper headlines on October 29, 1929, were filled with stories from New York about the great crash of the stock market. Nine million shares traded hands in one day, with losses totalling $14 billion.

For many Marylanders, the stock market losses seemed far away. But as the months passed, industries stopped building new plants and buying new machinery. Instead of investing in manufacturing, they began to sell off their inventories of goods already produced and lay off their extra workers. At first the depression hit hardest at working people in cities.

In 1930 the Baltimore Association of Commerce reassured the city that its "industry as a whole [was] in good shape," even though several important parts of the economy were working at only 70 percent of their normal levels. In Baltimore, several factors at first delayed the hard times that were hitting the rest of the nation. Because mortgages were often paid off in five years, many citizens owned their own homes and could not be put on the streets by foreclosures and evictions.

The city's diverse economy also prevented the depression from hitting all at once. The rate at which business dropped off varied from one plant to another, and not all workers were laid off at one time. Maryland banks, like the Maryland government, were fiscally conservative. Many of their holdings were city and federal bonds, which were more secure than riskier investments. Relatively few Baltimore banks failed, but those that did often took people's lifetime savings down with them.

POPULATION CHANGES, 1910–1940

During the 1920s some farmers switched from growing grain to milking cows; some watermen turned from oystering to crabbing. But many more farmers and watermen migrated to the cities, where they became wage earners in the growing industries. Many of those who moved to the cities seeking work were black.

When hard times came, new urban dwellers often had the most difficulties finding and keeping jobs. They were less likely than older city residents to own their own homes. They were also far away from family or friends who could help them with food or lodging. During the depression the pattern of migration to Maryland cities continued, but migration itself slowed down significantly.

Growth of Unemployment in Maryland

Although it came more slowly, when the Great Depression did come to Maryland, it caused great distress to every part of the state. Women and blacks were the first to lose their jobs. By 1931 almost one-third of all union workers were unemployed, and another one-third could find only part-time work. By Christmas of 1933, 23,000 families in Baltimore, 1 family out of every 6, were on relief.

Unemployment also grew in the counties, reaching a high of 46 percent in Somerset County during the winter of 1933–34. People without jobs began to draw on their savings to pay for necessities. Even so, between 1930 and 1935, the value of goods sold at retail to Maryland citizens dropped from $619 million to $462 million. Unemployed people could not afford to go shopping.

In September 1931, the Baltimore Trust Company, the second largest bank in Baltimore, with assets of $85 million and a 32-story skyscraper, closed its doors. The Central Trust Company of Frederick, with assets of $8 million, went bankrupt and closed its eleven branches. This closing caused 14 other, smaller, banks in western Maryland to fail. People whose life savings were in other banks began to panic and withdraw their money.

Most bankruptcies were not caused by individual withdrawals, but by the sudden demands on banks by large account holders. If a bank could not meet the demand, it paid what it could pay and then closed. In all, 3 nationally chartered and 15 state chartered banks in Maryland failed before March 4, 1933. On that day, the new president, Franklin D. Roosevelt, declared a bank holiday and closed all banks across the nation. This action was to give the federal government a chance to restore order.

Private Efforts to Provide Relief

A few Marylanders could not face the crisis. One bank manager shot himself. An Italian immigrant who was unemployed climbed up onto the Calvert Street Bridge in Baltimore City and jumped into the Jones Falls. But most people found some way to cope with hard times.

Many tried to make do with individual resources. Families used up their savings. Adult children moved back in with their parents. Fewer people got married, and fewer babies were born. People who had migrated to the cities looking for work returned home to the farm if they could.

Families tried to eat less food or less expensive food. Social

Jennings in Garrett County became a ghost lumbertown during the depression, which hit rural areas of the state especially hard.

During the depression, all the members of the Bettinger family of Garrett County lived together in this cabin.

Maryland and the Great Depression   235

Although these early 1930s food prices seem low compared to today's, many people could not afford such items during the depression.

workers in Baltimore reported that many children were coming to school without eating breakfast. Some children could not come to school at all, because they did not have enough clothing or shoes.

The depression was caused by economic forces that were beyond the control of individuals, and traditional means of helping people soon proved to be inadequate. In Maryland, as in much of the United States, relief for people who did not have jobs was organized initially at the local level. Most people believed that relief of poverty was a private, rather than a government, responsibility. Private charitable agencies distributed most of the relief funds in the early years of the depression.

In 1930 the largest of Baltimore's relief agencies, the Family Welfare Association, spent $200,000; in 1931 it spent $600,000; and in 1932 it spent $3,400,000. The police became middlemen in the distribution of charitable contributions for the needy. They redistributed food and fuel to families and provided meals at local station houses.

Although the most pressing need was in the city of Baltimore, unemployment and the need for relief expenditures also put a burden on private charities in the counties. Many of the counties had no agencies to provide unemployed families with funds for food, fuel, or rent. By June of 1933, 1 of every 17 inhabitants in the counties was on relief. Many of the mines in Garrett and Allegany counties were closed. Two-thirds of all blacks in Elkton were unable to find any work at all.

State and Local Relief Efforts

Unemployment continued to rise, and relief needs grew. Social worker Anna D. Ward, writing for the Family Welfare Association, urged the city and the state governments to meet the needs of those affected by the depression. But Governor Albert C. Ritchie believed strongly in the principles of a balanced budget and local responsibility. Baltimore's newly elected Democratic mayor, Howard W. Jackson, was a "businessman's businessman." Both men were influenced by worried property holders, who did not want their taxes to be raised.

Nevertheless, when the depression began, the city and the state expanded public works projects. They speeded up construction of roads and schools in order to provide jobs for the unemployed. The city responded before the state did in providing desperate city residents with food, fuel, and shelter. First it lent $150,000 to the Citizens' Emergency Relief Committee. Then, in March of 1932, Mayor

ALBERT C. RITCHIE: FOUR-TERM GOVERNOR

When Albert Ritchie graduated from the Johns Hopkins University in 1896, the yearbook predicted that he would be elected president of the United States by one vote and then reelected for life. Although he was only in the running for the presidency in 1924 and 1928, he did win the governorship of Maryland in 1919 by a narrow margin, and he was reelected three more times.

The role that Albert C. Ritchie played in the campaigns against prohibition and women's suffrage illustrates well both his skillful control of Maryland politics and his political philosophy. Ritchie entered politics in his native city of Baltimore in 1911. He became attorney general of Maryland in 1915. After he was elected governor in 1919, he remained the symbol of moderately progressive Maryland Democratic politics for the next decade and a half.

He believed in the responsibility of the state to solve its own problems, and he opposed legislation like prohibition that interfered in individual rights. He also believed that the state must operate economically and efficiently to allow individual citizens and businesses to prosper. His programs succeeded well until the depression. Then, his opposition to the New Deal cost him many of his earlier supporters. In 1934 he failed to win a fifth term as governor.

Jackson met with Governor Ritchie and proposed that the state lend the city money, which would be backed by bonds. The loan would enable Baltimore to fund relief directly.

By this time, the U.S. government, under Republican President Herbert Hoover, was beginning to accept some responsibility for solving the problems of the depression. But Governor Ritchie thought that states ought to take care of their own people. Maryland relied on property taxes for its relief programs. As the depression continued, however, property owners were less able to pay these taxes.

In 1933 Ritchie finally decided to apply for federal help, because other states were getting their share. "All hands agreed we ought to get all we can get" of federal money, he told reporters. Responsibility for meeting the costs of relief from unemployment had gradually shifted from individuals, to charitable organizations, to city and state, and, finally, to the federal government.

Under the direction of the National Recovery Administration (NRA), industries drew up codes to reduce competition and to help speed recovery. Companies who signed the codes could display the Blue Eagle emblem of the NRA.

Maryland and the New Deal

Early in 1933 a new administration took office in Washington which changed America's approach to the enormous problems of the depression. Under President Franklin D. Roosevelt, the national government created programs to provide relief for hungry families, to help the poor find employment, and to promote industrial and agricultural prosperity. An expanded federal government and its work force spilled over from the District of Columbia into nearby Maryland counties. This initiated suburban growth there, which increased rapidly during World War II.

The National Government Takes Charge

The New Deal programs created by Roosevelt's Democratic administration covered a variety of areas. Government-sponsored agencies experimented with ways to gear industry up to produce again. They set up a licensing and inspection system to insure that banks lent money wisely and to assure citizens that their savings were safe. They limited the production of farm goods in an effort to help raise the farmers' income.

For a great many people who could not find jobs in private industry, government agencies provided work relief. The purpose of these jobs was to give the unemployed work rather than charity, usually on public projects like roads or parks. The New Deal programs allocated money to the states as direct relief for people who were unable to work. They created new towns of inexpensive housing near areas where work could be found. They brought electricity to rural areas, and they provided regular incomes for the elderly.

Almost all of these programs created a great deal of controversy. The federal government became involved in many aspects of local government. When federal money was used to build roads, federal employees set rules about how hiring was to be done and what kinds of roads were to be built. Federal codes were drawn up by different industries in order to reduce the risks of competition and to get companies back on their feet financially. The federal government also insisted that labor unions have some say in the codes and required companies to deal fairly with unions.

To reduce farm production and thereby raise prices paid to farmers, the federal government paid farmers to plow under crops or to keep land idle. This caused outrage among city dwellers who were unable to afford enough food for their families. Labor unions in the

The Federal Farm Security Administration made loans available to rural clients in Maryland. FSA supervisors in 1941 showed this La Plata farmer how to replace his dangerous shallow well in a barn lot with a deeper, safer one.

city thought that the city pay rate of $45 per month for work relief was too low. Employers on the Eastern Shore argued that the lower scale there was twice the regular local wage rate.

The federal government required state and local governments to contribute to direct relief. State and federal officials quarreled constantly over how much money the state should contribute. Rural members, who controlled the state legislature, were particularly reluctant to provide as much as the federal agencies said they should. They believed that any able-bodied man who really wanted to could find work. Federal programs, in their view, set dangerous precedents. They argued that people would expect higher pay for unskilled labor, or would too easily accept public relief payments without working at all.

Early New Deal Work Relief Programs

In spite of the controversy, the New Deal had a profound effect on Maryland. The programs that affected the largest number of Marylanders most directly were the work relief programs. The state and the Baltimore City government had already put some citizens to work by creating public jobs. Through the Public Works Administration (PWA), the Civil Works Administration (CWA), and the Works Progress Administration (WPA), the federal government hired tens of thousands of Maryland residents.

The PWA was designed to complete large-scale projects. By July

THE CIVILIAN CONSERVATION CORPS

The most popular New Deal Program in Maryland was the Civilian Conservation Corps (CCC). Through this program, young men between the ages of 18 and 25 from families on relief were recruited into work camps. There they did manual labor to conserve national and state forest land. In exchange for labor, the CCC sent $22 a month to these men's families. This helped many households get off the relief rolls. Sending these fully grown young men, who had large appetites, to camp also cut food costs for their families.

Young men in CCC camps were treated like army recruits. They were vaccinated, assigned to a company that was ruled over by a sergeant, marched around, and ordered to perform calisthenics. Many poor Baltimore families believed that the country was expecting war and was "taking these men to train for the first draft." But the 21,000 young Maryland CCC corpsmen fought a different kind of war, a war against mosquitoes, fires, erosion, and vandalism in the parks and public lands of the state.

The Civilian Conservation Corps hired young men to work outdoors on projects in Maryland. Here, CCC men are using local stone to build a copy of an 1827 monument that had fallen into disrepair in Washington Monument State Park. The original monument had been erected by the citizens of Boonsboro in just one day.

1934, 14 Maryland counties had proposed to Governor Ritchie public works projects worth $13 million. Baltimore City presented plans to spend an additional $16.1 million. Most of the state-sponsored PWA projects were roads, including a new major highway from Baltimore to Philadelphia. But PWA did not hire all the people who needed jobs, and it required more skilled than unskilled workers. At the height of PWA activity in Maryland, only 3,899 people were on the public works payroll.

The CWA and WPA programs were intended to put the maximum number of people to work. Created in 1933, CWA was an experiment in federal work relief. Half of the 51,000 Maryland workers hired for its projects came directly from the relief rolls. The other half were people who needed jobs but were not yet so destitute that they qualified for relief. In 1935 CWA was replaced by a more permanent agency, the WPA.

The Works Progress Administration

Before it was dismantled in 1943, the WPA spent $58 million in Maryland. At one time or another, nearly one-fifth of all the workers in the state were on its payroll. Local communities provided equipment and supplies, and the WPA paid workers' salaries. The small number of women who qualified for WPA work were in its Service Division. Black women trained as domestics. Both black and white women worked in "sewing rooms," where they learned the skills of the garment industry. Some of the clothing they made was given away in the general relief program.

The WPA Service Division also conducted a historical records survey, repaired library books all over the state, and held nursery school and adult education classes. A small group of WPA workers surveyed, measured, and photographed historical Maryland buildings as part of the Historical American Buildings Survey.

The majority of Maryland WPA workers were unskilled male laborers, who worked on construction projects in the Operations Division. Few local communities had resources to provide them with modern tools. The work they did was accomplished by manpower, rather than by machinery. Using wheelbarrows and shovels, WPA workers on the Eastern Shore and in western Maryland built or improved 1,300 miles of roads. In villages all over the state, they built miles of curbs and sidewalks. Other community-sponsored WPA projects improved local parks and playgrounds.

Many communities used WPA funds to build sanitary sewer systems. When WPA work was done, outhouses disappeared from the back alleys of towns from Garrett County to Worcester County.

Aerial view of Greenbelt, 1941.

GREENBELT

Maryland was the home of one of the most ambitious New Deal projects: the city of Greenbelt. New Deal planners thought that federally funded "greenbelt towns" could solve several problems. Building the towns near large cities would provide work for the urban unskilled unemployed, and the new homes would provide inexpensive housing for working poor people. These homes would be in a healthy suburban atmosphere, rather than in the inner city. Fathers would be close to their work, but children would be surrounded by trees, parks, and gardens.

Better communities, it was thought, would emerge from advance planning. Schools, stores, movie houses, libraries, gasoline stations, beauty parlors, would all be in a "town center," where everyone could gather. Only three such towns were ever built. Greenbelt, Maryland, was the first and most successful.

Greenbelt was begun in 1935 on 12,000 acres located 12 miles from Washington. It was close to Beltsville, where a federal Agricultural Research Center provided jobs for Greenbelt residents. Completing the town took two and a half years and employed more than 13,000 people. The federal government became the town's landlord, renting each of the 885 homes for, on the average, $31.23 per month. Tenants for the new town were carefully chosen from over 5,700 applicant families.

In 1942, when Maryland became a center for wartime industries, housing had to be found for war workers. One thousand additional "defense housing" units were built in the undeveloped areas of Greenbelt. In September of 1945, when the war was over, the federal government sold the row houses to a cooperative of Greenbelt tenants.

Long, straight sidewalks along tree-shaded streets provided safe places for children to play. The look of Maryland's small towns was transformed. On the Eastern Shore, WPA workers cleared out drainage ditches and tidal rivers and built retaining walls to stop shoreline erosion. A new public pier was built in Baltimore. Other workers built flood walls along the rivers of Garrett and Allegany counties after disastrous floods in 1936.

Politics, Labor, and Blacks during the Thirties

New Deal programs brought Maryland citizens some relief from the depression. But the changes also disrupted Maryland's political balance. Moreover, as national programs were put into effect in the state, laborers used strikes to demand overdue improvements in their status. Maryland blacks also raised challenges to discrimination, and then took them to federal courts.

Political Changes in Maryland

In Maryland, one of the most popular measures passed by President Roosevelt and Congress did not create a new program, it ended an old one. The new president had promised to end prohibition, and Congress moved immediately to pass the Twenty-First Amendment. Maryland voters, particularly in Baltimore, voted overwhelmingly to pass it and repeal the ban on drinking.

The end of prohibition also changed the state's political leadership. In 1934, when Ritchie ran again for governor, prohibition was a dead issue and many Marylanders were still unemployed. Ritchie had insisted on a state's right to solve its own unemployment problems without federal interference, a stance that alienated many of his former supporters.

His Republican opponent, Harry W. Nice, promised to seek full Maryland participation in New Deal programs. Nice won by a narrow margin, but the Democrats won most of the other election-day contests. Without Ritchie's strong leadership, the state legislature became dominated by financially conservative rural delegates from southern Maryland and the Eastern Shore. They blocked state tax increases that were needed to fund the New Deal programs that they opposed.

Organized Labor Makes Gains

From the beginning of the New Deal, President Roosevelt had insisted that organized labor ought to have a say in important economic decisions. Labor unions had been particularly hard hit by the loss of jobs for their workers. They won an important national victory in 1935 with the passage of the Wagner National Labor Relations Act. This act guaranteed labor the right to organize and bargain collectively. In Maryland, the struggle to establish a strong position for labor led to a series of strikes during the 1930s.

Some of labor's demands were voiced by organizers in a new national union. Before 1937, most skilled Maryland workers were members of craft unions that belonged to the American Federation of Labor. Many unskilled workers in the large industries in Maryland which manufactured rubber, textiles, and automobiles were not represented by any union. The Congress of Industrial Organizations (CIO), which organized in Maryland in 1937, represented workers on an industrywide basis rather than on the basis of a single craft.

Young CIO labor leaders fought for collective bargaining rights in the large industries that had no unions. CIO–United Textile Workers and CIO–United Rubber Workers obtained union recognition, better wages and hours, and better working conditions at large plants in Cumberland. In Baltimore, the CIO–United Auto Workers succeeded in organizing General Motors. Not all union successes were won by CIO unions. When 2,000 poorly paid workers walked out of the Phillips Packing Company canning plant in Cambridge, they asked the AFL to organize and represent them.

In most of these strikes, violence on both sides heightened tensions. Earlier, the government had often intervened on behalf of industry when struggles between labor and management had led to violence. But in each of these Maryland strikes, the federal government's National Labor Relations Board (NLRB) enforced the right of workers to organize an independent union. The NLRB insisted that the company bargain in good faith. Maryland working men in this way became active supporters of the Democratic party, whose policies had won them significant economic gains.

Change for Blacks Comes Slowly

The people who benefited least from state and national programs during the New Deal were Maryland's black citizens. The greatest unemployment, both in Baltimore City and on the Eastern Shore,

Black women demonstrated on Pennsylvania Avenue in Baltimore to urge patrons to shop only in stores that hired black employees.

was among blacks. The tensions that accompanied economic hard times often exploded in racial prejudice and racial violence.

A special study commissioned by the National Urban League in 1935 revealed that Baltimore blacks were concentrated in the poorest sections of the city, crowded into deteriorating housing. They suffered such high rates of tuberculosis that one section of the ghetto was known as Lung Alley. Many were segregated in the lowest-paying jobs, usually those involving manual labor or difficult or unpleasant services. A large percentage of black women worked for low wages as domestic servants, leaving their own homes and children to care for the homes and children of white families. Because the work was steady, these were considered good jobs.

Black leaders protested depression conditions in a number of ways. Some political leaders, like the former Republican Baltimore City Councilman William Fitzgerald, switched to the Democratic party to help win New Deal benefits for blacks. During Roosevelt's presidency the majority of black voters changed their allegiance from the Republican to the Democratic party, primarily for economic reasons.

The National Association for the Advancement of Colored People

(NAACP) and several other local groups, under the leadership of Lillie Mae Carroll Jackson, began to fight the problem of black unemployment directly. They boycotted and picketed stores that would not hire black workers in the black community along Pennsylvania Avenue. They urged people to buy only where they could work. Merchants responded by hiring black workers.

During the 1930s black citizens in Maryland did make some important gains in education for their children. Although schools were still segregated, Maryland schools for black children had already improved dramatically during the 1920s. In 1916, there was only one black high school in the entire state, Baltimore Colored High School. By 1921, 10 black high schools enrolled 300 children. In 1928, 989 black Maryland pupils attended schools that offered a high school academic and vocational curriculum. Eleven Maryland counties bused nearly 500 black children across county lines to enable them to get a high school education—but in segregated high schools. Despite the improvements, by 1940 only 3½ percent of all black students completed high school.

The state spent less money to support black schools than it spent for white schools. In 1935 the state spent $48.01 for educating a black student, compared to $67.61 for a white student. Black teachers were paid lower salaries than white teachers. During the 1930s, the black churches, the Maryland NAACP, and the *Baltimore Afro-American*, three powerful community institutions, all fought the inequity. Challenges in the courts finally won a federal injunction against the practice.

Segregation Is Challenged

If secondary education for blacks was improving but still poor, higher education was worse. Only the private (Methodist-connected) Morgan College provided a four-year liberal arts program. Bowie State Teacher's College, founded in 1867, was the only state school for blacks. Princess Anne Academy, owned by Morgan, did not have even a two-year college curriculum until 1927. Coppin Normal School was run by Baltimore City to provide black teachers for its schools. There was no provision for professional education.

In the spring of 1935 a black Baltimore resident named Donald Murray, an honors graduate from Amherst College in Massachusetts, applied to the all-white University of Maryland Law School for admission and was refused. The state argued that it had provided equal professional educational opportunities by creating in 1933 a scholarship fund for blacks to attend out-of-state professional schools. The NAACP hired Baltimore lawyer Thurgood Mar-

shall to argue Murray's case. He showed that no money had been
put into that scholarship fund and that no scholarships had been
awarded.

The federal judge agreed with the NAACP that Maryland had
failed to provide the legally required "separate but equal" education for Murray, and he ordered the University of Maryland Law
School to admit Murray. Murray quietly took his seat in classes in
the fall of 1935, and he graduated with an excellent record in 1938.
He was the first black student to integrate a state university south
of the Mason-Dixon line in the twentieth century.

In some ways the victory was a hollow one. For the next 15 years,
only the law school admitted blacks. The state became fearful that
it would be required to integrate other parts of the university.
Maryland did purchase Morgan College from the college's trustees,
but the state continued to maintain a segregated state college
system.

World War II and the End of the Depression

Renewal of war in Europe in 1939, not New Deal programs, ended hard times in Maryland and the nation. World War II placed heavy military and industrial demands on the people of Maryland. People from rural counties and nearby states flocked to Baltimore to work in war industries. Housing for new workers and the creation of new industries surrounded Baltimore with a new ring of suburbs. Growth of the federal government and the military brought more people to the Washington suburbs. Factories making aircraft and weapons rapidly expanded, bringing new life to smaller cities like Frederick and Cumberland. Farms became more productive and more mechanized, producing greater quantities of food with a smaller work force.

War Begins Again in Europe

Americans watched uneasily from 1935 onward as Germany under Adolf Hitler and Italy under Benito Mussolini rearmed and advanced into neighboring countries. Baltimore's German community had begun cautiously to celebrate its heritage again in the late 1920s as memories of World War I faded. But by the late 1930s most Germans in Maryland were as alarmed at Hitler's actions in Europe as other Americans were. They were careful to identify themselves as Americans of German descent. By the time Hitler invaded Czechoslovakia, German-language broadcasts on WCBM had been dropped because of loss of advertising.

For Americans, the war began, not in Germany, but in the Pacific. On December 7, 1941, Japan bombed the American naval base at Pearl Harbor, in Hawaii. Americans, including Marylanders, entered World War II more united and better prepared for war than they had been in 1917.

Wartime Industrial Growth in Maryland

Maryland industrial expansion began long before its military participation in the war. In 1937 industries like Bethlehem Steel and the Glenn L. Martin Company were already beginning to receive orders from overseas nations preparing for war. The emperor of Japan bought ships in Baltimore, and England ordered airplanes. When it became clear that the United States would take part in the

The Glenn L. Martin Company supplied bombers for the United States and its allies in World War II. Jobs created by the war helped end the depression.

war on the side of England and France, industrial activity speeded up even more.

The federal government invested $185 million to construct defense plants throughout Maryland. The government also made sure that factories in Baltimore, Cumberland, and Frederick received raw materials to manufacture steel and rubber, build ships and airplanes, and refine oil. Maryland eventually filled war production contracts totalling more than $5½ billion.

This enormously expanded wartime production ended unemployment, the most stubborn problem of the depression. The largest growth in employment was in two industries that had been only moderately important in Maryland before the war: the aircraft industry and shipbuilding. Total aircraft industry employment in 1940 was 11,000. By 1943, 50,000 people, many of them women, were making airplanes in Baltimore and Hagerstown plants. The Glenn L. Martin Company alone employed 37,000 workers.

In 1940, shipbuilding employed 4,000 workers. Three years later, 77,000 laborers were employed as shipbuilders. Forty-seven thousand workers at Bethlehem Steel's Fairchild Shipyards built more than 500 Victory and Liberty Ships. Wartime production adapted

WOMEN'S WORK IN WARTIME

Women were heavily recruited by the U.S. Employment Service for war work. Unemployed homemakers in neighborhoods near war plants were promised good pay and government-funded day care centers for their children if they would come to work. Recruiters also tried to make the work sound familiar, or *feminine*. At the Fairchild Aircraft Plant in Hagerstown, promotional signs extolled the superior ability of women to do the "delicate" work of riveting aircraft wings. The caption on a 1943 photograph of white women cleaning train passenger cars says they "are replacing men who have dropped the brushes and picked up guns. The ladies found it no harder than cleaning the woodwork at home."

Women cleaning a passenger car of the B & O Railroad.

Woman riveting airplane wings at Fairchild Aircraft plant in Hagerstown.

automobile assembly-line techniques, cutting the time needed to launch a ship from 110 days down to 52.

Women and Blacks as War Workers

Industries that were struggling to meet defense contracts could not find enough men to fill their production lines, so they turned to women for their labor supply. Posters told women that it was their patriotic duty to work in war industries. As more and more men were drafted or volunteered for the armed services, the proportion of women in the work force grew. As they had in World War I, women learned to do many jobs that traditionally had been limited to men. Women became welders and riveters, and they operated heavy cranes and drove trucks.

For blacks, the war opened up economic opportunities that decades of protest against discrimination had been unable to create. Before the war, less than 8 percent of black Baltimoreans worked in factories. Many industrial managers believed that they were incapable of doing the more skilled work of running complicated machinery. Federal Fair Employment Practices Committee members attempted to overcome this prejudice. When persuasion failed, President Roosevelt issued an executive order to force industry to employ blacks.

The U.S. government followed a policy allowing no discrimination in the employment of workers in defense industries because of race, creed, color, or national origin. This clause was included in all defense contracts. By the time Germany surrendered in May 1945, the number of blacks working in industry had more than doubled. The percentage of blacks in the industrial work force in the Baltimore area reached 17.6 percent. But the improvement was only a wartime phenomenon. Black employment in the industrial force began dropping off as war production ended. In the postwar years, the hopes of blacks who had experienced better times and the fears of whites over loss of their privileged position would result in more and more direct confrontation.

Demographic Changes during the War

Wartime demand for labor not only brought women and blacks within the cities into the work force, it also drew new people to the cities. The civilian population of Baltimore grew by 134,000 people between April 1940 and November 1943. The total migration of workers into the city in the war years equalled 210,000. Many of these people came from other parts of Maryland. Additional workers seeking industrial employment came from North Carolina, Virginia, West Virginia, and Pennsylvania.

These new workers and their families needed housing, transportation, and educational services, and Baltimore scrambled to satisfy the needs. By the end of 1944, 28,000 wartime housing units had been built. Many war workers lived in makeshift trailer parks near the Martin Company plants on the deltas on the outskirts of the city. Long lines formed at laundries, and buses and trolleys heading in and out of the city were crowded. In Baltimore's inner harbor, sightseeing boats were converted to marine buses to transport workers from crowded city neighborhoods to the Bethlehem Steel Shipyards. Defense plants built day-care centers for the children of women who had come to Baltimore to find jobs. Public schools went on double shifts to accommodate all the new children.

At the same time, directing the enormous worldwide war effort caused a growth of the federal government's civilian work force. These workers and their families began to seek housing in Montgomery and Prince George's counties near Washington, D.C. All these population shifts, or demographic changes, complicated the political split between rural counties, the new suburbs, and urban Baltimore.

Soldiers and Civilians in Wartime Maryland

Thousands of Marylanders who worked overtime in war industries also followed closely the radio and newspaper reports from Europe and the Pacific. Many wondered if their sons or daughters, husbands, or brothers and sisters were involved in battle. Wartime shortages and rationing affected everyone, even those who had no relatives fighting in the war.

Maryland Military Participation in World War II

Maryland sent 242,023 men and women into service in the armed forces. At the end of the war, 4,375 of them were dead or missing. Many of the deaths in World War I were due to disease, but most of the World War II dead were killed in action or died of wounds and injuries suffered in battle. White Marylanders for the most part served in one of six army military units. The 29th Infantry Division, made up of armed National Guard units from Maryland, Virginia, Pennsylvania, and the District of Columbia, formed an important part of the Allied European invasion force at Omaha Beach on D-Day.

In addition, Marylanders formed five general hospital units in the army: the 18th and 118th, from the Johns Hopkins Medical School; the 42d and 142d, from the University of Maryland Medical School; and the 56th, organized by Baltimore physicians, which served as a front-line hospital in Europe. The others provided medical care in the Pacific theater of war, serving in India, the Fiji Islands, Australia, Manila, and Leyte in the Philippines.

Both the political and the military establishment were still committed to complete segregation in the armed services at the outbreak of World War II. They accepted the idea that equality within separate units was possible, just as blacks were coming to the conclusion that separation was inherently unequal and therefore not acceptable. Black Marylanders were not trained in hometown units, like their white counterparts, but were scattered throughout the army. Over the opposition of many military leaders, President Roosevelt promised that black volunteers and draftees would play a combat role in all branches of the armed services. The president was responding to persistent criticisms of segregation and discrimination in the armed forces voiced by the black press, including Baltimore's *Afro-American*.

Since World War I many army and navy installations had been located in Maryland. By the end of World War II, military training bases, defense posts, testing sites, air fields, and medical centers were an even more important part of the state's economy. Five hundred million dollars was spent in Maryland to expand older bases such as Fort Meade and to create new ones like Andrews Air Force Base. The army alone had 65 installations within the state. Most of them were small offices consisting of maintenance or service units. Others, like Aberdeen Proving Ground, covered hundreds of thousands of acres and became small cities in themselves.

Civilian Life during Wartime

Every aspect of life in Maryland was affected by the war effort. Tires, gasoline, and food were rationed. Families turned to home gardens and public transportation for the duration of the war. Classes in canning and preserving food were taught to homemakers, many of whom also worked in war industries. To relieve the manpower shortage, older children worked after school. They stocked

PRISONERS OF WAR IN MARYLAND

Not all of the military installations in Maryland were used for training American troops. As early as March 1942, Japanese, German, and Italian enemy aliens were interned in stockades at Fort George C. Meade. As wartime demands for labor became harder to meet, German and Italian prisoners of war (POWs) were allocated to Maryland farms and industry to meet the need. At one point 18 camps in Maryland were furnishing POW labor. Ten thousand prisoners spent up to three years in Maryland before being repatriated or sent home, at the end of the war.

The use of German prisoners as farm labor saved the Maryland tomato crop in 1943. At Fort Meade, Italian prisoners worked very diligently in labor gangs. To improve their morale, Major General Philip Hayes asked Baltimore's Italian community to provide entertainment similar to that provided for American troops by the USO. When some 300 Italian-American girls over age 18 arrived at Fort Meade to participate in the dances, the American Legion protested that the prisoners were being "coddled."

Ration books defined wartime limits on purchases of sugar, gasoline, and other goods. For instance, consumers could buy only as much gasoline as their windshield sticker allowed ("A" stickers got a minimal supply).

grocery store shelves, waited on tables, set pins in bowling alleys, and cared for children whose mothers worked in war plants. High school boys and girls even volunteered to spend their Saturdays and summer vacations as farm laborers to harvest valuable crops.

Black and white college girls and women war workers volunteered as hostesses at USO dances for GIs far from home. Theaters and restaurants donated free tickets to servicemen to use on their off hours. Women all over the state rolled bandages for the Red Cross, knit wool sweaters to be distributed to servicemen, and participated in letter-writing campaigns to boost the morale of American soldiers. Newspaper advertisements promoted scrap metal collection drives. War bonds once again became the patriotic way for civilians to save the extra money they earned working overtime in war plants.

The news of "Victory!" in Europe in June 1945, and the atomic end of the war in the Far East in August 1945, brought Marylanders thronging into the streets in celebration. But postwar readjustment threatened that unity. By October 1945, nearly 40,000 war workers had been laid off. Returning soldiers entering the job market were given priority over women and blacks who had entered the work force during wartime.

Men who came home from war found that their wives and families had managed to run their affairs without a man in the house. Reunited families often faced unexpected strains. Thousands of women happily quit their war jobs and turned their attention to children and housework. But other women had become accustomed to working at a full-time job and earning decent pay. They wanted to stay in the work force. Blacks had fought for equal treatment in the armed services and against an enemy that had carried racism to murderous extremes. They returned home determined to work for equal treatment and an end to racism in civilian life.

1945: A Pivotal Year

Maryland and the nation had lived through the crises of war, depression, and a second war. Everyone longed for better times. As the crowds cheered V-J Day, they looked ahead, hoping for peace and prosperity.

Maryland at the end of 1945 was poised between its complex

On August 14, 1945 (V-J Day), Balti-moreans crowded the streets to cele-brate the end of World War II.

past, with all its rapid growth, and an uncertain future. The consolidation and growth of the preceding 30 years, as well as the stubborn loyalty to old ways and a colorful and unique Maryland identity, set the framework within which the postwar years would develop.

MARYLAND		THE NATION AND THE WORLD
First suburban department store opens in Silver Spring	**1946**	Beginning of a national "baby boom"
Democrat William Preston Lane, Jr., becomes governor	**1947**	Truman Doctrine and Marshall Plan
Ober Law	**1949**	NATO formed Communist revolution in China First Soviet nuclear test
	1950–1953	Korean War
Republican Theodore R. McKeldin becomes governor	**1951**	
Chesapeake Bay Bridge opens	**1952**	
	1953	Republican Dwight D. Eisenhower becomes president
Baltimore public schools desegregated	**1954**	*Brown* v. *Topeka Board of Education*
Maryland Port Authority created	**1955**	
Harbor Tunnel opens	**1957**	Soviet satellite Sputnik launched
Democrat J. Millard Tawes becomes governor	**1959**	
Charles Center construction begins in Baltimore	**1961**	Democrat John F. Kennedy becomes president
	1962	Cuban Missile Crisis
	1963	John F. Kennedy assassinated; Lyndon B. Johnson becomes president
	1964	Civil Rights Act
	1965	Voting Rights Act
Republican Spiro Agnew becomes governor Convention attempts to revise Maryland Constitution	**1967**	
Baltimore riots	**1968**	Martin Luther King, Jr., and Robert F. Kennedy assassinated
Democrat Marvin Mandel becomes governor	**1969**	Republican Richard M. Nixon becomes president Spiro Agnew becomes vice-president First man walks on the moon
	1973	Agnew resigns vice-presidency End of the Vietnam war
Calvert Cliffs nuclear power plant built	**1974**	Nixon resigns presidency Republican Gerald Ford becomes president
Governor Mandel indicted for bribery	**1975**	
	1977	Democrat Jimmy Carter becomes president
Democrat Harry Hughes becomes governor	**1979**	
	1981	Republican Ronald Reagan becomes president
	1982	Sandra Day O'Connor becomes first woman appointed to the Supreme Court
	1985	Chesapeake Bay preservation legislation

CHAPTER 7

Maryland since World War II, 1945 to the Present

The patterns of life which had begun early in the century continued in Maryland in the years after World War II. At the same time, there was much that was new. The movement of people away from the farms and into cities and suburbs increased. The Industrial Revolution went through its last stages and then was replaced by an Information Revolution as the technology of computers and television dominated work and play. New bridges across the Bay, as well as highways throughout the state, tied Maryland's communities closer together. In politics, the old bosses and organizations were replaced by new groups and leaders from the cities and suburbs. The history of the state and the nation in these postwar years contain strong parallels: Maryland changed in much the same way that the United States changed.

Return to Peace and Prosperity

When President Harry S. Truman announced the Japanese surrender at 7 P.M. on August 14, 1945, the people of Maryland joined the rest of the nation in celebration. For many, the greatest joy would be the return home of their family and friends. Others rejoiced that the democracies of the world had defended their way of life. Everyone welcomed the end to years of worry and sacrifice. President Truman declared a two-day holiday for federal workers in recognition of their efforts during the war. For the first time since December 7, 1941, Marylanders looked forward to waking up in a nation at peace.

The Postwar World

After the initial excitement died down, the return to a normal life began in earnest. Street lights came on again at night, ration lines disappeared from gas stations, and scarce consumer products began to reappear on store shelves. Families could again buy rubber tires for their cars and bicycles. Women could buy nylon stockings again, and more fresh meat appeared in the local grocery stores.

But for those who remembered clearly that the war had followed the Great Depression of the 1930s, peacetime brought fears that unemployment would return and spending money would decrease. The government canceled billions of dollars of contracts in defense industries like shipbuilding, ammunition manufacturing, and airplane construction. By October 1945, about 45,000 defense workers in Maryland had been laid off, and 35,000 soldiers had returned home to begin to look for work. Many women who had spent the war years employed in factories, government offices, and part-time defense jobs were encouraged to go back to doing housework. While some were happy to return to the role of wife and mother, others were not. They regretted the loss of income and the opportunity for a career.

The fears that Marylanders might have had about their future in the postwar world were quickly set aside as the state began a new period of growth and development. They would soon discover that the years ahead would be among the most prosperous the state had ever experienced. Instead of returning to depression, Maryland's economy improved. The wartime industries began to convert their factories from armaments to automobiles and from gunboats to consumer products.

Bethlehem Steel at Sparrows Point stopped building ships for war and began scrapping them instead, to get steel for buildings and bridges. Westinghouse, which had been making torpedoes and weapons, switched to making electrical equipment for industrial use. Western Electric began to make parts for the new televisions, and factories that had made airplanes during the war began making products for the booming housing market.

Local and state governments helped the economy, too. In the four years following the end of World War II the state's Department of Public Works spent over $28 million on new projects. Construction of Friendship Airport cost the state $3 million, and $10 million was spent for new schools to serve a growing population. Slum clearance and public housing projects also created jobs for workers in Baltimore and other Maryland cities. Many materials manufac-

Assembly-line production of automobiles provided employment for many people in the post–World War II period.

tured in Maryland or shipped from Baltimore's port overseas made their way to help rebuild war-torn Europe. The high wages and nearly full employment of the war years continued for the next quarter of a century in Maryland and much of the nation. Fear of a postwar depression was replaced by confidence in a more prosperous future.

The Baby Boom

One reason the post–World War II years were so prosperous was the baby boom. Between 1946 and 1964 the birth rate in the United States rose well above expected levels. Maryland's population increased 11.6 percent during the 1940s, from 1,821,244 to 2,343,001. Between 1950 and 1960, however, it grew 32.3 percent, and by 1970 by another 26.5 percent. The state's population in 1980 stood at 4,216,446.

This population increase set off a buying binge. At first the demands were for diapers, baby food, and bassinets. Later this generation would need more schools, clothes, and toys. Mass consumer markets developed to provide education and housing and playthings such as hula hoops, Slinkys, Barbie dolls, Silly Putty, and Davy Crockett coonskin caps. In the late 1940s and 1950s shopping centers sprang up across the state and the nation to serve a prosperous new generation.

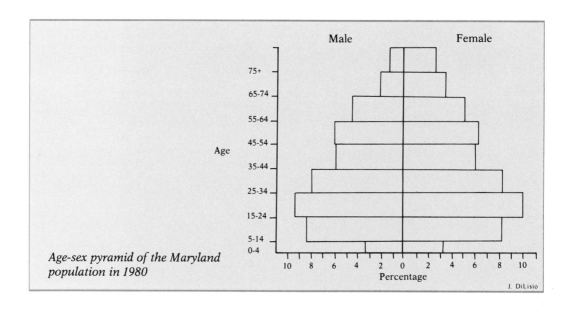

Age-sex pyramid of the Maryland population in 1980

There was a boom in births in Maryland, but the population of the state increased after 1946 for other reasons, as well. It was a good place to work and raise a family. Maryland became the fifth leading state in attracting new residents from other parts of the nation. Most came from nearby Middle Atlantic states like New York, New Jersey, and Pennsylvania. Others came from the Middle West and the Deep South, seeking an environment that offered economic opportunity, a favorable climate, and good schools.

Transition from Rural to Urban to Suburban

Whether native-born or migrant, the residents of Maryland in the 1940s and 1950s followed certain patterns of movement within the state. Movement at first was generally from countryside to city; later, movement was from city to suburb.

The greatest rural shift was away from the farms of western and southern Maryland and toward the large urban corridor. This corridor stretched across the center of the state from Wilmington, Delaware, through Baltimore and on to Washington, D.C. At midcentury no county had more than 20 percent of its residents living on farms. By 1980 more than 80 percent of all Marylanders lived within the Baltimore-Washington metropolitan area.

Even outside the main urban corridor, smaller cities like Cumberland and Hagerstown in the west or Cambridge and Salisbury on the Eastern Shore drew population off the farms at a steady rate. Young adults were attracted to these growing regional centers by the jobs they offered, which had shorter hours and better pay than jobs in agriculture. The advantages of city life—a variety of stores, recreational and cultural facilities, and modern schools—appealed to the majority.

The Urban Crisis

The movement of Marylanders from country to city after the war continued a trend that had begun more than a century earlier. Since the early nineteenth century, urban life had attracted new residents. In the 1950s, however, a new change occurred. As the cities grew older, their cores began to decay, and people began to leave the cities, just as earlier they had left the farms.

Maryland's urban crisis of the postwar period pointed up the economic and racial divisions that still plagued society. As the cities had grown in the first half of the twentieth century, their problems had become more intense. Overcrowded or unsafe housing, uncollected garbage, poor sanitation, rising crime rates, pollution, and heavier tax rates were all unpleasant features of Maryland's larger cities by midcentury. Those who could afford it moved outward toward the more spacious urban fringe or beyond, to the suburbs. Left behind, usually, were the poor and the black. By the 1950s Baltimore and other Maryland cities had become "two cities" divided by economic and racial barriers.

Early Attempts at Urban Renewal

Large cities across the nation looked for ways to change the trend toward decay. One solution to this urban crisis was demolition. Believing that new was always better, Baltimore began tearing down slum housing. This early attempt to solve urban problems by destroying old buildings, however, soon proved to be a failure. New public housing projects quickly developed the same problems of overcrowding and poor sanitation. Worst of all was the loss of the sense of community. Many residents of Baltimore became angry when old neighborhoods were torn apart and replaced with concrete expressways.

By the 1960s the outward flight of middle-class whites had become almost a stampede. In 1962, before federal civil rights and housing laws were passed, Baltimore County was 96.5 percent white, but Baltimore City had the second largest percentage of black residents in any American city, ranking behind Washington,

in the inner city

in the inner city
or
like we call it
home
we think a lot about uptown
and the silent nights
and the houses straight as
dead men
and the pastel lights
and we hang on to our no place
happy to be alive
and in the inner city
or
like we call it
home

Lucille Clifton, *Good Times* (New York: Random House, 1969).

Suburban developments grew up around the superhighways designed for high-speed automobile traffic. This now-familiar sight was unknown before World War II.

WASHINGTON SUBURBS

The Maryland suburbs of Washington, D.C., were among the fastest growing areas of the state after 1945. Returning war veterans and new government workers flocked to the attractive countryside of Montgomery and Prince George's counties. Rockville, Wheaton, College Park, Bladensburg, and other communities at first were "bedroom suburbs."

By the 1950s business, government, and industry followed the population shift to the suburbs. Silver Spring was the site of the state's first shopping center. In the 1950s the federal government spread into suburban Maryland with the National Institutes of Health in Bethesda, the Atomic Energy Commission headquarters in Germantown, and the Bureau of Standards in Gaithersburg. Private corporations like IBM, Comsat Corporation, Control Data, Bechtel, Kodak, and Xerox all established new offices and factories in Rockville along Route 270. By the 1980s these Maryland suburbs had become a key part of Washington's growth.

D.C. The median income of county families was $7,098, compared to $5,659 in the city. Baltimore also had twenty times more people receiving welfare than did the suburban counties. People in Cumberland and Hagerstown were moving toward the suburbs, too, and race was not a factor there.

Riots between discontented blacks and their white landlords in the late 1960s brought the urban crisis to the point of explosion. National Guard troops had to be called in to halt the looting and burning of sections of Baltimore after the 1968 assassination of Martin Luther King, Jr., in Memphis. Racial violence also struck the normally peaceful town of Cambridge on the Eastern Shore. The crime rate increased, the number of welfare recipients grew, and the conflict between ethnic and racial groups seemed to reach a peak in the early 1970s, at the height of the war in Vietnam. By the early 1970s critics across the nation warned of the death of America's older central cities.

The situation improved only after the Vietnam war ended and the federal government enforced fair housing laws passed to prevent racial discrimination by real estate companies, mortgage bankers, and developers. By 1980 the number of nonwhites in suburban Baltimore had risen to 24 percent of the total population there. Prince George's and Montgomery counties, located near Washington, had similar increases in nonwhite residents.

Suburbia

Middle-class whites looked for newer homes and better schools far away from the more crowded centers of the cities. Few had any desire to return to the countryside, but the suburbs and, eventually, whole new towns offered them what they considered a better type of urban life. The cities of Baltimore and Washington had peaked in the 1940s, and then, like the rural areas, they began to decline steadily. By 1970 Baltimore no longer ranked among the nation's ten largest cities. Too much of its population had fled from the city into the suburban counties of Anne Arundel, Baltimore, Harford, and Howard. Similarly, Washington lost residents to nearby Montgomery and Prince George's counties. Howard County, lying between the two cities, grew the fastest of all, especially after the new town of Columbia was built.

Those who left the city were escaping the crowded conditions of urban life and the fear of rising crime and taxes, but they also hoped to find in suburbia more space, more privacy, and more control over their lives. Parents sought good schools, clean streets, and neighbors whose values were similar to their own. While some critics said the suburbs were dull and monotonous places, the thousands who moved there saw them as safe havens for a home and peaceful lives.

The rapid growth of Maryland's suburbs resulted also from the closeness of Baltimore and Washington. When the beltways around both cities were completed in the 1960s, industries, businesses, and consumers moved to suburban counties. Transportation in the suburbs was easier, and land and taxes were cheaper. The federal government encouraged the move by providing money for new housing through the G.I. Bill, a bill to help veterans get reestablished after the war, and by constructing more highways. Later, new subway systems made movement between city and suburb even easier. Washington launched its Metro in 1978 and Baltimore followed in 1983.

To serve the growing population of suburban consumers, the shopping center appeared as a new phenomenon on the American scene. The Hecht Company opened its first suburban store in 1946 in Silver Spring, and one year later Edmundson Village opened in Baltimore with a variety of shops and ample parking to serve its customers. Later, the covered mall, of which Harundale Mall was the first in Maryland in 1958, became both a social and a shopping center.

New Towns

The shift of population also led to the creation of entirely new urban centers. Americans had always been fascinated with new town planning, and Maryland was one of the leading states in this type of urban experimentation.

For example, during the New Deal of the 1930s, President Roosevelt's administration tried to create an environment that blended together the best of city and country life in Greenbelt. In 1960 the Levitt Company opened Bowie, a residential community for middle-class and working class families. By 1968 Bowie boasted nearly 33,000 residents, mainly commuters to nearby Washington and Annapolis.

A more complete model town was Columbia, in Howard County. Started by developer James W. Rouse, Columbia opened in the mid-1960s and rapidly grew to 57,000 residents by 1980. This new town, which received national attention, was a carefully planned mixture of village clusters, shopping centers, and industrial sites. Racial mixing was more successful than economic mixing; about 20 percent of Columbia's population is nonwhite.

By the 1970s the interest in finding better ways of urban living

JAMES ROUSE: URBAN PIONEER

James W. Rouse, who was born in 1914, is a native of Easton, Maryland. A graduate of the University of Maryland Law School, he became a key figure in the state's urban growth. He built his first shopping center in Talbottown. In 1958 his company created Harundale Mall, the first enclosed shopping mall in Maryland. Rouse was a leader in bringing together private businessmen and public officials in new projects like Baltimore's Charles Center. Both the Village of Cross Keys and his Harborplace project in downtown Baltimore won praise from city planners and the general public. Rouse's new town of Columbia has been one of the largest and most talked about experiments in community planning in the twentieth century.

James Rouse has combined social activism with his business ventures. His urban malls have been designed to draw people of all incomes and racial backgrounds to the central city. His residential projects have encouraged racial integration in pleasant surroundings. A man of imagination and business success, Rouse left the company he established to head the Enterprise Foundation, a nonprofit organization. Its goal is to raise funds to house the urban poor.

Columbia, the planned new town in Howard County, gained national acclaim for developer James Rouse.

led to a revival of some of Maryland's older towns. Small towns began to discover a new vitality that emphasized their historic past and their unique character. Towns on the Eastern Shore, like Easton, St. Michaels, and Salisbury, gradually developed new life as centers for tourism and recreation. New highways made long-distance commuting easier. Cities of western Maryland, like Frederick, began to attract residents who found the larger suburbs monotonous or crowded. Industries and businesses also found Maryland's smaller towns and cities attractive.

The Urban Renaissance

Despite the fact that many critics predicted the death of America's large cities, there was a new effort to revive them. The failures of urban renewal and slum clearance in the 1950s taught the planners, politicians, and citizens valuable lessons. By the end of the decade business and political leaders in Baltimore joined forces. They sought to revive Baltimore's port and downtown core and to renew and renovate urban residential housing.

Baltimore

In 1955, under the leadership of men like James Rouse, the Greater Baltimore Committee was formed. This group of local businessmen collected financial resources, hired an urban planner, and began to define their objectives. They first sought to restore Baltimore's port to a prominent place in the nation's economy. Second, they planned to improve the area's transportation facilities, which served the port and the city. Third, they hoped to construct a new civic center. And lastly, they called for a more comprehensive plan for urban renewal.

The construction of Charles Center in the heart of the business district symbolized the new outlook. Planned by the Greater Baltimore Committee in 1958 and designed by the internationally known architect Mies van der Rohe, this complex of high-rise offices, apartments, and stores reflected Baltimore's self-confidence and expectations for renewed growth. The carefully designed plazas and elevated walkways once again made the center of the city an interesting and pleasant place to work and shop.

At the same time Charles Center was being built, a cluster of state office buildings was constructed on North Howard Street. Together these two major projects illustrated the value of cooperation between private and public sectors.

In 1963 Mayor Theodore McKeldin announced an even larger plan to revitalize Baltimore's inner harbor. Once again private capital and public planning combined to renew 240 acres around the harbor at a cost of $200 million. Even the federal government joined in by granting the city $19 million in 1964 to help start the inner harbor redevelopment.

When Harborplace opened in 1981, it attracted 18 million visitors in the first year. By the 1980s the Inner Harbor of Baltimore was one of the most attractive city centers in the country. It contained the National Aquarium, a convention center, and several hotels, as well as the older attractions, like the Maryland Science Center and the battleship *Constellation*.

The urban renaissance had an equally important consequence for Baltimore's residential neighborhoods. The key to progress again proved to be close cooperation between private and public interests. Progress was slow during the 1950s, but in 1968 the Department of Housing was formed. Robert D. Embry, Jr., the first

Baltimore's revitalized Inner Harbor draws residents and tourists alike to shop, eat, and enjoy themselves. Baltimore had a highly successful urban renaissance in the 1980s.

commissioner of this new city department, became a key figure in the improvement of the city's housing.

Luckily, much of Baltimore's older housing, particularly its unique row houses, had not been destroyed by earlier projects for urban renewal. In 1973 Baltimore was one of the first cities in the nation to begin an urban homesteading program. The city government acquired houses from delinquent taxpayers and sold them to the public for one dollar. By 1980 over 500 houses had been reclaimed under this program. Other government-supported programs helped restore nineteenth-century neighborhoods and funded new housing projects.

By the 1980s Baltimore, Maryland's largest urban center, was being described as a very "liveable" city. Urban planners from all over the country visited Baltimore, not only to view the spectacular Inner Harbor, but, more importantly, to observe how neighborhood life had been preserved. The strong involvement of citizens through community organizations was often pointed to as a key factor. Likewise, the strong leadership of mayors Theodore McKeldin, Thomas D'Alesandro III, and William Donald Schaefer was recognized. Although Baltimore still suffered serious difficulties with unemployment, poverty, occasional racial conflict, urban crime, and pollution, it had achieved a new sense of pride and confidence in progress.

Across the State

Although Baltimore received the most national attention for its renewal efforts, many of Maryland's cities underwent planned changes. Some, like Annapolis, Easton, and Frederick, emphasized preservation of historic buildings. Others, like Cumberland and Cambridge, turned to new construction. As in Baltimore, these efforts usually combined public and private resources and interests.

As the capital of Maryland since 1694, Annapolis had a rich heritage to preserve. Nevertheless, local groups that hoped to restore the historic district along the city's waterfront and around the State House faced strong opposition. Private developers saw greater profits in building new, efficient buildings than in restoring the old. More serious was the racial conflict that arose when poor blacks who lived in the small homes in the central area were displaced by the urban renewal movement. By the late 1970s Annapolis had restored much of its historic core and had become a favorite stop for tourists.

In Easton similar conflicts occurred between blacks and whites, and between preservationists and those who wanted to build anew. Through careful zoning laws Easton was able to retain its colonial heritage. New construction usually followed a style that matched that of the past.

In the western part of the state, Cumberland experienced much of the same conflict over urban renewal that other Maryland cities faced. Through the 1950s and early 1960s Cumberland's population declined as unemployment increased. In 1973, under the direction of the city's Urban Renewal Agency, the local and federal governments joined resources to restore 83 acres in the downtown area. Twenty-one million dollars were spent tearing down or restoring old buildings and constructing new ones.

The urban renaissance in Frederick began in 1973, after Ronald N. Young was elected mayor. By combining historic preser-

As mayor of Baltimore, William Donald Schaefer worked for cooperation between the government and the private sector to benefit the city.

In an area reserved for pedestrians in downtown Cumberland, patrons buy vegetables in an outdoor market.

The old and the new exist side by side in Cambridge. Traditional workboats are tied up in view of new residences along the city's waterfront.

vation of buildings like the Roger Brooke Taney House and the Barbara Fritchie House with new construction, Frederick was able to revive its downtown area. A new county courthouse in the center of the city and an attractive park along Carroll Creek kept businesses and residents from fleeing to the suburbs.

Cambridge on the Eastern Shore was another Maryland city that fought urban decline with planned restoration. Cambridge rebuilt sections of its downtown shopping area and constructed new luxury townhouses along its waterfront in order to achieve what local planners called the "Bay Country look."

The Technological Revolutions

Wherever Marylanders lived in this second half of the twentieth century, they saw their world grow smaller and their lifestyles become more alike. Rapid changes in transportation and communications reduced the separations and differences that had made some parts of the state so unique. Before World War II, the watermen of the Chesapeake Bay had little in common with the farmers near the Appalachian Mountains. But bridges, highways, and television and communications networks brought them closer together.

The Transportation Revolution

For years Marylanders had argued the pros and cons of building a bridge across the Chesapeake Bay. Opponents cited the immense cost of such a project, fear for the bay's ecological balance, and threats to the fishing industry. Finally, Governor William Preston Lane, Jr., made the dream a reality by introducing a state sales tax of two cents for every dollar spent by consumers. Construction of the bridge began on October 1, 1949.

The spectacular Chesapeake Bay Bridge opened with a ribbon-cutting ceremony on July 30, 1952. Former Governor Lane and Governor Theodore McKeldin led 10,000 celebrants in song as the band played "Maryland, My Maryland." The bridge was one of the largest public works projects in Maryland ever undertaken up to that time; it cost $112 million. Almost 2 million travelers passed over the bridge in its first year of use. By 1980 the state had to open a second, parallel, span.

With their annual traffic surpassing 10 million travelers by 1982, the bridges over the Bay had a tremendous impact on Maryland's Eastern Shore. A boom in real estate, retail sales, land development, and tourism changed the traditionally rural lifestyle of the region. In addition to the hundreds of thousands of weekend and holiday visitors to the beaches, new permanent residents came to build homes along the shore. Towns like Salisbury and Cambridge saw modest growth, while Ocean City grew more like a boom town.

OCEAN CITY

The Chesapeake Bay Bridge brought tremendous changes to Maryland's Eastern Shore. Ocean City, which had been a small town before World War II, blossomed into the state's major resort by the 1960s. Even fierce Atlantic hurricanes like the one in 1962 did not stop the rapid development of Fenwick Island, where Ocean City is located. Each year tourists from Maryland and many other states spend millions of dollars enjoying the beaches and pleasures of Ocean City.

Political leaders joined hands at the opening of the William Preston Lane Memorial Bridge (the Chesapeake Bay Bridge) in 1952. From the left are Maryland Governor Theodore R. McKeldin, Delaware Governor Elbert N. Carvel, William Preston Lane, Millard Tawes, and Baltimore Mayor Thomas D'Alesandro, Jr.

Several generations of Maryland children have enjoyed this merry-go-round, installed at Trimper's amusement park in Ocean City at the turn of the century.

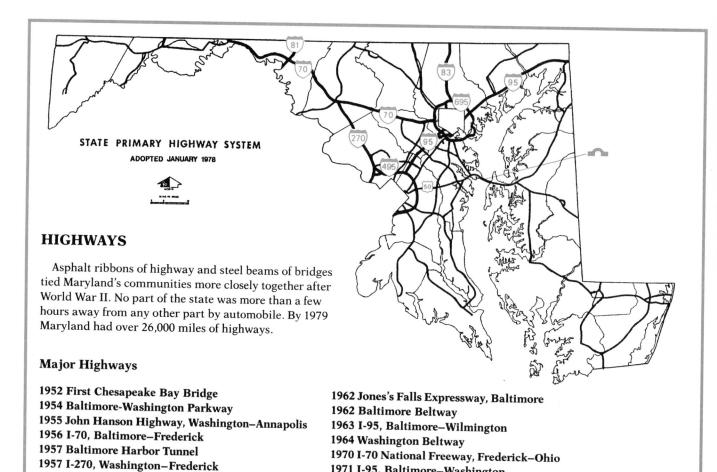

HIGHWAYS

Asphalt ribbons of highway and steel beams of bridges tied Maryland's communities more closely together after World War II. No part of the state was more than a few hours away from any other part by automobile. By 1979 Maryland had over 26,000 miles of highways.

Major Highways

1952 First Chesapeake Bay Bridge
1954 Baltimore-Washington Parkway
1955 John Hanson Highway, Washington–Annapolis
1956 I-70, Baltimore–Frederick
1957 Baltimore Harbor Tunnel
1957 I-270, Washington–Frederick
1959 I-83, Baltimore–Harrisburg

1962 Jones's Falls Expressway, Baltimore
1962 Baltimore Beltway
1963 I-95, Baltimore–Wilmington
1964 Washington Beltway
1970 I-70 National Freeway, Frederick–Ohio
1971 I-95, Baltimore–Washington

Similarly, a new network of highways drew Maryland's western and central cities closer together. Beginning with the Baltimore-Washington Parkway, which opened in 1952, and continuing for the next 30 years, the state and federal government built an interstate system that linked all parts of the region. Beltways around Baltimore and Washington and local expressways helped commuters to travel ever-greater distances from home to work with ease.

The dependence on highways and the automobile meant that mass public transportation tended to decline. In Baltimore streetcars were replaced by buses. The city's train stations fell into a state of decay. By 1980 about 1.2 million Marylanders commuted to work by car, but only 170,000 used public transportation. Maryland, like the rest of the nation, became a society on wheels, despite unpleasant side effects like air pollution and traffic congestion.

Development in Ocean City has generated controversy. New high-rise buildings have brought more people and greater prosperity to the resort, but scientists and environmentalists fear these buildings along the dune line will spell eventual destruction for the unprotected barrier island.

New highways, such as Route 48 past Cumberland, were constructed in response to the postwar transportation boom, easing access to major parts of the state.

More successful than efforts at mass transit was air travel. In 1972 Friendship Airport was purchased by the state for $36 million. It was renamed Baltimore-Washington International Airport in 1973. Smaller airports, like the Hagerstown Municipal Airport or the Wicomico County Airport at Salisbury, served other areas of the state. Along with the rest of the nation, Marylanders accepted air travel as a normal part of their business and personal worlds.

The Information Revolution and the Loss of Isolation

New communications networks, like transportation systems, drew the people of Maryland closer together. By 1980 Marylanders shared information in 14 daily newspapers, 80 weekly papers, 10 television stations, and 50 AM and 50 FM radio stations. These communications facilities were supplemented by newspapers and television stations in the District of Columbia. Multiple-channel cable television systems and new technologies in telephone and computer communications promised to expand the available information facilities even more in the last two decades of the twentieth century.

By the 1980s few homes in any part of the state were not influenced by the revolution in communications. Coal miners' families in western Maryland and watermen's families on Smith Island could receive the same news and watch the same television network entertainment shows. Fashions, taste in entertainment, political opinions, and general lifestyles in rural Maryland, small towns, suburbs, and large cities were all shaped by the powerful forces of the new information technologies.

The Modernization of Farm Life

The impact of the new technology in Maryland could be seen in the farmer's way of life. At the end of World War II it was still possible to find a few farmers in rural Maryland plowing their fields with teams of oxen. Even by the early 1950s, just over half of the state's farms had electricity, and about the same number used modern machinery like tractors and trucks.

Once the technological revolution began, however, change was rapid. Besides using new machinery, farmers used more artificial fertilizers, insect controls, hybrid seeds, and selective breeding. Although the number of farms in Maryland declined by about half between 1950 and 1970, productivity increased greatly. Farmers became more like businessmen, depending heavily on price sup-

Farmers in southern Maryland still grow tobacco and sell it at auction.

ports from the federal government and joining organizations like the Farm Bureau to improve their economic condition.

Maryland's agricultural production was a mixture of the old and the new. Tobacco farmers still brought their crops to auction at Hughesville, Waldorf, or Upper Marlboro, as their ancestors had done. Corn, wheat, and barley remained the typical field crops of central Maryland, and livestock was raised. Dairying made up 70 percent of the total farm production for Frederick County. Eastern Shore truck farming supplied nearly 80 percent of Maryland's vegetable crop in 1978. Newer to the state's agriculture was the production of broiler chickens. By 1978 Maryland produced over 900 million pounds of chickens, making it the sixth largest producer in the nation.

Maryland's New Economy

In the post–World War II years Maryland's growth and change was clearest in its economy and in the way its people made a living. Not only did farming become less important, but there was also a gradual shift away from industry and other blue-collar jobs

THE PORT OF BALTIMORE

Baltimore's port is the economic center of the state. More than 4,000 ships each year bring imports into Maryland from around the world and export the state's coal, grain, steel, machinery, and other goods. It is one of the six largest ports in the United States. An important advantage Baltimore has is that it is farther west than any other East Coast port. Railroad, highway, and airport facilities connect Baltimore to the rest of the nation.

In addition to thousands of jobs, the port's activities create over $50 million for the state in taxes each year. The ability to handle container ships helped the port add nearly $1 billion to Maryland's economy by the 1980s. Without the port, Maryland would not be one of the most prosperous states in the nation.

A ship passes Fort McHenry as it leaves the port of Baltimore.

and toward a greater dependence on jobs in services, government bureaucracy, and new technology.

The Port of Baltimore

At the heart of Maryland's economy was the port of Baltimore. When the United States passed the Marshall Plan in 1948 to help rebuild Europe after the war, millions of tons of materials passed through Baltimore. The Korean War of the early 1950s also resulted in much activity for Maryland's busy port. Baltimore built an international trade that sent coal to Japan, grain to India, and steel and fertilizer to Brazil. In return, Baltimore received iron ore from Venezuela, copper from Chile, and textiles from the Far East. By 1966 studies showed that port activities contributed over $1½ billion to Maryland's economy.

Every ship that passed into and out of Baltimore needed many services. Pilots, who guided vessels through the channel; radio and radar operators; tugboat captains; and longshoremen, who loaded and unloaded cargo, were directly involved. There was work for clerks, customs and immigration officials, ship cleaners and repairers, and doctors, who quarantined vessels that carried disease. In the port, there was also a need for inspectors, truck drivers, warehouse managers, bankers, and foreign language interpreters.

The Pride of Baltimore, *a clipper ship, visited ports around the world as a goodwill ambassador promoting the state of Maryland.*

The port was not only Maryland's largest industry, but in 1980 it was one of the six largest ports in the United States.

The activities of this busy center are controlled by the Maryland Port Authority. Its job is to coordinate the interests of the state, the city, and private business in order to make the port more efficient. In 1977 it opened the World Trade Center to house the services of international businesses, bankers, and government officials. The port activity is a good example of the way Maryland's economy depends on the relationship between public and private interests.

To promote trade and extend the reputation of Baltimore and its port, the city built the *Pride of Baltimore*, an authentic clipper ship. The ship, which tragically sank in a sudden squall in 1986, was a symbol of Maryland's close connection with the sea.

Blue-Collar Workers

Those people who work with their hands and make a product are called blue-collar workers. Others, who work in offices or provide certain services, are called white-collar workers. Gradually after World War II, as prosperity continued and new technology was introduced, white-collar workers replaced blue-collar workers as the majority.

At the end of World War II, when Maryland industries changed back to peacetime production, blue-collar workers found the most jobs in the metal and food industries. In Baltimore large corporations like Bethlehem Steel, Martin-Marietta Aircraft, and Kennecott Refining built ships and made railroad rails, metal barrels, petroleum products, parts for airplanes, and steel for buildings or bridges. Three out of every four blue-collar workers in the state were employed by factories in the Baltimore metropolitan area.

On the Eastern Shore men and women earned a living by canning food in Cambridge, making men's clothing in Salisbury, or producing explosives in Elkton. In western Maryland blue-collar workers found jobs in Cumberland at the Kelly-Springfield Tire Company, in Allegany County at the Westvaco paper mills, or in Hagerstown making Mack trucks. Many of these industries in both Baltimore and elsewhere were located in industrial parks outside the cities. Industry, like its workers, became more suburbanized after the war.

Watermen and Miners

More unique than Maryland's farmers are the watermen. Although urban growth and industrial pollution had taken a heavy toll on the Bay's production, there were still 17,504 licensed watermen and waterwomen in Maryland in 1978. Most important among the fishermen's catch are the hardshells: oysters, clams, and crabs. Hardy Marylanders harvest more than 2 million bushels of oysters each year and millions of dollars worth of other seafood. The Chesapeake Bay is still the world's largest producer of the Atlantic blue crab.

Rivalry between Maryland and Virginia for Chesapeake seafood continued in the years after World War II. Finally, a new agreement, drawn up in 1958, helped to reduce conflict and divide the oyster catch between Maryland and Virginia. Although in the late twentieth century the annual catch of oysters, crabs, and other seafood was only a fraction of what it was earlier in the century, it still contributed nearly $20 million to Maryland's economy.

Mining was one of the state's oldest industries, and it continued to be important in this period. Various stone, sand, gravel, and limestone were mined and quarried. Bituminous coal, soft coal that yields pitch or tar when it burns, is one of the state's most valuable resources. Five major coal basins lie in Garrett and Allegany counties, the most important being George's Creek basin. Modern coal mining is dominated by a few large coal companies that supply fuel to urban utilities companies. The international oil

Above, left: *Watermen, operating tongs by hand, harvest oysters. Tongers and dredgers have been rivals for decades. Below: Watermen can bring in more oysters with a large dredge than they can with hand tongs. By law, watermen must operate dredges under sail, and they can only use dredges in specified areas. Above, right: Watermen harvesting clams from the bottom of the Chesapeake Bay. The Bay provides employment for many Marylanders.*

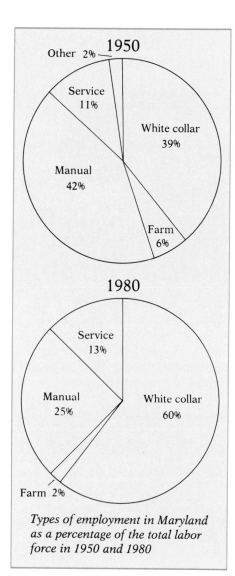

1950

Other 2%
Service 11%
White collar 39%
Manual 42%
Farm 6%

1980

Service 13%
Manual 25%
White collar 60%
Farm 2%

Types of employment in Maryland as a percentage of the total labor force in 1950 and 1980

embargo of 1973 emphasized the importance of America's coal resources and encouraged new efforts to improve Baltimore as a coal-exporting port.

White-Collar Workers

Although many GIs returning home in the 1940s went to work in Maryland's factories, others went into nonmanufacturing occupations. Maryland reflected the national trend as its economy grew less dependent on heavy manufacturing and more dependent on services and white-collar work. By 1950 one out of every two wage earners held a nonmanufacturing job, and in 1980 the proportion was closer to two out of every three.

There were several reasons for this change in the state's economy. The baby boom between 1946 and 1964 created huge demands for all kinds of new services, from medical care to education. Since this was a time of prosperity, too, many workers were needed to serve the vast consumer market. Clerks, salespersons, appliance repairmen, insurance and real estate agents, waiters and waitresses, car dealers, and many others helped satisfy the demand for more consumer goods and services.

Maryland's economy also changed as more women entered the labor market, during the 1960s and after. There was a trend toward greater independence and equality for women throughout the nation, and the numbers of women employed outside the home dramatically increased. After 1960 the percentage of women in the work force grew three times faster than the rate of increase for men. Most of these women worked in service or nonmanufacturing occupations. As more women than ever before graduated from Maryland's universities and colleges, they entered the professions of doctor, lawyer, and teacher, or they found jobs in business corporations.

By far one of the largest employers of the postwar decades was government. At all levels—local, state, and federal—the number of jobs multiplied several times over. The growth of government services that began during President Roosevelt's New Deal in the 1930s continued on a large scale. Both Republicans and Democrats supported the growth of government services. After accepting responsibility for the health, welfare, and security of all citizens, the government had to increase the size of its bureaucracy to meet all the needs.

Since Maryland was so close to the nation's capital, it probably benefited more than most states from the large increase in federal jobs. The large Social Security complex near Baltimore and the many military bases in the state were large employers of Maryland white-collar workers. Many residents of Prince George's, Montgomery, and Howard counties worked in federal offices in Washington, D.C. By 1980 nearly one out of every four wage earners worked for the government. The federal government employed 145,000, the state 80,000, and local governments another 150,000. The largest private employer, Bethlehem Steel, had about 40,000 workers.

The New Technology and a New Middle Class

Another change in Maryland's economy after 1945 came about as the result of new technology. When the war ended, few Marylanders were familiar with either television or computers. Children born in the 1970s and 1980s, however, would find it hard to imagine life without these and other technological "necessities." Children of the eighties could awaken to stereo music from their digital clock radio, eat a breakfast that had been heated in a microwave oven, and rush off to a school where learning was assisted by electronic calculators, microcomputers, video cassettes, and slide projectors. Their parents withdrew money from electronic banktellers or used plastic credit cards to buy groceries in stores with automatic price scanners, made appointments by mobile telephones, and conducted business with computers and word processors. The older Industrial Revolution had been replaced by a newer Technological or Information Revolution.

These revolutionary changes meant new ways of earning a living. Many people who had been employed in older types of manufacturing had to retrain in order to take jobs in new companies. Between 1970 and 1975, for example, over 40,000 jobs disappeared from the manufacturing sector of the state's economy. At the same time, new jobs were created in other areas.

The most impressive concentration of new industries was along I-270 near Rockville and Gaithersburg. Nicknamed "Satellite Alley," this area between Washington and Frederick was the home of telecommunications, electronic, biomedical, and genetic engineering companies. Comsat, IBM, Hewlett-Packard, General Electric, American Satellite, and Litton Bionetics all had offices and laboratories there. The National Institutes of Health, the Department of Energy, and the National Bureau of Standards were also located in this area, where they could draw on the knowledge of many research firms. The Goddard Space Flight Center of the National

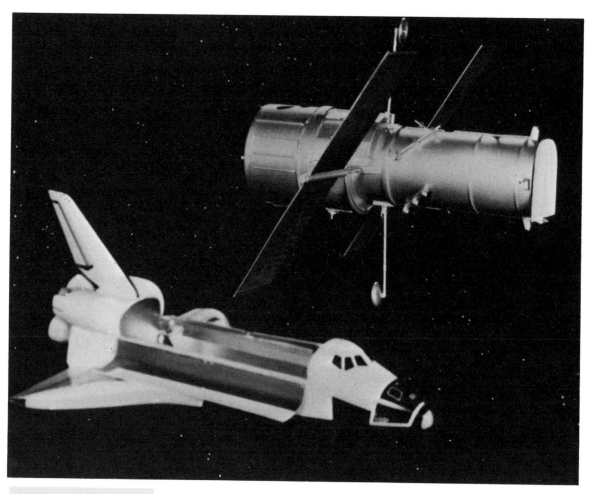

Maryland is also part of America's space age. The Space Telescope Science Institute, located at the Johns Hopkins University, helped in the development of the Hubble Space Telescope, seen in the upper right of the picture.

Aeronautics and Space Administration, in Greenbelt, the Johns Hopkins Applied Physics Laboratory, near Columbia, and several army and navy research centers helped to make Maryland one of the leading states in the new technological economy.

For most Marylanders the changes in the economy meant a higher standard of living. As the number of white-collar and government workers increased, observers pointed to the rise of a new middle class. The typical Maryland family of the second half of the twentieth century was better educated, made higher wages, and spent more on consumer and luxury goods than their ancestors. The average income for families steadily rose, reaching $26,521 by the 1980 census. This was more than double what it had been only a dozen years earlier. In per capita income, income for each person, Maryland ranked thirteenth in the nation. Maryland's standard of living was among the best in the nation.

Postwar Politics

Maryland's politics reflected the changes in the nation as much as its economic growth did. The decline in power of the old political bosses, the rise of a new middle-class bureaucracy, and the tremendous growth of both government spending and services are a part of Maryland's history after 1945. The unreasonable fear of communism, the conflict over civil rights, and the spread of corruption that plagued the nation also could be found in Maryland.

The Politics of Growth

The first major change came after William Preston Lane, Jr., was elected governor in 1946. With the war over, he wanted to turn the state's attention to the need for better public services. New schools were needed to serve the baby boom's children. New highways and bridges had to be built to connect different parts of the state. Better health care and welfare programs were needed for the state's sick and poor. This demand for more government services was a continuation of the trend started before the war by Roosevelt's New Deal.

The problem Governor Lane faced, however, was that more services meant more money. A bridge across the Bay, new state mental hospitals, higher salaries for teachers, and 1,100 miles of new highways were all expensive. Maryland's budget increased from $60 million to over $200 million during Lane's administration. To pay for the new programs and facilities, he persuaded the General Assembly to pass his two-cent sales tax in 1947. Unfortunately for Governor Lane, this tax also cost him reelection in 1950. Although the public wanted more services, it did not want to pay for them.

McCarthyism in Maryland

Maryland shared in the Cold War between the United States and the Soviet Union. The late 1940s and early 1950s was a time of fear in both the state and the nation. Americans feared the threat of communism. In Washington, Senator Joseph McCarthy of Wisconsin led the movement to rid the government of subversives, people who worked to overthrow the government. He used scare tactics and unfairly accused people of being Communists.

McCarthy seemed to be more interested in gaining power and recognition for himself than in finding the truth about the people he accused. "McCarthyism" became the term later used to refer to the practice of depriving people of their rights through false accusation.

In Maryland the fear of communism was particularly strong. Although in fact there were very few Communists in the state, Maryland passed the infamous Ober Law in 1949 requiring public officials and teachers to take an oath stating that they were loyal to the United States. Even the Boy Scouts called for an investigation to make sure there were no subversives in their organization.

Maryland also had a particular interest in anti-Communist activities because several of its residents played major roles in national events. Alger Hiss, a former high-ranking official in the State Department, was accused by Whittaker Chambers of being a Communist. Both Hiss and Chambers were from Maryland. The whole nation closely followed the dramatic trial in which Hiss was convicted of perjury, lying while under oath in court.

Another Marylander, Owen Lattimore, who taught at the Johns Hopkins University School of International Relations, was accused of being a Communist by Joseph McCarthy. When Senator Millard Tydings of Maryland conducted an investigation and concluded that McCarthy was a fraud, Marylanders were shocked. In the next election, in 1950, the voters agreed with McCarthy, who campaigned actively against the reelection of Tydings, and voted Tydings out of office. The fear of subversives had become a powerful force in Maryland politics.

By the mid-1950s the anti-Communist hysteria faded. The public and politicians alike began to realize that there was more to fear from ignoring people's civil liberties than there was to fear from communism in America. The steady leadership of President Dwight D. Eisenhower at the national level and capable government at the state level restored people's confidence.

The Politics of Stability

In the 1950 election Maryland voters chose Theodore R. McKeldin as governor. Although Maryland was usually a Democratic state, the people switched to the Republican McKeldin because they opposed any further increases in taxes. The truth was that the new governor would continue many of the programs started by Governor Lane and would increase government spending and services even more. Patuxent Institute at Jessup, Clifton T. Perkins State Hospital, and the Western State Hospital near Hagerstown were all built during McKeldin's administration. More money was spent on education, including a new campus for Coppin State College. New state office buildings were constructed in Baltimore and Annapolis, and the state spent $130 million to complete the Harbor Tunnel Expressway System.

In many ways Governor McKeldin's administration in Maryland was similar to that of President Dwight Eisenhower's in the 1950s. Both men were well liked. Although they were Republicans, they continued and expanded the Democratic attitude that the government is responsible for the security and well-being of its citizens.

In 1958 Maryland voters returned to tradition by electing a Democrat as governor again. Two years later the nation would follow by electing John F. Kennedy president. The state's new governor was J. Millard Tawes from Somerset County on the Eastern Shore. Long-time comptroller of the treasury, Tawes was experienced in state politics. He continued the expansion of government by adding departments, like the Department of Economic Development, and a Regional Planning Council to the state government. He encouraged the expansion of the state's education system and promoted new industry and business.

Tawes was not a dynamic leader, but some of his actions were controversial nevertheless. For example, he initiated reform that brought legislative reapportionment, which is the redistribution of representatives among equal numbers of voters. This reapportionment of the state legislature brought voting power more in line with the growth of cities and suburbs.

It was during Tawes's administration that Maryland finally phased out of existence the last slot machines in the state. And Maryland was one of the first states south of the Mason-Dixon line to pass a Public Accommodation Law requiring equal treatment for blacks in public places. Governor Tawes also took the lead in attacking economic problems by inviting the governors from 11 states to come to Annapolis for the Conference of Appalachian Governors. On the whole, the administrations of both Theodore McKeldin and Millard Tawes were effective in leading Maryland through the growth years between 1951 and 1967.

The Rise of Spiro Agnew

One of the most famous names in all of Maryland politics in the second half of the twentieth century is Spiro Agnew. Agnew symbolized in many ways the changes that had occurred in Maryland and national politics. He was the product of the new middle-class, suburban America. He attended Forest Park High School in Baltimore, graduated from the University of Baltimore Law School, and eventually set up a modest law practice in suburban Towson. His rise in politics was casual and undistinguished, as he moved from

Governor McKeldin hosts Queen Elizabeth II of England at a University of Maryland football game in October 1957.

THEODORE R. MCKELDIN: POPULAR REPUBLICAN

Theodore Roosevelt McKeldin was a most unusual Maryland Republican. He won election twice as the mayor of Baltimore, in 1943, and 1963, and he served two terms as governor of Maryland, from 1951 to 1959.

The son of an Irish immigrant father and a German-American mother, the Baltimore-born McKeldin was a master of popular politics. A moving orator and a true humanitarian, he won the support of many workers, blacks, and liberals who normally voted Democrat. He benefited from splits within the Democratic party, and on occasion he received help from some of that party's leaders.

Like President Dwight Eisenhower, McKeldin was a liberal Republican. He supported a program to improve the state highway system. He encouraged the creation of the Maryland Port Authority to improve the state's economy. He worked with black leaders like Lillie Mae Carroll Jackson to implement civil rights programs. In 1952 McKeldin, the only Republican governor south of the Mason-Dixon line, gave the speech nominating Dwight Eisenhower for president at the Republican National Convention in San Francisco.

president of the Dumbarton Junior High School PTA to a seat on the county zoning appeals board. When he won the race for Baltimore County executive in 1962, it was because no other Republican would agree to run and because the Democrats, who usually controlled the county, were split.

Agnew's election as governor in 1966 was again a case of being at the right place at the right time. Running on a campaign that called for honest government, he defeated the racially conservative Democratic candidate, George P. Mahoney. Mahoney's slogan was "Your home is your castle—defend it." Everyone knew he meant that blacks should not be encouraged or permitted to move into the all-white suburbs of Baltimore and Washington. Since his narrow-minded racial views drove away the liberal Democrats, Mahoney lost the 1966 election to Agnew by a vote of 455,318 to 373,543.

During his first two years in office, Agnew was a reasonably successful governor. He supported bills in the General Assembly to reform income taxes, control water pollution, and acquire Friendship Airport for the state. He even supported civil rights legislation requiring open housing.

To improve government efficiency, Agnew called for a constitutional convention. In 1967 voters elected special delegates to a meeting to revise Maryland's 100-year-old constitution. The purpose was to streamline and modernize the state government. The proposed reforms would strengthen the governor's authority, improve the court system, and lengthen sessions of the legislature. The public voted not to accept the new document, however. The fears that the new constitution might lead to higher taxes and that it gave the state power to join Baltimore City and Baltimore County into one government were enough to defeat it. Later, many of the reforms proposed by the constitutional convention were adopted separately by the General Assembly.

Agnew's plan for a new constitution had been defeated, but plans for entering national politics were waiting in the wings. Once again he benefited from being in the right place at the right time. Richard Nixon, the Republican nominee for president, chose Agnew as his vice-presidential running mate. In 1968 Agnew had the reputation of being a moderate Republican who looked good in public. Nixon would use Agnew as his spokesman for stronger law and order, and as a defender of his administration.

The Politics of Corruption

The first four years of Agnew's vice-presidency went well. He acquired a reputation as a sharp-tongued speaker who criticized the liberal opponents of Nixon's policies. But after the ticket's reelection in 1972, Agnew's career came to an abrupt and disgraceful end. An investigation of corruption among public officials in Baltimore County uncovered a pattern of bribery in Agnew's administration. Even as vice-president he had continued to accept bribes, called kickbacks, in return for political favors.

Agnew resigned as vice-president after this information became known. Later he was required by the courts to pay back to the state nearly $250,000 for the alleged kickbacks. Involvement in corruption was another example of the similarity between Maryland's politics and the politics of the nation. Within a year, Richard Nixon was forced to resign the presidency.

Unfortunately for Maryland, Agnew's successor as governor was also stained by charges of corruption. Chosen by the legislature to fill the vacancy as the state's chief executive, Marvin Mandel seemed well suited for the job. He was a product of Baltimore politics who had worked his way up the ladder until he became Speaker of the House of Delegates. In January 1969 he became governor of Maryland.

During his first two years in office, Mandel demonstrated his skills as a politician. Ninety-three of the 95 bills proposed by the governor's office were passed. Mandel achieved many of the reforms that had been lost when the proposed constitution was rejected. First of all, the governor's cabinet was revised and streamlined. Twelve departments were created: Agriculture, Budget, Economic Development, General Services, Health, Licensing, Natural Resources, Personnel, Planning, Police and Corrections, Transportation, and Welfare.

Like his predecessors, Mandel continued to increase the number of services offered to citizens. He supported bills to increase Medicare payments, protect consumers, expand the court system, and increase home rule for county governments. The new office of lieutenant governor, similar to a vice-president but at the state level, was also approved by the legislature. Unfortunately, Maryland's first lieutenant governor, Blair Lee III, would be required to step into the governor's role when Mandel became tangled in a web of corruption.

In November 1975 Governor Mandel was indicted, formally accused by a grand jury, for accepting bribes. He was accused of accepting $415,000 in gifts from friends. In return, the indictment

Harry Hughes, a democrat, served two terms as governor of Maryland.

said, he had influenced the passage of bills in the legislature that would help these friends. After a lengthy and confusing trial, Mandel was convicted, and in July 1980 he went off to serve 15 months in prison. He was only the third governor in the nation's history to be convicted of a crime while in office, and the first one in 43 years.

Once again Maryland had reflected the nation in its history. The years of the Agnew and Mandel scandals were also the years of the Watergate scandal in Washington. But just as the nation recovered from the corruption of the Nixon administration, so, too, did the state return to honest government. Both Blair Lee III, who served as governor for one and a half years after Mandel's conviction, and Harry Hughes, who was elected in 1978 and again in 1982, had good records. After the controversies of the Agnew and Mandel administrations, many voters welcomed the quiet manner of Harry Hughes. Nevertheless, even the reputation of the less controversial Hughes administration was marred by the collapse of several of the state's savings and loan companies.

The late seventies and early eighties were a time of limitations rather than expansion. The postwar era of growth and prosperity seemed to be coming to an end. Instead of the usual confidence in the future, Americans had doubts. Sources of fuel and natural resources seemed to be dwindling. Fighting in the Middle East, Africa, and Central America threatened the peace and security of the world. Concern over inflation and unemployment undermined social and civil rights reforms. Governor Hughes, a former member of the General Assembly and past secretary of the Department of Transportation, had to answer the voters' demand for less spending, fewer government programs, and lower taxes.

The Challenge of Equality

The second half of the twentieth century was a time of significant change for black Marylanders. At the end of the war Maryland resembled southern states in its racial segregation and discrimination. By the 1980s, however, its schools and public places were integrated. Blacks held important positions in state and local government. And a greater percentage of blacks had joined the suburban whites in a middle-class style of life. Racial prejudice and bigotry were by no means gone from Maryland, but their influence was dramatically reduced.

The Black Revolution

The racism and Jim Crow laws that still prevailed in 1945 had been weakened by the war. Black migration into Maryland and especially into Baltimore increased because new jobs were plentiful in the wartime industries. Blacks and whites worked side by side. When the war was over and workers retrained for peacetime employment, blacks were most successful in service areas, such as state and federal jobs, or in jobs with city services and utilities, such as bus drivers or telephone company employees.

The improvement in job opportunities, however, was overshadowed in the 1940s by overcrowding, poor housing and sanitation, lack of recreation facilities, and segregated schools. Blacks still were not allowed to try on clothes in many department stores or to eat in white restaurants. As a border state, Maryland was a mixture of racial traditions and liberal change. Although blacks had pressed for reforms before the war, they now picked up the pace.

The University of Maryland was pressured to accept more blacks into its law school and professional programs in 1947. That same year Baltimore appointed its first black police sergeant. Over the next seven years Maryland's barriers to racial equality gradually weakened. In 1949 Baltimore's first black plumber received his license, and both the Baltimore County and the Frederick County medical societies admitted black physicians. Even on the Eastern Shore, where the tradition of segregation was more rigid, the hospitals at Cambridge and Salisbury opened their doors to black doctors.

The election of Theodore McKeldin as governor was an important event for the growing black revolution. He became a strong spokesman for racial equality. Governor McKeldin appointed blacks to most state commissions and to several courts. Robert B. Watts became the first black traffic court magistrate, and George L. Russell was made the first magistrate-at-large of Baltimore. In 1952 McKeldin appointed a new Maryland Commission on Interracial Problems and Relations.

In the black community, several leaders appeared. One of the most prominent was Lillie Mae Carroll Jackson, the head of the local branch of the National Association for the Advancement of Colored People. Her organization became a powerful force in breaking down the barriers in black hiring, housing, and the use of public facilities. Others who stepped forward to take leading roles were Walter Carter and Edward Chance of the Congress of Racial Equality (CORE), Furman Templeton of the Baltimore Urban League, and Carl Murphy, owner of the *Afro-American*. Thurgood

LILLIE MAE CARROLL JACKSON: CIVIL RIGHTS LEADER

Lillie Mae Carroll Jackson was born on May 25, 1889, in West Baltimore. Her father had been a household slave for Charles Carroll of Carrollton, according to family history. Lillie Mae Carroll was a teacher until 1910, when she married Keiffer Jackson.

In the 1930s she became one of the leading black activists for civil rights in Maryland. She served as the head of the state's branch of the National Association for the Advancement of Colored People for 35 years. She led the fight to employ black clerks in supermarkets and stores, and for Baltimore to hire black policemen, firemen, and bus drivers.

Together with Carl Murphy, editor of the *Afro-American* newspaper, she helped bring about the desegregation of the city's restaurants, department stores, and theaters. Her daughter, Juanita Jackson Mitchell, became the first black woman to graduate from the University of Maryland Law School. When Lillie Mae Carroll Jackson retired from the NAACP in 1970, she was widely recognized for her courage and her persistent fight for equal rights.

The Civil Rights Struggle

The Nation		Maryland	The Nation		Maryland
President Truman desegregates armed forces	1948	St. John's College admits first black resident student	March on Washington	1963	Cambridge Riot Verda Welcome becomes first black woman elected to state Senate Public Accommodation Law Demonstrations at Gwynn Oak Amusement Park
	1951	Commission on Interracial Problems and Relations established			
	1952	Fords Theatre in Baltimore desegregated Baltimore municipal swimming pool desegregated	Civil Rights Act	1964	
Brown v. *Topeka Board of Education*	1954	(September) Baltimore City public schools desegregated First blacks elected to General Assembly	Voting Rights Act	1965	
			Thurgood Marshall becomes first black appointed to the Supreme Court	1967	
Montgomery, Alabama, bus boycott	1955		Martin Luther King, Jr., assassinated	1968	Baltimore Riot Maryland Commission on Human Relations organized
	1956	Baltimore Fair Employment Ordinance		1969	Maryland Commission on Afro-American History and Culture established
Sit-ins in Greensboro, North Carolina	1960	Sit-ins at College Park, Baltimore, and Salisbury	Supreme Court upholds busing as a way to achieve integration	1970	
				1973	Busing begins in Prince George's County

Marshall, who later became the first black American appointed to the Supreme Court, got his start fighting for equal civil rights in Maryland.

School Desegregation

In 1954 the Supreme Court ruled in the test case *Brown* v. *Topeka Board of Education* that the doctrine of "separate but equal" has no place in American education. Schools had been legally segregated throughout the South, but they had never been equal in practice. Earlier challenges had questioned the lack of equality, but segregation per se was the target of Thurgood Marshall and the other NAACP lawyers. The Supreme Court's unanimous decision stated that to separate children by race "generates a feeling of inferiority as to their status in the community that may affect their hearts and minds in a way unlikely ever to be undone."

In Maryland the decision received mixed reactions. Baltimore City immediately declared that it would accept the court's ruling and began admitting students to schools without considering race. Baltimore County delayed school integration until 1955. Residents of Montgomery County asked the state Board of Education in 1955 to reverse its ruling that would send 32 blacks to a formerly white school. Most colleges in Maryland admitted black students, although some were not enthusiastic about the change. H. C. (Curly) Byrd, a past president of the University of Maryland who had resisted earlier integration reform, ran for governor against McKeldin in 1954 on a campaign platform that opposed desegregation.

After the first steps toward desegregation, the real progress for racial equality was slow. One problem was that children attended the schools near their homes, so as long as blacks and whites did not live together in the same neighborhoods, schools continued to be largely segregated. By 1978, because of white flight to the suburbs, two-thirds of Baltimore's schoolchildren were black. In 1954 less than half of them had been black. The other problem was the continuing presence of racial prejudice. At Deale, in Anne Arundel County, for example, a black physician was forced by threats of violence to withdraw his son from a white elementary school.

Pressure from black parents and community leaders sometimes led to improvements. New schools were built and curricula were strengthened. In the 1970s, beginning with Prince George's County in 1973, the courts ordered children to be bused to achieve better racial balance. But the progress toward racial equality in education as well as in jobs and housing was slower than many had hoped.

The New Militancy

By the 1960s the lack of significant progress led to greater frustration and a more militant level of protest. Organized demonstrations, like those to integrate Baltimore's Gwynn Oak Amusement Park in 1963, were a sign that black Marylanders were growing impatient. Even more disturbing to whites were the riots that occurred in Cambridge that same year.

A new state law that prohibited discrimination in hotels, restaurants, and other public places had exempted the counties of the Eastern Shore. Frustrated with the slow pace of change, peaceful protestors became more militant in the summer months. Sit-ins and demonstrations led to mass arrests and growing anger on both

Clarence Mitchell, Jr. (right), a longtime Maryland resident, headed the Washington office of the National Association for the Advancement of Colored People for many years. Here he meets with Roy L. Wilkens, who was head of the organization during the early civil rights struggles.

sides. On the night of June 11, 1963, fighting broke out between black and white citizens of Cambridge. Stores were firebombed, cars were overturned, and several people were wounded by gunfire. Peace was restored only when National Guard troops were called in. The violence that occurred in Cambridge was a forewarning of the riots that would continue in Maryland and throughout the nation for the rest of the decade.

In 1964 Congress passed the Civil Rights Act in an attempt to correct some of the racial inequality. The most important part of the bill outlawed discrimination in hotels, motels, restaurants, theaters, and other public places. Other parts of it increased the federal government's authority to stop discrimination in schools, elections, and the workplace. The following year the Voting Rights Act strengthened the protection against voting rights abuse. As a result, by the end of 1965 black registration in the Deep South had increased by 40 percent. Marylanders took leading roles in the battle for civil rights. Clarence Mitchell, Jr., for example, played a key role in persuading congressmen to vote for the new legislation. A graduate of Douglass High School in Baltimore, Mitchell made a career of working for better civil rights laws. As the director of the NAACP's Washington bureau, he was a strong lobbyist for the new guarantees against discrimination in the 1960s. Even with the successes of the civil rights movement, however, the decade continued to be characterized by protest and violence.

The worst year was 1968. The year's first crisis occurred at Bowie State College, where students boycotted classes to protest the ne-

glect of the historically black school by state authorities. When the students attempted to take over the college, Governor Agnew called in state troops and had the protesters arrested.

More serious rioting broke out in April 1968 after the assassination of Dr. Martin Luther King, Jr. Baltimore blacks, frustrated by overcrowded housing, high unemployment, and poverty-level incomes, took out their anger in violent protest. Stores were looted and buildings were firebombed. After four days of rioting the casualties included 6 people dead, 700 people injured, 1,000 businesses destroyed, and over 5,000 people arrested.

Violence returned to Cambridge in the summer of 1968. H. Rap Brown, a nationally known black radical leader, encouraged local residents to protest the poor living conditions and inadequate schools. Before the rioting ended, two square blocks of Cambridge had been burned. This was the last of the major racial violence in Maryland.

In the 1970s public attention turned away from the civil rights struggle. Concern for the economy and protest over the war in Vietnam distracted reformers. Also, by the 1970s, civil rights legislation was beginning to have some effect. Federal and state laws made discrimination in jobs and housing more difficult. And black Marylanders had more spokespersons. By 1973 there were 14 blacks in the House of Delegates and 4 in the state Senate. Parren Mitchell, the first black admitted to the University of Maryland's graduate program in sociology, took on a leading role in the U.S. House of Representatives.

Above, left: Many people protested against U.S. military involvement in Vietnam. In this photograph, Maryland veterans and others are demonstrating at Charles Center in downtown Baltimore.

Above, right: Parren J. Mitchell (right), the first black member of the U.S. House of Representatives from Maryland, became the dean of the state's congressional delegation in 1985. He is pictured with Herbert L. Jones, vice-commander of the military Order of the Purple Heart.

The Challenge of Equality   291

Environmental Concerns

One of the issues that grew as a public concern after the late sixties was deterioration of the environment. The fact that Maryland's population doubled between 1945 and 1980 was the basic problem. The land, air, water, and energy resources were placed under heavier use. Discharges of waste grew at a rapid rate and increasingly fouled the environment.

Preservation of the Land

As early as 1945 the state had two agencies that were responsible for the environment. A Water Pollution Commission joined the older Health Department in trying to regulate pollution from industries and urban communities. These two agencies gave Maryland a headstart over most other regions. In 1955, for example, Maryland was the first state to pass a strip mining law. Through this law, companies that mined coal by stripping the top layers of soil away were required to restore the land to its original condition.

Maryland also began early to protect its land by creating state parks and forests. State protection of wildlife led to an increase in the numbers of deer, turkeys, and other animals in Maryland's woodlands. Cities and counties helped by establishing parks and playgrounds for tennis, baseball, soccer, swimming, and picnicking.

By the late 1960s, however, Marylanders along with the rest of the nation realized that greater measures were needed to stop the deterioration of the environment. Rachel Carson, originally from Maryland, aroused concern with her book *The Silent Spring*. She warned of the dangers of the pesticides and chemicals that were polluting America's land and water, and she showed how they killed wildlife and endangered human health.

In 1968 Maryland responded to the need for better control by establishing the Department of Natural Resources. This government department coordinated the actions of all the state agencies that regulated parks, forests, and wildlife and that tried to solve pollution problems. It helped get new laws to control oil spills, chemical dumps, industrial pollution, and even noise pollution. The creation of the Environmental Protection Agency by the federal government in 1970 was another important step toward better control.

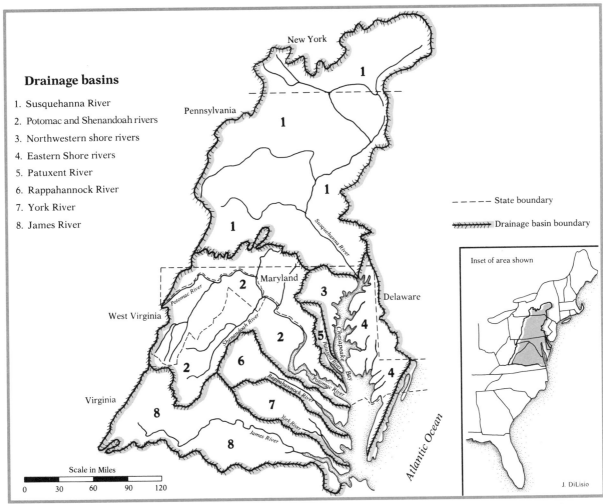

Drainage basins

1. Susquehanna River
2. Potomac and Shenandoah rivers
3. Northwestern shore rivers
4. Eastern Shore rivers
5. Patuxent River
6. Rappahannock River
7. York River
8. James River

- - - - State boundary

╫╫╫╫╫ Drainage basin boundary

Inset of area shown

J. DiLisio

Major drainage basins of the Chesapeake Bay system

Efforts to Save the Bay

Of special concern in Maryland was the deterioration of the Chesapeake Bay. Described as the state's greatest natural resource, the Bay was declining because it was being so heavily used by industry and the growing population. Pollution of the Bay came from several sources. Cities and towns dumped millions of gallons of untreated sewage into its waters. Industrial wastes included chemicals, oil, grease, and metals. Commercial shipping and recreational boating contributed more pollution. Even farmers were to blame, because their pesticides, herbicides, and chemical fertilizers eventually washed down to the Chesapeake. The Water Pollution Control Commission, created by the legislature in 1947, had little effect on the steady deterioration.

Only after 1960 did Maryland begin to make any progress toward saving the Bay. The Department of Natural Resources under the direction of former Governor Tawes and then James B. Coulter pushed tougher legislation through the General Assembly. These state laws, combined with federal action by the Environmental Protection Agency, helped to slow the decline in quality of the Bay. The Maryland Environmental Service helped towns and cities improve their waste-disposal systems.

Although Maryland and its neighboring states did much to slow the rate of deterioration, new studies in the 1980s showed that more needed to be done. Estimates on population growth in the Bay region predicted an increase from 3.6 million to 9 million people by the end of the century. Because water was needed for industry, homes, and irrigation, the Bay would not receive as much fresh water as it had in the past. The salinity, the amount of salt, of the Bay's water would increase, threatening the health of oysters, crabs, and fish. More money, knowledge, and public commitment would be needed to save the Bay for future generations.

Sources of Energy

Concern for the environment included a concern for diminishing sources of energy. At the end of World War II, Maryland largely depended on coal mined in the nearby Appalachian Mountains. By the late 1960s the Baltimore Gas and Electric Company, the Potomac Electric Power Company, Potomac Edison, and Delmarva Power and Light, major suppliers of energy in the state, had begun to use oil and natural gas in addition to coal. By the 1970s Maryland imported fuel for energy from all over the world. Oil came from Venezuela, and natural gas was piped and tanked in from Texas, Algeria, and the Arctic Sea. Coal still came from the mines of West Virginia.

Unfortunately, this dependence on international sources also raised the cost of Maryland's energy. At the same time, more people used more energy. Prices gradually increased to many times the prices of the 1940s. Baltimore Gas and Electric, which spent $25 to $30 million for fuel supplies per year in the 1950s, was spending about $250 million each year by the 1970s.

Some of the increased cost for energy came from the construction of the nuclear power plant at Calvert Cliffs in 1974. As one of the largest power-producing plants in the world, this new facility supplied 11 percent of the state's energy by 1979. The new source of energy brought with it fear of nuclear accidents and radiation pollution.

The Calvert Cliffs nuclear power plant provides plentiful energy, but many people fear that it and other nuclear plants will one day lead to a nuclear disaster.

Life in Modern Maryland

As Maryland passed its three hundred and fiftieth anniversary in 1984, its citizens looked back on their past. There was much to celebrate and to point to with pride. Marylanders liked to suggest that their state was a reflection of the nation as a whole. It had scenic variety, from mountains to seashore. As a border state, it had both northern and southern characteristics. Best of all, Marylanders pointed out, Maryland was a good place to live.

Education

For many, the key to a good life was education. Like other states, Maryland faced the need for more and better schools. The postwar baby boom swelled the demand for classroom space, teachers, and books. The sales tax begun by Governor Lane provided the revenue

Rosa Ponselle thrilled opera audiences worldwide with her beautiful soprano voice. In 1952 she became the artistic advisor to the fledgling Baltimore Opera Company. Under her guidance the company, and many young singers, gained prominence.

needed for buildings and better teachers' salaries. Enrollment in public schools increased by more than 50 percent during the 1950s, and salaries in education also rose by about that percentage.

In this period there was also an ongoing debate over the quality of education. When the Soviet Union put the first satellite into space in 1957, Americans worried that the United States might fall behind in engineering and the sciences. Student rebellions and demonstrations on college campuses in the late 1960s, however, turned public opinion against education. By the 1970s the economic recession undermined efforts to improve the quality of schools.

In Maryland there was a modest attempt to expand the opportunities for higher education. With Governor Tawes's support in the 1960s, the University of Maryland system, including campuses in Baltimore County and on the Eastern Shore, grew to almost 37,000 students. Six state colleges were combined under a single board of trustees and enrolled 17,000 students. Towson State University grew to be the second largest university in the state. By 1978 the 20 community colleges around the state had 28,000 attending classes. About 42 percent of all Maryland students attended college.

Arts and Culture

The post–World War II era saw an increase in the cultural opportunities for Marylanders. Each of the two-year and four-year colleges offered classes, exhibits, lectures, and other activities for adults. Baltimore and Washington were the dominant cultural centers, but all of Maryland's smaller cities also expanded their cultural activities during this period.

Baltimore's urban renaissance in particular included a new blossoming of the arts. The Morris Mechanic Theatre, for example, was a popular part of Charles Center in the heart of the city. Dozens of small theaters and dramatic groups drew audiences from the entire metropolitan area.

Maryland's growth in the arts and culture was the result of both private and public efforts. In 1967 Governor Agnew appointed a Maryland Arts Council, whose budget by 1979 reached $1.7 million. These public dollars joined private funds to offer Marylanders a better quality of culture and entertainment. The Meyerhoff Symphony Hall, built with a large contribution by philanthropist Joseph Meyerhoff, opened in 1981 in Baltimore. It was symbolic of the enthusiasm for the arts which existed in the last half of the twentieth century.

The Merriweather Post Pavilion in Columbia, the Harford Opera

Company in Bel Air, the Weinberg Center for Performing Arts in Frederick, the Washington County Museum of Fine Arts in Hagerstown, and the rebuilt Peale Museum in Baltimore were other examples of renewed support for culture. Music by groups like the Montgomery Symphony Orchestra and theatrical performances by local companies in College Park or Salisbury offered Marylanders alternatives to the national artists who came to the metropolitan areas.

Maryland became better known, too, as a home for writers. John Barth, a Johns Hopkins University professor, gained a national reputation with his novels *The Sot-Weed Factor*, *Giles Goat-Boy*, and *The End of the Road*. Anne Tyler's novels, such as *The Clock Winder*, were also read by a national audience. Poetry in particular seemed to suit the Maryland environment. Gilbert Byron became the best-known poet of the Eastern Shore. In Baltimore, poetry flourished in the 1970s and 1980s with many excellent writers like Lucille Clifton and Josephine Jacobsen, who became poet in residence at the Library of Congress. A Maryland Writers Council gave support to the state's literary talents.

Lucille Clifton, Poet Laureate of the state of Maryland from 1979 to 1985.

Sports and Recreation

As Maryland's population increased after World War II, demand for more recreation and sports facilities also grew. Outdoor play and relaxation were always favorites among Marylanders. Blessed with a diverse environment, they could choose between the mountains of western Maryland and the beaches of the Atlantic and the Chesapeake. In Allegany and Garrett counties the favorite pastimes were skiing, fishing, hunting, camping, and hiking. On the Eastern Shore, horse shows, yacht regattas, log canoe races, and hunting geese and ducks were the traditional sports. After the Chesapeake Bay Bridge was built, taking in the sun and waves along the beaches of Maryland's Atlantic Coast brought pleasure to hundreds of thousands each weekend.

Baltimore's rebuilt downtown harbor became a major recreation site in the 1970s. The City Fair, started under Mayor Thomas D'Alesandro III, attracted crowds of half a million. Ethnic festivals, children's concerts, and parades made the urban landscape a playground for Marylanders.

Maryland also had two of the most successful spectator sports teams in America. When the Baltimore Colts won "the greatest game ever played" to become the National Football League champions in 1958, Maryland had a new set of folk heroes. Johnny Unitas, Lenny Moore, Raymond Berry, Art Donovan, and Gino

TWO FAMOUS MOMENTS IN SPORTS

Before leaving Maryland in March 1984, the Baltimore Colts delighted football fans everywhere with great players and heart-stopping games. In this photograph of what is perhaps the landmark game in the National Football League, Hall-of-Fame quarterback Johnny Unitas drops back to unleash one of his patented "bombs." The underdog Colts won the 1958 title game in overtime, 23 to 17. Played in New York against the Giants, this game, many people say, established football as a national professional sport, and placed Baltimore, and Maryland, atop the American sports scene for the first time.

Long acknowledged as one of baseball's most solid organizations, the Baltimore Orioles have been a source of pride for Marylanders since they came to the city in 1954. The "O's" won their first World Series in 1966, defeating the heavily favored Los Angeles Dodgers four games to none. In this photograph, Dave McNally, Andy Etchebarren, and Hall-of-Famer Brooks Robinson celebrate the team's victory moments after outfielder Paul Blair caught the series-ending fly ball.

Marchetti—these were names that every schoolchild knew well in the Colts' glory days of the 1950s and 1960s.

Even more successful were the Baltimore Orioles. New to the city in 1954, the team won a world championship in 1966. In their first 25 years in Baltimore, they became the winningest team in all of baseball.

Marylanders loved tradition in their sports. One of the longest and richest traditions was the running of the Preakness. This event, held each May, gave Maryland an honored place in horse racing as a site of one of the Triple Crown races. The annual Hunt Cup Race and the popular jousting tournaments proved that Maryland's love of fine horses had not diminished since the seventeenth century.

From Past to Present to Future

The line from past to present moves inevitably toward the future. Maryland in 1985 was a vastly different place from Maryland in 1634. The colonial wilderness had been replaced by a modern industrial and technological society, with all of its advantages and all of its problems. The once sparsely populated land had grown crowded with the great variety of people that makes the United States unique among nations. Many challenges remain for Marylanders in the years to come. Some of them will simply be repetitions or continuations of old challenges. Others cannot yet be imagined.

The economy will have to adjust periodically to new conditions. This can deplete resources and cause unemployment. Social customs change all the time. Recent years have witnessed strong campaigns for greater equality, yet discrimination and inequities among the state's citizens still remain. Increasing population and past failure to care for the environment have put a strain on the natural resources that have served the state so well.

In some cases, the decision-makers of the future can benefit from the experiences of the past. Sometimes the failures of the past indicate what to avoid, while past successes give clues about how to proceed. Marylanders, while looking forward to the future, might occasionally glance backward, at the state's rich history.

On the Occasion of Maryland's 350th Birthday

from the Ark
of refuge,
from the Dove
of peace,
we have become.

we celebrate
three hundred fifty years
of learning.

turning
watermen and women,
hill folk and city,
into citizens.

safe now and at peace
in this proud state
named for a woman

we blend our brown
and yellow, red
and black and white
into a greater We.

Maryland,
heiress to refuge
and to peace,
We celebrate.
We praise.

Lucille Clifton
Poet Laureate of Maryland

Appendix A. Supplementary Maps

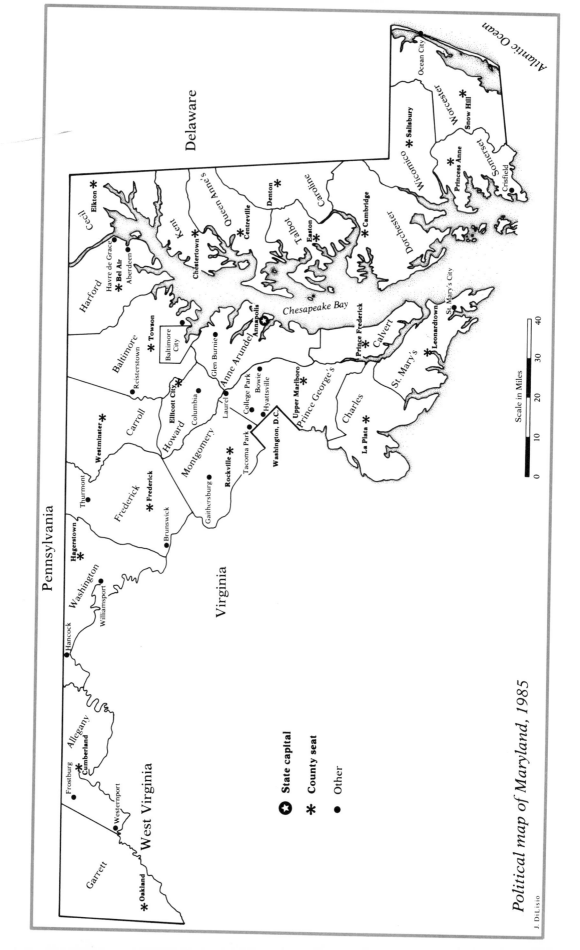

Political map of Maryland, 1985

J. DiLisio

State capital
County seat
Other

Scale in Miles
0 10 20 30 40

Atlantic Ocean

Delaware

Pennsylvania

Virginia

West Virginia

Chesapeake Bay

Cecil
Elkton

Harford
Havre de Grace
Bel Air
Aberdeen

Kent
Chestertown

Queen Anne's
Centreville

Caroline
Denton

Talbot
Easton

Cambridge
Dorchester

Wicomico
Salisbury

Princess Anne

Snow Hill
Worcester
Somerset
Crisfield

Ocean City

Baltimore
Towson
Baltimore City
Reisterstown

Anne Arundel
Annapolis
Glen Burnie

Prince Frederick
Calvert

St. Mary's City
St. Mary's
Leonardtown

Carroll
Westminster

Howard
Ellicott City
Columbia

Montgomery
Rockville
Gaithersburg
Tacoma Park

Howard

Laurel
College Park
Bowie
Hyattsville

Prince George's
Upper Marlboro

Washington, D.C.

Charles
La Plata

Frederick
Thurmont
Frederick
Brunswick

Hagerstown
Washington
Williamsport

Hancock

Allegany
Cumberland
Frostburg
Westernport

Garrett
Oakland

302

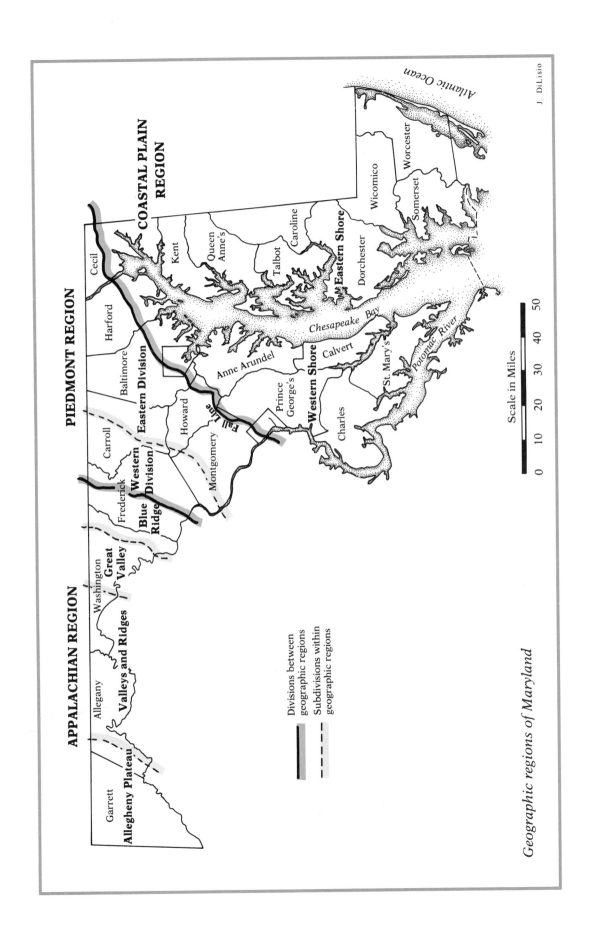

Geographic regions of Maryland

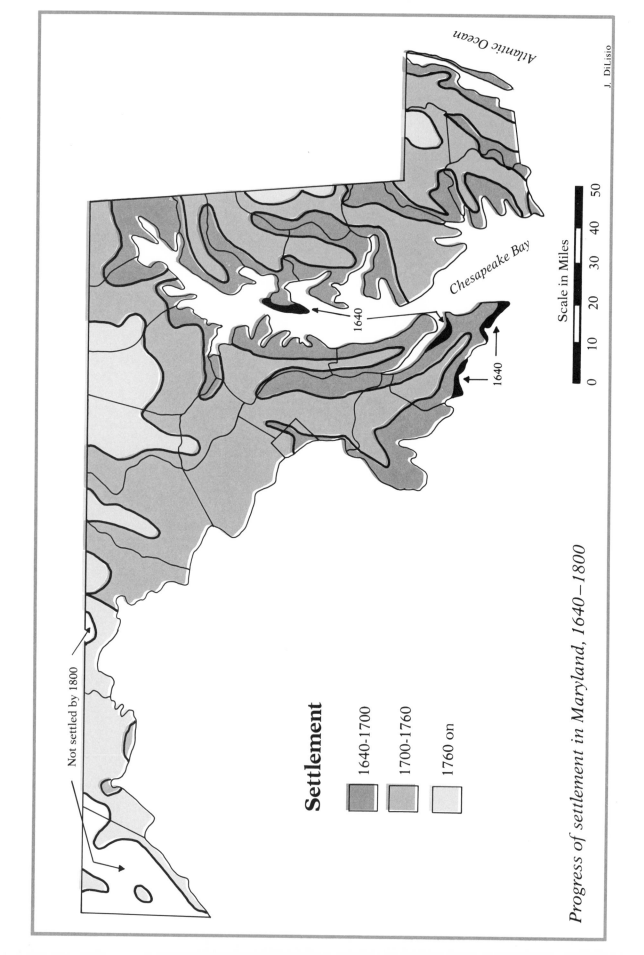

Progress of settlement in Maryland, 1640–1800

Atlantic Ocean

J. DiLisio

Chesapeake Bay

1640

1640

1640

Not settled by 1800

Settlement

1640-1700

1700-1760

1760 on

Scale in Miles

0   10   20   30   40   50

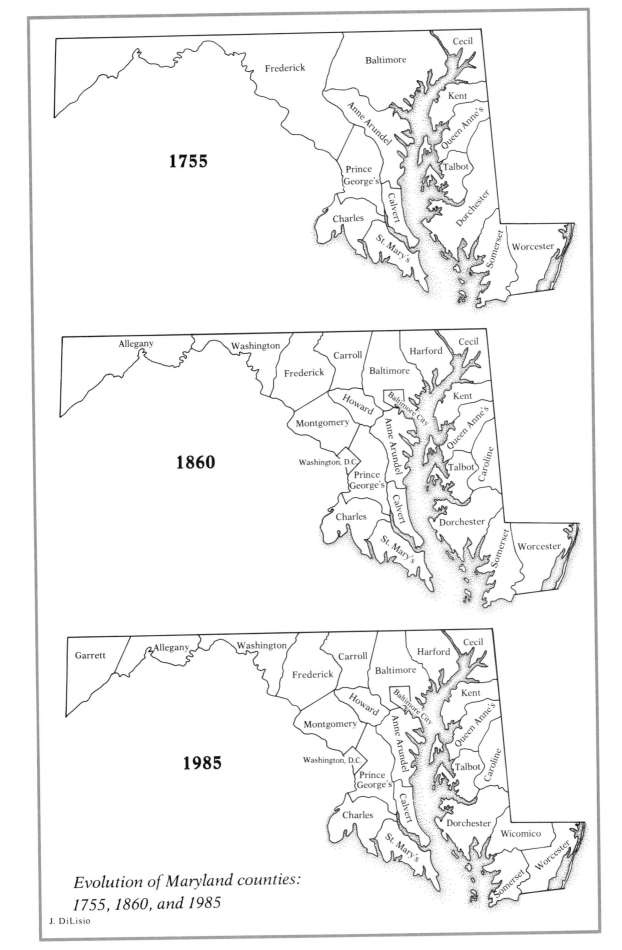

1755

1860

1985

Evolution of Maryland counties:
1755, 1860, and 1985

J. DiLisio

Appendix B. Governors of Maryland

Colonial Governors

1634–1647	Leonard Calvert
1647–1649	Thomas Greene
1649–1652	Captain William Stone
1652	Parliamentary Commissioners
1652–1654	Captain William Stone
1654–1657	Commissioners appointed by the Parliamentary Commissioners
1657–1660	Josias Fendall
1660–1661	Philip Calvert
1661–1676	Charles Calvert
1676	Jesse Wharton
1676–1679	Thomas Notley
1679–1684	Charles Calvert, Lord Proprietary
1684–1688	Benedict Leonard Calvert
1688–1689	William Joseph
1689–1690	John Coode
1690–1692	Nehemiah Blackiston
1692–1693	Sir Lionel Copley
1693	Sir Thomas Lawrence
1693	Sir Edmund Andros
1693–1694	Colonel Nicholas Greenberry
1694	Sir Edmund Andros
1694	Sir Thomas Lawrence
1694–1699	Sir Francis Nicholson
1699–1702	Colonel Nathaniel Blackiston
1702–1704	Thomas Tench
1704–1709	Colonel John Seymour
1709–1714	Major General Edward Lloyd
1714–1720	John Hart
1720	Thomas Brooke
1720–1727	Charles Calvert
1727–1731	Benedict Leonard Calvert
1731–1732	Samuel Ogle
1732–1733	Charles Calvert, Lord Proprietary
1733–1742	Samuel Ogle
1742–1747	Thomas Bladen
1747–1752	Samuel Ogle
1752–1753	Benjamin Tasker
1753–1769	Horatio Sharpe
1769–1776	Robert Eden

Governors Elected Under the Constitution of 1776 by the Legislature for One Year

		Party	Birthplace
1777–1779	Thomas Johnson	None	Calvert County
1779–1782	Thomas Sim Lee	None	Prince George's County
1782–1785	William Paca	None	Harford County
1785–1788	William Smallwood	None	Charles County
1788–1791	John Eager Howard	Federalist	Baltimore City
1791–1792	George Plater	Federalist	St. Mary's County
1792–1794	Thomas Sim Lee	Federalist	Prince George's County

		Party	Birthplace
1794–1797	John H. Stone	Federalist	Charles County
1797–1798	John Henry	Federalist	Dorchester County
1798–1801	Benjamin Ogle	Federalist	Anne Arundel County
1801–1803	John Francis Mercer	Democrat	Stafford County, Virginia
1803–1806	Robert Bowie	Democrat	Prince George's County
1806–1809	Robert Wright	Democrat	Queen Anne's County
1809–1811	Edward Lloyd	Democrat	Talbot County
1811–1812	Robert Bowie	Democrat	Prince George's County
1812–1816	Levin Winder	Federalist	Somerset County
1816–1819	Charles Ridgely of Hampton	Federalist	Baltimore County
1819	Charles Goldsborough	Federalist	Dorchester County
1819–1822	Samuel Sprigg	Democrat	Prince George's County
1822–1826	Samuel Stevens, Jr.	Democrat	Talbot County
1826–1829	Joseph Kent	Democrat	Calvert County
1829–1830	Daniel Martin	Anti-Jackson	Talbot County
1830–1831	Thomas King Carroll	Jackson Democrat	Somerset County
1831	Daniel Martin	Anti-Jackson	Talbot County
1831–1833	George Howard	Anti-Jackson	Anne Arundel County
1833–1836	James Thomas	Anti-Jackson	St. Mary's County
1836–1839	Thomas W. Veazey	Whig	Cecil County

Governors Elected by the People for Three Years Under the Constitution of 1776 as Amended in 1837

1839–1842	William Grason	Democrat	Queen Anne's County
1842–1845	Francis Thomas	Democrat	Frederick County
1845–1848	Thomas G. Pratt	Whig	Georgetown, D.C.
1848–1851	Philip Francis Thomas	Democrat	Talbot County
1851–1854	Enoch Louis Lowe	Democrat	Frederick County

Governors Elected Under the Constitution of 1851 by the People for Four Years

1854–1858	Thomas Watkins Ligon	Democrat	Prince Edward County, Virginia
1858–1862	Thomas Holliday Hicks	Native American	Dorchester County
1862–1866	Augustus W. Bradford	Unionist	Harford County

Governor Elected Under the Constitution of 1864 by the People for Four Years

		Party	Birthplace
1866–1869	Thomas Swann	Unionist-Democrat	Alexandria, Virginia

Governors Elected Under the Constitution of 1867 by the People for Four Years

1869–1872	Oden Bowie	Democrat	Prince George's County
1872–1874	William Pinkney Whyte	Democrat	Baltimore City
1874–1876	James Black Groome	Democrat	Cecil County
1876–1880	John Lee Carroll	Democrat	Baltimore City
1880–1884	William T. Hamilton	Democrat	Washington County
1884–1885	Robert M. McLane	Democrat	Wilmington, Delaware
1885–1888	Henry Lloyd	Democrat	Dorchester County
1888–1892	Elihu E. Jackson	Democrat	Somerset County
1892–1896	Frank Brown	Democrat	Carroll County
1896–1900	Lloyd Lowndes	Republican	Clarksburg, West Virginia
1900–1904	John Walter Smith	Democrat	Worcester County
1904–1908	Edwin Warfield	Democrat	Howard County
1908–1912	Austin L. Crothers	Democrat	Cecil County
1912–1916	Phillips Lee Goldsborough	Republican	Cambridge
1916–1920	Emerson C. Harrington	Democrat	Dorchester County
1920–1935	Albert C. Ritchie	Democrat	Richmond, Virginia
1935–1939	Harry W. Nice	Republican	Washington, D.C.
1939–1947	Herbert R. O'Conor	Democrat	Baltimore City
1947–1951	William Preston Lane, Jr.	Democrat	Washington County
1951–1959	Theodore R. McKeldin	Republican	Baltimore City
1959–1967	J. Millard Tawes	Democrat	Somerset County
1967–1969	Spiro T. Agnew	Republican	Baltimore City
1969–1979	Marvin Mandel	Democrat	Baltimore City
1979–	Harry Hughes	Democrat	Talbot County

SOURCE: Information from the *Maryland Manual*, courtesy of the Maryland State Archives.

Glossary

Abolitionists: People who wanted to end slavery.

Anglican church: The Church of England. This was the legally established church in Maryland from 1692 until the American Revolution. An established church is supported by public monies collected from the taxpayers. After the revolution, the Anglican church became the Protestant Episcopal Church and existed on an equal basis with all other churches.

Antebellum: Before the Civil War.

Australian ballot: The long ballot listing all the candidates in an election. This allows truly secret voting. It replaces the one-party ballot, which, when it was carried to a voting box, made a voter's choice obvious to all observers.

Baby boom: The rapid increase in the birth rate between 1946 and 1964.

Blockade runner: A ship or person who tries to go through a blockade. A blockade is a shutting off of a place or a region by hostile troops or ships.

Capital: Assets that produce income. In the colonial economy, these included crops, livestock, laborers, buildings for storing crops and sheltering animals, orchards, and farm equipment.

Charter: The document that confirmed the grant of the colony of Maryland to Cecilius Calvert. The charter defined the powers given to Lord Baltimore as the colony's proprietor.

Colonization: The establishment of a colony in territory that is distant from the homeland of the colony's settlers.

Consolidation: Merging together of many companies into a few or one.

Continental army: Established in June 1775. The regular troops of the American army during the War for Independence. General George Washington served as commander in chief of the Continental army. The number of troops in this army never amounted to more than 25,000. The Continental army was disbanded in 1784.

Contraband: Unlawful or prohibited trade or smuggled goods. During the Civil War, a slave who fled to or was smuggled behind Union lines.

Country and Court parties: Neither was a political party in the modern sense. The Country party consisted of a group of men who united on various issues in opposition to the proprietor and his officials in Maryland. Proprietary supporters made up the Court party.

Demagogue: A political leader who gains power and popularity by arousing the emotions, passions, and prejudices of the people.

Demography: The study of people, their distribution and their characteristics.

Direct relief: Funds or goods given to the poor without obliging them to work in exchange for the funds or goods.

Diversification: A usually desirable economic strategy, in which many different kinds of industry are operating. In Baltimore, factories manufacture items ranging from clothing and soap to iron and steel, and other factories refine oil. Thus, Baltimore has a diverse economy.

Electors: People who are elected in order to select other officers of government. The Senate established under the first Maryland Constitution was selected by electors. The use of electors meant that the senators were not directly elected by the people, which was intended as a check on excessive democracy.

Embargo: An order from the central government stopping all foreign commerce in and out of the ports.

Enfranchisement: The act of admission to citizenship, especially the right to vote.

External tax: A term used to describe duties, or taxes, charged on items of commerce. External taxes were charged on most items imported into the American colonies from England. The selling price of these goods already included the amount of the tax.

Extralegal government: A government that functions but is not based on existing law. The convention government that came into being in Maryland in 1774 was extralegal; the legally established government was that of the proprietor under the charter of Maryland.

Foreclosure: The forcible sale of farm, home, or business properties when the owners are unable to meet mortgage payments.

Freemen: In colonial Maryland, men who had paid for their own passage to the new world and thus enjoyed full legal rights. As indentured servants worked off their terms of service, they, too, became freemen.

General Assembly: The state legislature, or representative branch of the Maryland government. *See also* Lower House; Upper House.

Gentry: The upper class, usually the large planters in the counties, as well as government officials, professional men, and merchants. Gentry families controlled most local offices and filled most of the seats in the Lower House of the Assembly.

Graft: Money acquired dishonestly, in exchange for political favors.

Habeas corpus: A legal expression first used in medieval England meaning, literally, "you have the body." In law it is a written requirement that a court decide the legality of a prisoner's detention.

Harlem Renaissance: The term used to describe a remarkable flowering of the arts in the black community in the 1920s. Although it originated in the Harlem section of New York, the phrase came to include black cultural and artistic accomplishments throughout the nation.

Impressment: The practice or act of forcing into service men or property for the use or service of the public.

Indentured servant: A servant who signed a legal agreement, known as an indenture, agreeing to serve for a term of years in exchange for passage to the colonies. The term generally ranged between three and five years.

Indict: Formally accuse by a grand jury.

Internal improvements: A term describing transportation projects, such as roads, turnpikes, canals, and railroads. The issue of internal improvements became controversial because some politicians argued that the federal government ought to help pay the cost of internal improvements, while others believed the projects should be left in the hands of the state or private interests.

Internal tax: Taxes charged on goods and services at the time of sale or use. The Stamp Act was an internal tax, because it required that tax stamps be purchased for various commodities and documents filed in court.

Inventory: Stock of goods already produced or acquired, and held in reserve or in storage until needed for sale or use.

Iron-clad oaths: The oaths used in the Civil War which included swearing that you had never given aid or support to the Confederate government.

Ku Klux Klan (KKK): A secret organization formed after the Civil War to terrorize newly freed slaves. It experienced a major national revival during the 1920s, when its campaign of hatred was extended to immigrants, Catholics, and Jews.

Lieutenant governor: Similar to a vice-president, but at the state level.

Lower House: In colonial times, the elected branch of the General Assembly. In the eighteenth century, the Lower House consisted of four representatives from each county and two from Annapolis. Baltimore gained two delegates under the first state constitution.

Loyalist: A person who remained loyal to England during the War for Independence. Also called a tory.

Manor: A large holding of land, carrying special privileges. In colonial Maryland, the owner could call himself lord of his manor and could hold special manorial courts.

Manumission: A legal act freeing a slave.

Mercenary: A foreigner hired to serve in another country's army. In the War for Independence, England used many mercenaries, most of whom came from Germany.

Mobilization: Getting men and military equipment ready to enter the war.

Moveable wealth: Wealth in the form of moveable goods such as furniture, silverware, or farm animals.

Nativism: Anti-Catholic, anti-immigrant prejudice; especially prevalent in the 1850s in Maryland.

Naturalization: The process by which foreign-born immigrants to the United States become citizens.

Nonexportation: Refusal to export goods abroad. Although the colonies were heavily dependent on exporting goods for income, nonexportation was added to nonimportation to heighten the economic impact of the protest against English policies.

Nonimportation: Refusal to import goods from abroad. In the years before the War for Independence, it was used to bring economic pressure against England. Nonimportation hurt English merchants who specialized in exporting goods to the colonies.

Nonpartisan: Not controlled by any single political party; beyond party interests.

Parliament: The legislative branch of British government, consisting of a hereditary House of Lords and an elected House of Commons.

Party convention: The party convention came into use during the Jacksonian era to nominate candidates to run for office. An official nomination was designed to discourage independent candidates and to unify various factions behind a party's choice.

Patronage: The power to appoint to office or grant political favors. Patronage jobs are ones received through political favoritism.

Peonage: The system of bond labor that some white Marylanders tried to install after emancipation. Blacks were to be forced to work for individuals and could not leave the employ of their "master."

Per capita income: Income for each person.

Perjury: Lying while under oath in a court of law.

Philanthropy: The practice of helping mankind, especially through gifts and acts of service.

Pogrom: An organized massacre or attack on Jews, especially in czarist Russia.

Primary election: The election to choose the nominees of each party to run in the general election. Voters choose among all candidates seeking nomination by one party. Primary elections put this choice in the hands of the voters instead of the party leaders.

Privateers: Privately armed ships licensed by the government to attack and harass an enemy's commerce. During the War of 1812, the American government licensed privateers, many of which sailed from Baltimore.

Progressives: Reformers in the late nineteenth and early twentieth centuries. They were especially concerned with ending political corruption and improving social conditions.

Prohibition: The political reform movement for the passage of an amendment to the U.S. Constitution forbidding people to sell or consume alcoholic beverages. It also refers to the period of time in which that amendment (the Eighteenth) was in effect.

Propaganda: Biased appeals to emotional fears, often used in time of war to portray an enemy as evil or uncivilized.

Proprietary official: An officer, such as the governor, who was appointed by the proprietor to oversee his affairs and protect his interests in the colony.

Proprietary party: This party was made up of men who supported the proprieter in colonial politics. Most were loyal to the proprietor because he had appointed them or members of their families to high-paying offices. (Same as the Court party.)

Proprietor: A person who has legal title to some property. Maryland's proprietor was Lord Baltimore, the owner of the colony. The charter of 1632 gave Maryland to Cecilius Calvert, second Lord Baltimore, and his heirs forever.

Quitrent: A small monetary payment made by the owner of land to the person who originally granted title to the land (the proprietor). It took the place of certain obligations, holdovers from the feudal system, that would have been owed the proprietor.

Ratification: The act of confirming or approving. For example, the Treaty of Paris ending the War for Independence was negotiated and signed by representatives of each country involved in the war, but before the treaty could take effect it had to be formally confirmed or approved by the appropriate authorities in each country. Congress ratified the Treaty of Paris for the United States.

Reapportionment: The distribution of representatives among equal numbers of voters.

Referendum: The submission of a law to a direct vote by the people for approval or rejection.

Seasoning: A period of adaptation to a new land, often a time of hardship and great adjustment. Some colonial settlers and slaves did not survive the time of seasoning.

Separate but equal: A provision of a Supreme Court decision in the case of *Plessy* v. *Ferguson* in 1896. The court ruled that it was legal to provide segregated facilities for blacks, so long as they were of equal quality to those for whites. In practice the facilities tended to be separate and unequal.

Sharecropper: A person who farms another person's land in return for a set portion of the crop.

Silting: The choking up of a body of water by fine particles of earth.

Social Darwinism: A belief that the fittest people will survive and prosper, while the weak will fall by the wayside. This was an especially popular philosophy in the late nineteenth and early twentieth centuries. It was often used by the rich to justify their wealth and explain away poverty as the result of being "unfit" to prosper in the new industrial society.

Subsistence: The ability of a farm or plantation to produce virtually everything that its residents need for survival. Subsistence farmers or planters did not produce extensively for a market and earned little, if any, profit.

Subversives: Persons who work to overthrow the government.

Suffrage: The right to vote.

Tayac: The leader of a group of Indian tribes. Europeans thought of him as the Indians' "emperor."

Tenant: A person who farms another person's land and pays an annual rent. In colonial Maryland the rent was often collected in tobacco or wheat.

Truck farming: The growing of vegetables and fruits to be marketed nearby, generally in close urban areas. Produce is usually taken to market by trucks.

Union shop: A workplace in which unions enroll all of the workers and represent their interests in bargaining with the owners.

Upper House: In colonial times, the appointed branch of the General Assembly. Upper House members were chosen by the proprietor and served at his pleasure. Members of the Upper House also served as the governor's advisory council. Now members of the Upper House, or Senate, are elected by popular vote.

Work relief: Government-created jobs whose purpose is to give the unemployed work rather than charity. It usually refers to public works projects like roads or parks.

Further Reading

The following list of reading is not meant to be all inclusive. Interested students will discover a wealth of information at county historical societies, local libraries, the Maryland Historical Society in Baltimore, the Maryland Hall of Records in Annapolis, and through other local groups and associations. Newspapers, magazines, government documents, and papers of organizations as well as county and local histories available through these sources will fill in some of the detail that more general works do not cover.

Chapter 1 Maryland's Formative Years, 1634–1763

Carr, Lois Green, and David W. Jordan. *Maryland's Revolution of Government, 1689–1692*. Ithaca, N.Y.: Cornell University Press, 1974.

Carr, Lois Green, Russell R. Menard, and Louis Peddicord. *Maryland . . . at the Beginning*. Annapolis, Md.: Maryland Department of Economic and Community Development, 1984.

Clemens, Paul G. E. *The Atlantic Economy and Colonial Maryland's Eastern Shore: From Tobacco to Grain*. Ithaca, N.Y.: Cornell University Press, 1980.

Earle, Carville V. *The Evolution of a Tidewater Settlement System: Hallow's Parish, Maryland, 1650–1783*. Chicago: Department of Geography, University of Chicago, 1975.

Greene, Jack P., and J. R. Pole, eds. *Colonial British America: Essays in the New History of the Early Modern Era*. Baltimore: Johns Hopkins University Press, 1984.

Land, Aubrey C. *Colonial Maryland—A History*. Millwood, N.Y.: KTO Press, 1981.

Middleton, Arthur Pierce. *Tobacco Coast: A Maritime History of Chesapeake Bay in the Colonial Era*. Baltimore, Md.: Johns Hopkins University Press, 1984.

Porter, Frank W., III *Maryland Indians: Yesterday and Today*. Baltimore, Md.: Maryland Historical Society, 1983.

Quinn, David, ed. *Early Maryland in a Wider World*. Detroit: Wayne State University Press, 1982.

Smith, Daniel B. *Inside the Great House: Planter Family Life in Eighteenth-Century Chesapeake Society*. Ithaca, N.Y.: Cornell University Press, 1980.

Stiverson, Gregory A. *Poverty in a Land of Plenty: Tenancy in Eighteenth-Century Maryland*. Baltimore: Johns Hopkins University Press, 1978.

Tate, Thad W., and David L. Ammerman, eds. *The Chesapeake in the Seventeenth Century: Essays on Anglo-American Society*. Chapel Hill, N.C.: University of North Carolina Press, 1979; New York: Norton, 1980.

Chapter 2 The Revolutionary War Era, 1763–1789

Barker, Charles A. *The Background of the Revolution in Maryland*. New York: Archon Books, 1967.

Clarkson, Paul S., and R. Samuel Jett. *Luther Martin of Maryland*. Baltimore, Md.: Johns Hopkins Press, 1970.

Haw, James, et al. *Stormy Patriot: The Life of Samuel Chase*. Baltimore, Md.: Maryland Historical Society, 1980.

Hoffman, Ronald. *A Spirit of Dissension: Economics, Politics, and the Revolution in Maryland*. Baltimore, Md.: Johns Hopkins Press, 1973.

Land, Aubrey C., Lois Green Carr, and Edward C. Papenfuse, eds. *Law, Society, and Politics in Early Maryland*. Baltimore, Md.: Johns Hopkins University Press, 1977.

Papenfuse, Edward C. *In Pursuit of Profit: The Annapolis Merchants in the Era of the American Revolution, 1763–1805*. Baltimore: Johns Hopkins University Press, 1975.

Papenfuse, Edward C., et al., eds. *A Biographical Dictionary of the Maryland Legislature, 1635–1789*. 2 vols. Baltimore, Md.: Johns Hopkins University Press, 1979–84.

Risjord, Norman K. *Chesapeake Politics, 1781–1800*. New York: Columbia University Press, 1978.

Skaggs, David C. *Roots of Maryland Democracy, 1753–1776*. Westport, Conn.: Greenwood, 1973.

Steffen, Charles G. *The Mechanics of Baltimore: Workers and Politics in the Age of Revolution, 1763–1812*. Urbana, Ill.: University of Illinois Press, 1984.

Stiverson, Gregory A., and Phebe R. Jacobsen, *William Paca: A Biography*. Baltimore, Md.: Maryland Historical Society, 1976.

Chapter 3   Maryland in the New Nation, 1789–1850

Browne, Gary. *Baltimore in the Nation, 1789–1861*. Chapel Hill, N.C.: University of North Carolina, 1980.

Cassell, Frank A. *Merchant Congressman in the Young Republic: Samuel Smith of Maryland, 1752–1839*. Madison, Wis.: University of Wisconsin Press, 1971.

Crowl, Philip A. *Maryland during and after the Revolution*. Baltimore, Md.: Johns Hopkins Press, 1943.

Garitee, Jerome R. *The Republic's Private Navy*. Middletown, Conn.: Wesleyan University Press, 1977.

Graham, Leroy. *Baltimore: The Nineteenth-Century Black Capital*. Washington, D.C.: University Press of America, 1982.

Livingood, James W. *The Philadelphia–Baltimore Trade Rivalry, 1780–1830*. Harrisburg, Pa.: Pennsylvania Historical and Museum Commission, 1947.

Lord, Walter. *The Dawn's Early Light*. New York: W. W. Norton, 1972.

Preston, Dickson J. *Young Frederick Douglass: The Maryland Years*. Baltimore: Johns Hopkins University Press, 1980.

Ridgway, Whitman H. *Community Leadership in Maryland, 1790–1840: A Comparative Analysis of Power in Society*. Chapel Hill, N.C.: University of North Carolina Press, 1979.

Risjord, Norman K. *Chesapeake Politics, 1781–1800*. New York: Columbia University Press, 1978.

Renzulli, L. Marx. *Maryland: The Federalist Years*. Rutherford, N.J.: Fairleigh Dickinson University Press, 1972.

Sanderlin, Walter S. *The Great National Project: A History of the Chesapeake and Ohio Canal*. Baltimore, Md.: Johns Hopkins Press, 1946.

Wright, James M. *The Free Negro in Maryland, 1634–1860*. New York: Columbia University Press, 1921.

Chapter 4   Maryland in Peace and War, 1850–1870

Baker, Jean H. *Ambivalent Americans: The Know Nothing Party in Maryland*. Baltimore, Md.: Johns Hopkins University Press, 1977.

———. *The Politics of Continuity: Maryland Political Parties from 1858 to 1870*. Baltimore, Md.: Johns Hopkins University Press, 1973.

Berlin, Ira, et al., eds. *The Black Military Experience*. Cambridge, Mass.: Cambridge University Press, 1982.

Douglass, Frederick. *Life and Times of Frederick Douglass*. New York: Collier Books, 1962.

Evitts, William. *A Matter of Allegiances: Maryland from 1850 to 1861*. Baltimore, Md.: Johns Hopkins Press, 1974.

Fields, Barbara Jerome. *Slavery and Freedom on the Middle Ground: Maryland during the Nineteenth Century*. New Haven: Yale University Press, 1985.

Radcliffe, George. *Governor Thomas Hicks of Maryland and the Civil War*. Baltimore, Md.: Johns Hopkins Press, 1901.

Wagandt, Charles. *The Mighty Revolution: Negro Emancipation in Maryland, 1862–1864*. Baltimore, Md.: Johns Hopkins Press, 1964.

Chapter 5   A New Century, 1870–1917

Callcott, Margaret Law. *The Negro in Maryland Politics, 1870–1912*. Baltimore, Md.: Johns Hopkins Press, 1969.

Crooks, James B. *Politics and Progress: The Rise of Urban Progressivism in Baltimore, 1895–1911*. Baton Rouge, La.: Louisiana State University Press, 1968.

Cushing, Harvey. *The Life of Sir William Osler*. Oxford: Oxford University Press, 1925.

Hart, Richard H. *Enoch Pratt: The Story of a Plain Man*. Baltimore, Md., Enoch Pratt Free Library, 1935.

Hirschfeld, Charles. *Baltimore, 1870–1900: Studies in Social History*. Baltimore, Md.: Johns Hopkins Press, 1941.

Kent, Frank. *The Story of Maryland Politics, 1864–1910*. Baltimore: Thomas and Evans Printing, 1911.

Lambert, John. *Arthur Pue Gorman*. Baton Rouge, La.: Louisiana State University Press, 1953.

Mencken, H. L. *The Vintage Mencken*, ed. Alistair Cooke. New York: Vintage Books, 1959.

———. The Young Mencken: The Uncollected Writings, ed. Carl Bode. New York: Dial, 1973.

Stenerson, Douglas C. *H. L. Mencken: Iconoclast from Baltimore*. Chicago: University of Chicago Press, 1971.

Thom, Helen Hopkins. *Johns Hopkins: A Silhouette*. Baltimore, Md.: Johns Hopkins Press, 1929.

Chapter 6 Prosperity, Depression, and War, 1917–1945

Anderson, Karen. *Wartime Women: Sex Roles, Family Relations, and the Status of Women during World War II*. Westport, Conn.: Greenwood, 1981.

Argersinger, JoAnn Eady. "Baltimore: The Depression Years." Ph.D. diss. George Washington University, 1980.

Arnold, Joseph L. *The New Deal in the Suburbs: A History of the Greenbelt Town Program, 1935–1954*. Columbus, Ohio: Ohio State University Press, 1971.

Bland, Randall W. *Private Pressure on Public Law: The Legal Career of Justice Thurgood Marshall*. Port Washington, N.Y.: Kennikat Press, 1973.

Brown, Dorothy. "Maryland between the Wars." In *Maryland, A History: 1632–1974*, edited by Richard Walsh and William Lloyd Fox. Baltimore, Md.: Maryland Historical Society, 1974.

Callcott, George. *A History of the University of Maryland*. Baltimore, Md.: Maryland Historical Society, 1966.

Fenderson, Lewis H. *Thurgood Marshall: Fighter for Justice*. New York: McGraw-Hill, 1969.

Kimberly, Charles M. "The Depression and the New Deal in Maryland." Ph.D. diss. American University, 1974.

Kirwin, Harry W. *The Inevitable Success: Herbert R. O'Conor*. Westminster, Md.: Newman Press, 1962.

Maryland Historical Society, War Records Division. *Maryland in World War II*. Baltimore, Md.: Maryland Historical Society, 1950–58.

Reid, Ira De A. *The Negro Community of Baltimore*. Baltimore, Md.: Urban League, 1935.

Chapter 7 Maryland since World War II, 1945 to the Present

Bambrilla, Robert, and Gianni Longo. *Learning from Baltimore*. New York: Institute of Environmental Action, 1979.

Bard, Harry. *Maryland: State and Government*. Centreville, Md.: Tidewater Publishers, 1974.

Brooks, Richard O. *New Towns and Communal Values: A Case Study of Columbia, Md*. New York: Praeger, 1974.

Callcott, George. *Maryland, 1940–1980*. Baltimore, Md.: Johns Hopkins University Press, 1985.

Jacobs, Bradford. *Thimbleriggers: The Law v. Governor Marvin Mandel*. Baltimore, Md.: Johns Hopkins University Press, 1984.

Lippman, Theo, Jr. *Spiro Agnew's America: The Vice-President and the Politics of Suburbia*. New York: W. W. Norton, 1972.

Maryland Historic Trust. *New Life for Maryland's Old Towns*. Annapolis: Department of Economic and Community Development, 1979.

Maryland Population Data. Baltimore: Maryland Department of State Planning, 1981.

Thompson, Derek, Joseph W. Wiedel, and Associates. *An Economic and Social Atlas of Maryland*. College Park, Md.: University of Maryland, 1974.

Warner, William. *Beautiful Swimmers: Watermen, Crabs, and the Chesapeake Bay*. New York: Penguin, 1976.

Witcover, Jules. *A Heartbeat Away: The Investigation and Resignation of Vice President Spiro T. Agnew*. New York: Viking, 1974.

General Works

Arnold, Joseph. *Maryland: Old Line to New Prosperity*. Northridge, Calif.: Windsor Publications, 1985.

Bode, Carl. *Maryland*. New York: Norton, 1978.

Brackett, Jeffrey. *The Negro in Maryland*. Baltimore, Md.: Johns Hopkins Press, 1889.

Brooks, Neil A., and Eric G. Rockel. *A History of Baltimore County*. Towson, Md.: Friends of the Towson Library, 1979.

Capper, John, Garrett Power, and Frank Shivers, Jr. *Chesapeake Waters: Pollution, Public Health, and Public Opinion, 1602–1972*. Centreville, Md.: Tidewater Publishers, 1983.

Cunz, Dieter. *The Maryland Germans*. Princeton, N.J.: Princeton University Press, 1948.

DiLisio, James. *Maryland: A Geography*. Boulder, Col.: Westview Press, 1983.

Everstine, Carl N. *The General Assembly of Maryland, 1634–1776*. Charlottesville, Va.: Michie Company, 1980.

———. *The General Assembly of Maryland, 1776–1850*. Charlottesville, Va.: Michie Company, 1982.

Fein, Isaac M. *The Making of an American Jewish Community: The History of Baltimore Jewry from 1773 to 1920*. Philadelphia: Jewish Publication Society of America, 1971.

Greene, Suzanne Ellery. *Baltimore: An Illustrated History*. Woodland Hills, Calif.: Windsor Publications, 1980.

Harvey, Katherine A. *The Best Dressed Miners: Life and Labor in the Maryland Coal Region, 1835–1910*. Ithaca, N.Y.: Cornell University Press, 1969.

Helmes, Winifred G., ed. *Notable Maryland Women.* Centreville, Md.: Tidewater Publishers, 1977.

MacMaster, Richard K., and Ray Eldon Hiebert. *A Grateful Remembrance: The Story of Montgomery County, Maryland.* Rockville, Md.: Montgomery County Government and Historical Society, 1976.

Maryland Manual. Annapolis: Maryland State Archives, latest edition.

Olson, Sherry H. *Baltimore: The Building of an American City.* Baltimore, Md.: Johns Hopkins University Press, 1980.

Papenfuse, Edward C., and Joseph M. Coale III. *The Hammond-Harwood House Atlas of Historical Maps of Maryland, 1608–1908.* Baltimore, Md.: Johns Hopkins University Press, 1982.

Papenfuse, Edward C., Gregory A. Stiverson, Susan A. Collins, and Lois Green Carr, eds. *Maryland: A New Guide to the Old Line State.* Baltimore, Md.: Johns Hopkins University Press, 1976.

Preston, Dickson J. *Talbot County: A History.* Centreville, Md.: Tidewater Publishers, 1983.

Scharf, J. Thomas. *Chronicles of Baltimore.* Baltimore, Md.: Turnbull Brothers, 1874.

———. *A History of Baltimore City and County.* Philadelphia, Pa.: Louis H. Everts, 1881.

———. *A History of Maryland.* 3 vols. Baltimore, Md.: John B. Piet, 1879.

———. *A History of Western Maryland.* 2 vols. Philadelphia, Pa.: Louis H. Everts, 1882.

Stegmaier, Harry, Jr., David Dean, Gordon Kershaw, and John Wiseman. *Allegany County: A History.* Parsons, W.Va.: McClain Printing Company, 1976.

Tilghman, Oswald, comp. *A History of Talbot County, Maryland, 1661–1861.* 2 vols. Baltimore, Md.: Williams and Wilkins, 1915.

Walsh, Richard, and William Lloyd Fox, eds. *Maryland: A History 1632–1974.* Baltimore: Maryland Historical Society, 1974.

Warner, Nancy M., Ralph B. Levering, and Margaret Taylor Woltz. *Carroll County, Maryland: A History, 1837–1976.* Westminster, Md.: Carroll County Bicentennial Committee, 1976.

Warren, Mame, and Marion E. Warren. *Maryland Time Exposures, 1840–1940.* Baltimore, Md.: Johns Hopkins University Press, 1984.

Weeks, Christopher, ed. *Between the Nanticoke and the Choptank: An Architectural History of Dorchester County, Maryland.* Baltimore: Johns Hopkins University Press, 1984.

Wennersten, John R. *The Oyster Wars of the Chesapeake Bay.* Centreville, Md.: Tidewater Publishers, 1981.

White, Frank. *The Governors of Maryland.* Annapolis, Md.: Hall of Records, 1971.

Williams, Thomas J. C. *A History of Frederick County, Maryland.* 2 vols. 1910; Baltimore: Regional Publishing Company, 1967.

———. *A History of Washington County, Maryland.* 1910; Baltimore, Md.: Regional Publishing Company, 1968.

Picture Credits

Chapter 1   Maryland's Formative Years, 1634–1763

Page 4: Maryland State Archives/ Artistic Property Commission (Annapolis); **5:** Maryland Historical Society (Baltimore); **8:** St. Mary's City Commission (St. Mary's City); **10:** Maryland Historical Society; **11:** Maryland Historical Society; **13:** St. Mary's City Commission and Dr. Cary Carson, artist; **15:** Maryland Tourism (Annapolis); **17:** Francis O. Chapelle (Baltimore); **23:** Maryland Historical Society; **27:** Maryland State Archives; **31:** Maryland Historical Society; **34:** Historical Society of Talbot County (Easton); **36:** Maryland Historical Society; **37:** Maryland Tourism; **38:** Maryland Historical Society; **43:** Maryland Historical Society; **44:** *left* and *right*, Maryland Tourism; **45:** *left*, M. E. Warren (Annapolis), and, *right*, Maryland Tourism.

Chapter 2   The Revolutionary War Era, 1763–1789

Page 50: Maryland State Archives (Annapolis); **51:** Frick Art Reference Library (New York City) and Mr. and Mrs. R. H. Dulany Randolph (Baltimore); **53:** *left*, Frick Art Reference Library and anonymous owner of the portrait, and, *right*, Maryland State Archives; **56:** Maryland State Archives; **57:** Maryland State Archives and Huntingfield Corporation (Rock Hall); **58:** Maryland State Archives; **62:** Maryland State Archives; **66:** *left* and *right*, Maryland State Archives; **67:** *left* and *right*, Maryland State Archives; **68:** The Historical Society of Pennsylvania (Philadelphia, Pa.); **71:** The Dietrich Brothers American Foundation (Chester Springs, Pa.) and Will Brown (Philadelphia, Pa.), photographer; **77:** Maryland State Archives; **78:** Maryland State Archives; **79:** *top*, Historical Society of Talbot County (Easton), and, *bottom*, M. E. Warren (Annapolis); **82:** Maryland State Archives; **83:** Maryland State Archives; **84:** Independence National Historical Park, National Park Service (Philadelphia, Pa.); **85:** Maryland State Archives.

Chapter 3   Maryland in the New Nation, 1789–1850

Page 99: The Peale Museum; **104:** Maryland Historical Society (Baltimore); **105:** Maryland State Archives (Annapolis); **107:** *top left*, G. Heileman Brewing Company, Inc. (Baltimore), and, *bottom* and *top right*, Maryland Historical Society; **113:** Research Library of the Washington County Historical Society (Hagerstown) and John R. Hershey, Jr. (Hagerstown); **115:** McKeldin Library, Special Collections, University of Maryland (College Park); **116:** Maryland Historical Society; **117:** John Work Garrett Collection, Special Collections Division, The Milton S. Eisenhower Library, The Johns Hopkins University (Baltimore); **121:** Maryland Historical Society; **122:** Chesapeake and Ohio National Historical Park, National Park Service (Sharpsburg); **123:** Maryland Historical Society; **125:** Maryland Historical Society; **127:** National Portrait Gallery, Smithsonian Institution (Washington, D.C.); **130:** Maryland Historical Society.

Chapter 4   Maryland in Peace and War, 1850–1870

Page 139: Maryland Historical Society (Baltimore); **141:** McKeldin Library, Special Collections, University of Maryland (College Park); **142:** Maryland Historical Society; **149:** Maryland Historical Society; **150:** The Library of Congress (Washington, D.C.); **151:** Maryland Historical Society; **157:** *top* and *bottom*, Maryland Historical Society; **163:** Maryland Historical Society; **165:** *top*, McKeldin Library, Special Collections, University of Maryland, and, *bottom*, National Archives (Washington, D.C.) and Alexander Gardner, artist; **166:** *top*, The Library of Congress, and, *bottom*, Maryland Historical Society; **168:** Suzanne Ellery Greene Chapelle (Baltimore); **171:** Maryland State Archives/Artistic Property Commission (Annapolis).

Chapter 5   A New Century, 1870–1917

Page 179: *top*, Allegany County Historical Society, Inc. (Cumberland), and, *bottom*, Maryland Tourism (Annapolis); **182:** The Peale Museum (Baltimore); **185:** *top*, The Edward L. Bafford Photography Collection, Albin O. Kuhn Library and Gallery, University of Maryland Baltimore County (Catonsville), and, *bottom*, Suzanne Ellery Greene Chapelle (Baltimore); **187:** Suzanne Ellery Greene Chapelle; **190:** *The Baltimore Sun* (Baltimore); **192:** The Library of Congress (Washington, D.C.); **194:** *top*, Suzanne Ellery Greene Chapelle, and, *bottom*, Maryland Historical Society (Baltimore); **196:** The Ferdinand Hamburger Jr. Archives, The Johns Hopkins University (Baltimore) and Alfred J. Miller, artist; **197:** Collection of the Washington County Free Library (Hagerstown); **198:** *top*, M. E. Warren (Annapolis), and, *bottom*, Mr. and Mrs. Herbert J. Null (Taneytown) and *Maryland: A Pictorial History* by Jacques Kelly (Baltimore); **199:** Collection of the Washington County Free Library; **200:** National Archives

(Washington, D.C.) and Lewis Hine, photographer; **203:** *top*, Allegany County Historical Society, Inc., and, *bottom*, The Library of Congress; **207:** Maryland State Archives/Artistic Property Commission (Annapolis); **208:** Enoch Pratt Free Library (Baltimore); **209:** Maryland Historical Society; **211:** Harry Sythe Cummings, Jr. (Baltimore) and Mrs. Louise Dorcas (Baltimore); **213:** Herman J. and Stacia Miller (Cumberland); **214:** The Library of Congress.

Chapter 6 Prosperity, Depression, and War, 1917–1945

Page 220: McKeldin Library, Special Collections, University of Maryland (College Park); **228:** Maxine B. Broadwater Collection; **230:** *top*, National Portrait Gallery, Smithsonian Institution (Washington, D.C.), and, *bottom*, The Library of Congress (Washington, D.C.); **231:** *left*, Maryland Historical Society (Baltimore), and, *right*, Gil Dunn (Stevensville); **232:** *top*, The Library of Congress, and, *bottom*, The Research Library of the Washington County Historical Society (Hagerstown); **235:** *top* and *bottom*, The Library of Congress; **237:** Maryland State Archives (Annapolis); **239:** The Library of Congress; **240:** Enoch Pratt Free Library (Baltimore); **242:** The Library of Congress; **245:** *Baltimore Afro-American* (Baltimore); **247:** The Library of Congress; **249:** Enoch Pratt Free Library; **250:** *left* and *right*, National Archives (Washington, D.C.); **255:** *The Baltimore Sun* (Baltimore).

Chapter 7 Maryland since World War II, 1945 to the Present

Page 259: *The Baltimore Sun* (Baltimore); **262:** M. E. Warren; **264:** M. E. Warren (Annapolis); **266:** Maryland Tourism (Annapolis); **267:** *top*, Office of the Mayor, City of Baltimore (Baltimore), and, *bottom*, Maryland Tourism; **268:** *The Baltimore Sun*; **269:** *left*, *The Baltimore Sun*, and, *right*, Ocean City, Maryland, Public Relations Division (Ocean City); **270:** Maryland State Roads Commission; **271:** *top*, Ocean City, Maryland, Public Relations Division, and, *bottom*, Richard O. Springer, Sr. (Cumberland); **273:** Maryland Tourism; **274:** M. E. Warren; **275:** Maryland Tourism; **277:** *top right*, Maryland Tourism, and, *bottom* and *top left*, M. E. Warren; **280:** The Johns Hopkins University Space Telescope Science Institute (Baltimore); **283:** McKeldin Library, Special Collections, University of Maryland (College Park); **286:** Maryland State Archives (Annapolis); **287:** Maryland Historical Society (Baltimore); **290:** *The Baltimore Sun*; **291:** *left*, *The Baltimore Sun*, and, *right*, Office of Representative Parren J. Mitchell (Washington, D.C.); **295:** *The Baltimore Sun*; **296:** Baltimore Opera Company, Inc. (Baltimore); **297:** *The Baltimore Sun*; **298:** *top*, The Indianapolis Colts (Indianapolis, Ind.), and, *bottom*, The Baltimore Orioles (Baltimore).

Index

Aberdeen, 201
Aberdeen Proving Ground, 253
Abolitionists, 125–27, 147–52, 154, 169
Act Concerning Religion, 19
Adams, John, 64, 101
Africa, 4, 25, 126–27, 148, 286
African Methodist Episcopal Church, 128
Africans, 24–25
African School, 128
Afro-American. See *Baltimore Afro-American*
Agnew, Spiro, 283–86
Agriculture, 9–10, 14, 16–17, 22–24, 26, 33–35, 40–45, 109–14, 122–24, 133, 135, 177–78, 200–202, 218, 221, 228, 231–33, 238, 272–73. *See also* Farmers; Farms
Agriculture, Department of, 285
Airplanes, 226, 249–50, 258, 276
Airports, 226, 258, 272, 274, 284
Alaska, 202
Alexandria, Va., 94, 104
Algeria, 294
Allegany County, 110, 112, 179, 181, 190, 195, 201–3, 213, 243, 276, 297. *See also specific towns*
Allen, Rev. Bennett, 54–55
All Saints' Parish, 54–55
American Federation of Labor (AFL), 192–93, 227, 244
American Legion, 253
American party. *See* Know-Nothing party
American Red Cross, 166, 254
American Satellite Co., 279
American Sugar Co., 226
Amherst College, 246
Andrews Air Force Base, 253
Anglicans, 18, 25, 27–29, 33, 46, 54–58, 67, 112, 128
Ann (brig), 126
Annapolis, 28, 32–33, 35, 39, 45, 50–54, 60–69, 76–79, 82–83, 91–92, 94, 114, 129–30, 138, 143, 155–56, 158, 181, 199, 211, 223, 263, 267, 282–83
Annapolis Convention, 92
Anne Arundel County, 14, 20, 25, 33, 35, 40, 54, 56, 110, 196, 199–200, 220, 225, 262, 289. *See also specific towns*

Annexations, 198–99, 225
Antietam, 162–65
Anti-Federalists, 93
"Antilon," 58
Appalachian Governors, Conference of, 283
Appalachian Mountains, 8–9, 38–39, 268
Appomattox, Va., 166
Apportionment, 77–78, 98, 132–33, 171, 210, 283
Arctic Sea, 294
Ark, 6–8, 12–13, 297
Armed Forces, British, 29, 64, 70–73, 75–76, 81–82, 100–108
Armed Forces, U.S.
  Confederate, 135, 161–67, 207
  post–World War II, 278, 280
  revolutionary, 64, 70–75, 81–82, 84–90
  Union, 135, 156–58, 160–68
  War of 1812, 100–108
  World War I, 217–22
  World War II, 248–55
Army. *See* Armed Forces
Articles of Confederation, 83–84, 92–93, 95
Artisans, 33, 35, 37, 39–41, 44, 73, 118, 130, 144
Asbury, Francis, 128
Ashmun Institute, 168
Assembly (colonial), 8, 15–16, 18–21, 28, 31–33, 35–36, 38–39, 51–53, 55–58
Association Assembly, 28
Association of Black Caulkers, 144
Association of Freemen of Maryland, 63
Atlantic Ocean, 3, 7, 109, 130, 225, 297
Atomic Energy Commission, 262
Auld family, 127, 146–47
Australia, 253
Australian ballot, 210, 213
Automobiles, 221, 225, 229–30, 244, 258–59, 269–71, 278
Avalon, 114
Avalon Iron and Nail Works, 123

Baby boom, 259–60, 278, 281, 295
Baltimore. *See also* Blacks; Immigrants and ethnic groups; Industry; Population; Trade
  Battle of, 105–8, 117

business and industry, 36, 56, 75, 109, 114–16, 118–19, 124, 142–43, 172, 177–78, 224–26, 233–35, 248–49, 265, 275–76
  and the Civil War, 156–63, 167
  colonial, 35–38, 50, 52–53, 56, 69, 74–75, 87, 114–16
  fire of 1904, 186–87
  nineteenth-century, 109, 111, 114–31, 133, 136–39, 142–50, 152–58, 168–72, 175–78, 180–98, 200–201, 207–15
  politics, 77, 98–99, 102, 108, 119, 133, 136–39, 154, 157–58, 171, 206–15, 236–37, 265–67
  port of, 36, 75, 87, 102, 105–8, 114–16, 143, 177, 225, 265, 274–75
  post-revolutionary period, 82, 94, 98–99
  during the Revolution, 74–75, 77, 87, 116
  riot of 1861, 156–58
  twentieth-century, 180–82, 186–98, 200–201, 207–15, 222–26, 228–31, 237, 239, 241, 243–46, 259–67, 270, 274–76, 278–79, 282–85, 287–91, 296–99
  and the War of 1812, 102–8
  in World War I, 217–22
  during World War II, 248–52, 254–55
Baltimore Afro-American, 190, 246, 253
Baltimore American, 170
Baltimore and Ohio Railroad, 123–24, 142, 171, 192, 196–97, 225, 227–28, 250
Baltimore Association of Commerce, 233
Baltimore Association for the Improvement of the Condition of the Poor, 144
Baltimore, Chesapeake, and Atlantic Railroad, 225
Baltimore City Fair, 297
Baltimore Colored High School, 246. *See also* Frederick Douglass High School
Baltimore Colts, 297–99
Baltimore County, 14, 20, 35–36, 40, 66, 91, 110, 146, 150, 159, 166, 173, 177, 181, 186, 198–200, 207, 225,

FEB 4 '87 C